Parametric Design
for Architecture

To Vassiliki, Maye and Sarah

Published in 2013
by Laurence King Publishing Ltd
361–373 City Road
London EC1V 1LR
Tel +44 20 7841 6900
Fax +44 20 7841 6910
E enquiries@laurenceking.com
www.laurenceking.com

A catalogue record for this book is available from the British Library

ISBN 978 178067 314 1
Designed by John Round Design
Printed in China

Parametric Design
for Architecture

WASSIM JABI

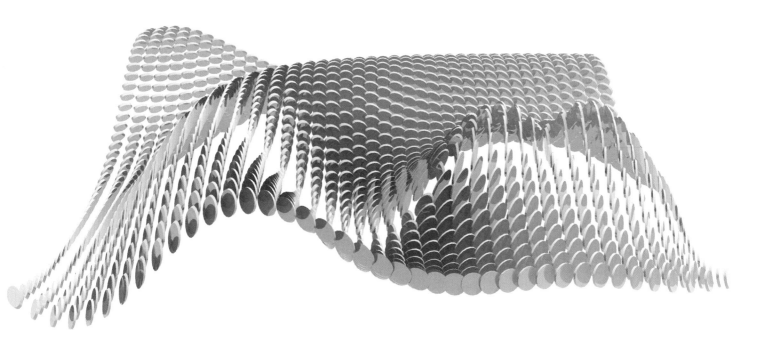

Laurence King Publishing

Contents

Related study material is available on the Laurence King website at
www.laurenceking.com

Preface

This book is, in part, the result of a particular frustration that I have harboured for many years. Like many of you, I love books about digital design, and I am always impressed by the wizardry of their beautifully illustrated projects and examples. But by the time I reach the concluding chapters, I am invariably frustrated to find that these books never reveal the mechanisms that yielded such spectacular results. The question on my mind – and which I am sure is often also on yours – is 'How did they do that?'

When I was approached to write a book about parametric design in architecture, I did not quite know what kind of book it would be, but I knew what kind of book it would not be. It would not resemble a magician's show, where the magic tricks are spectacular but the secrets of their creation are well kept. Instead, I wanted to write a book that would explain the algorithmic techniques in parametric design as well as analyze contemporary case studies that take advantage of such techniques. I also decided, perhaps against conventional wisdom, to include full source code for the examples I discuss. This presents three major problems (in addition to the fact that the included scripts may not be the most elegant or the most efficient). First, to paraphrase Robert Woodbury's words, books are a difficult medium in which to discuss computer code. I have to agree; books are not (yet) interactive and I am hoping electronic books will soon solve this problem. Second, there is a danger that inexperienced readers will simply copy the included scripts without investigating them. Third, the scripting environments for various 3D platforms differ in their syntax. There isn't enough space in a book of this type to present the scripts

for all popular scripting environments. However, one should keep an important fact in mind: parametric and algorithmic thinking is not about any one piece of computer software or any one particular syntax, but about logic, geometry, topology and interaction. If you approach this book with that idea in mind, then you will benefit from it regardless of the scripting environment and programming language it uses.

In the first two parts of this book, I decided to present the examples using two scripting environments: *Processing* and *MAXScript*. *Processing* is a free and open-source Java-based programming environment for visual designers. Its ease of use and simple interface make it suitable for the beginner scripter. It excels in 2D visual design without the need for any external plug-ins. That is why I chose it for the tutorial on generating the Fibonacci series and a golden rectangle. However, for advanced 3D parametric scripts, *Processing* pales in comparison to the power of *MAXScript* and that is why I use *MAXScript* for the remainder of the tutorials. I conclude the tutorials with a brief discussion of a new universal and hybrid programming language for design called *DesignScript* that was originated by Dr Robert Aish from Autodesk. *DesignScript*, although still in beta at the time of writing, promises to combine the power of several scripting and visual programming approaches. As in any other situation, always look at the problem at hand carefully and choose the best tool and environment for solving it.

To start experimenting with the ideas in this book, one of the first things you need to do is download *Processing* from http://processing.org. *MAXScript* is the built-in scripting language of Autodesk's *3ds Max*, a powerful engine for modelling, visualization and animation. At this point, even those of you who are familiar with those uses for *3ds Max* might be thinking, 'I didn't know *3ds Max* even has a scripting language.' In the field of parametric design in architecture, *MAXScript* is perhaps *3ds Max*'s best-kept secret. It is an extremely useful language that has the ability to expose and extend *3ds Max*'s functionality in powerful ways. I have to note here that I have no affiliation with Autodesk nor would I derive any benefit from recommending its software.

The fact that I have chosen *Processing*, *MAXScript* and *DesignScript* as the scripting platforms for the tutorials should be of little consequence. Any code, if well explained, can be generalized into an algorithm and that algorithm, in turn, can be re-written using a different syntax for a different system. In this book, I will give you both the code and the algorithms, first by presenting functional scripts for a particular platform, so that you can try them out and see immediate results,

fig. 1 A systematic design exploration of two parameters: tapering and twisting.

fig. 2 Soumaya museum, 2011, Mexico
City, Mexico, Fernando Romero.

and second by explaining them in detail, so that you can generalize and expand on them regardless of your computing environment. This book does not assume that you are a casual and passive reader, but an active one looking to solve a design problem in your practice or school using an algorithmic approach. However, becoming an expert in parametric design – and scripting in particular – is a journey that can take months, if not years. This book should be thought of as only one step in that process and a tool in your chest of resources.

This is a book for what I would call advanced beginners. To get the most of out it, you should already be familiar with 3D modelling and geometry. It does not include any discussion of what a coordinate system is, what vector maths is or what matrix transformations are. It covers the concepts of programming at a basic level that allows the reader to follow the tutorials, but not much more. To gain a better understanding in this area, I highly recommend three books in addition to this one: *Elements of Parametric Design* by Woodbury, *Architectural Geometry* by Pottman *et al*, and *Processing: A Programming Handbook for Visual Designers and Artists* by Reas and Fry. Yet, the tutorials in this book are purposely kept simple and self-contained so that they are instructional, clear and can be completed in one session without a need to reference outside resources.

Once you have mastered these tutorials, you are expected to find ways to expand and customize the provided code and use the presented ideas to suit your purpose.

Finally, you might be wondering why this book does not include any visual programming techniques. There are two reasons for that: a) the web is teeming with resources and ready-made examples for visual programming, and b) when you hit the limits of these systems and require customized code, you will find that there is a dearth of well-explained online resources for architects and visual designers. This is where books such as this one are most effective. They teach you the algorithmic logic behind built-in parametric and generative components so that you can write your own or augment them with custom scripting.

Before you embark on this journey, I want to offer my apology in advance for any errors or omissions in the book and for any lack of clarity you may encounter. Scripting, algorithmic thinking, parametric design, programming logic, geometry and trigonometry are all not easy things to absorb in the span of one book, but once you have mastered them they are incredibly powerful design tools. I wish you a productive and, most importantly, enjoyable journey.

Foreword by Robert Woodbury

To design well is to be in joyful flow. All good designers make copious – indeed massive – piles of media as they work. Somehow, from this mass of sketches, models and prototypes, something new emerges. To be a good designer, it has always been necessary to become an expert in the crafting of many different media, and today those crafts are mostly digital. Craft is always learned by doing and polished by practice, but these tacit acts are not sufficient. Designers must *know* the concepts that underlie the forms of media they use. In today's digital media, it is primarily symbols, algorithms and programs that form the language through which we come to know what we are doing. In this book, Wassim Jabi gives two gifts to the field of design. First, through many code examples, he builds a crucial and explicit practical knowledge that can be used to navigate the complex computer-aided design system. Second, he takes us on a wisely guided tour of contemporary design that has been shaped by the new parametric craft.

Be wary of the first gift – indeed you should be wary of any computer program so offered! Using code well requires thought and work. In the hurly-burly of design, you will be tempted to use Jabi's code quickly, as it is or with slight modification. This is fine, as long as you also, at some point, take the time to understand why the code works and, more importantly, why Jabi chose it and how he explains it. Try this. Explain it to yourself. If you think you understand it, explain it to a friend. If you can do that, use it

explicitly as the central form-making idea in a design. If you can do all these things, you are beginning to understand.

Be even more careful with the second gift! It shows you success, but not the hours of joyful work invested in it. Look beyond the surface glitz. Contemporary computer-aided design and visualization systems make enticing renderings easy. Look for depth, for places and forms in which parametric ideas meet the design situation to create the ineffable 'good' in 'good design'. Then try it yourself. Let parametric models tell you the most they can. To do this, you enter the cycle of design, in which you make, look, reflect, change and make some more. Eventually, you will find a resolution and will be a stronger designer for it.

There are too few books like this one. It lies between the mass of user manuals that show technique without design and the picture books that show design without technique. By joining the two, Jabi opens a gate to new possibilities. He does not – and cannot – show what lies beyond the gate. That is for you to discover, through joyful work with parametric design.

fig. 3 Antoni Gaudí's hanging chain catenary model at Casa Milà, Barcelona, Catalonia, Spain. Gaudí frequently used hanging chain models to derive the structure of his projects. View the image upside down to see how this model translates into the actual project.

Introduction

The architectural design process is almost always iterative. Designers create solutions that, in turn, pose new questions, which are then investigated to generate more refined or even entirely new solutions. Designers often use computer-aided tools to build models and help them visualize ideas. However, the vast majority of these models are still built in such a way that they are difficult to modify interactively. The problem becomes more severe when bespoke 3D models are geometrically complex. Changing one aspect of such a model usually requires extensive low-level modifications to many of its other parts. To address this problem, designers have begun using parametric design software, which allows them to specify relationships among various parameters of their design model. The advantage of such an approach is that a designer can then change only a few parameters and the remainder of the model can react and update accordingly. These derivative changes are handled by the software, but are based on associative rules set by the designer. Associative and parametric geometry, in essence, describe the logic and intent of such design proposals rather than just the form of the proposal itself. This kind of design both requires and helps to create powerful interactive tools that allow designers to explore and optimize a multitude of possibilities while reducing the amount of time it takes to do so in a rigorous manner. Engaging these parametric and algorithmic processes requires a fundamental mindset shift from a process of manipulating design representations to that of encoding design intent using systematic logic. Algorithmic thinking calls for a shift of focus from achieving a high fidelity in the representation of the appearance of a design to that of achieving a high fidelity in the representation of its internal logic. The advantage of algorithmic thinking is that it can build '... consistency, structure, coherence, traceability and intelligence into computerized 3D form'.[1] Parametrically and algorithmically built models can react with high fidelity to their real-life counterparts when subjected not only to user changes of geometric parameters, but also to structural forces, material behaviour and thermal and lighting variations, as well as contextual conditions. Because they accurately represent the internal construction logic of the structure at hand, parametric models can also be unfolded or translated into geometries that can be digitally fabricated. This powerful digital workflow of parametric form-finding that is influenced by design intentions as well as performance analysis and digital fabrication logic is one of the defining characteristics of current digital architectural practice. Contemporary architects, such as Patrik Schumacher, partner at Zaha Hadid Architects, have gone as far as coining *parametricism* as the name of a new movement in architecture following *modernism*. He writes: 'We must pursue the parametric design paradigm all the way, penetrating into all corners of the discipline. Systematic, adaptive variation and continuous differentiation (rather than mere variety) concern all architectural design tasks from urbanism to the level of tectonic detail. This implies total fluidity on all scales.'[2] He points out that the fundamental themes in parametric design include versioning, iteration, mass-customization and continuous differentiation. It is helpful to briefly define these terms.

Versioning

Borrowed from the software development field, the term *versioning* refers to the process of creating versions – or variations on a theme, if you will – of a certain design solution based on varying conditions. Parametric software allows the designer to create a prototype solution that, rather than being cast in a static CAD file format, is *wired* – almost as a string puppet would be. This wiring allows the design solution to be tweaked and manipulated, creating new versions when new forces and conditions arise.

Iteration

Again borrowed from the software development field (see a pattern here?), the term iteration refers to cycling through or repeating a set of steps. In the case of parametric architecture, iteration can, in principle, create variation at every pass through the same set of instructions. Examples may include varying the size and shape of a floor plate as one builds a skyscraper, or changing the angle of a modular cladding system as it is tiled over an undulating surface. In addition to producing variation, iteration can be a powerful tool for both optimization and for minimizing the time needed to achieve that optimization. Using a fluid parametric system, which can give immediate feedback, a designer can generate solutions and test them rapidly by iterating through many possibilities, each created with a different set of parameters.

Mass-customization

One of the main successes of the industrial revolution is the idea of mass production. Factories and robots are able to produce thousands of copies of the same prototype. However, given the advent of digital fabrication technologies, we are now able to change the manufacturing instructions between each object. Given that the process

---

1 Terzidis, K. *Expressive Form: A Conceptual Approach to Computational Design.* Routledge, 2003.
2 Schumacher, P. *Parametricism – A New Global Style for Architecture and Urban Design, AD/Architectural Design – Digital Cities*, Vol. 79, Iss. 4, July/August 2009

is parameterized and robotic, it often costs the same to mass-customize the manufactured products as it does to mass-produce the same quantity of identical products.

Continuous differentiation

Another borrowed term, this time from the field of calculus, continuous differentiation alludes to a feature of versioned, iterative and mass-customized parametric work that allows for difference to occur within a continuous field or rhythm. As opposed to mere variety, parametrically varied instances within an overall group, curve or field maintain their continuity to other instances before and after them while uniquely responding to local conditions.

The characteristics of a parametric design system

The question then becomes, what is a parametric design system, and how can it help improve the design process or more rigorously explore possible design alternatives? In addition to the themes defined above, all parametric design systems share several characteristics and have similar constructs: *object-orientation*, *classes* or *families*, *methods* and, of course, *parameters*. Let us briefly define these concepts.

Object-orientation

Modern parametric software usually uses an object-oriented approach in its design. Object-oriented programming is a well-established computer science topic that is beyond the scope of this book, but a brief description is in order.

The user interacts with a parametric system in a manner that reflects its internal algorithmic strucure, by creating and modifying *objects* such as circles, spheres, doors and walls.

A parametric system usually stores these objects in an object-oriented database that can be accessed, searched and modified.

Each object then has *values* that determine its *attributes*. For example, a circle will almost always contain an attribute called *centre* or *position* and another one called *radius* [**fig. 4**]. It will also probably contain an attribute called *name* that identifies the circle. It is usual for a certain value of an object to be represented with reference to the object and attribute with which it is associated. A popular notation is to use a full stop to separate an attribute from its parent object: *object.attribute*. Thus, if one wishes to reference the value of the radius of a circle named *circleC*, one might encounter the following term: *circleC.radius*. Similarly, the X-axis position of the same circle could be the X attribute of the position attribute of the circle, as in *circleC.Position.X*, and the Y-axis value could logically follow as *circleC.Position.Y*.

Values can either be constants (e.g. 100 m) or functions, which need to be evaluated to compute a final value. The power of a function in the value placeholder of an attribute is that it can derive its value from the values of other attributes, which can belong to other objects. Consider the following hypothetical function of a radius of a circle:

$$C.Radius = distance(PointA, PointB)$$

The above expression specifies that the radius of a circle is not a constant number, but is derived from the distance between two points (*PointA* and *PointB*). In such a case, we call the variable *C.Radius* a *dependent* variable as it depends on other values. We also describe such constructs as *associative* – as in *associative geometry*. Association of parameters with one another allows us to derive unknown entities from known ones. In the above example, if the distance between the two points ever changes, the circle's radius will change

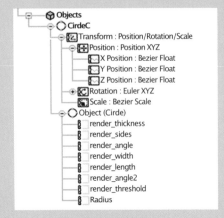

fig. 4 The attributes of a circle in Autodesk's *3ds Max* software.

fig. 5 A family of Scottish doors.

accordingly. We call this feature of updating the value of one object based on changes in other values *propagation*. Imagine a large network of wired or associated values. A change in one or few parameters would propagate through the whole network, modifying the values of attributes and changing the characteristics of the final design solution. This is the power of an associative parametric system. Objects, attributes and values are associated with one another and parameterized so that a change in the value of one parameter can have ripple effects throughout the design.

Families and inheritance

Objects that share certain characteristics can be organized as members of a *class* or *family* of objects. A class or family of *doors* **[fig. 5]**, for example, can contain many individual family members (hinged doors, sliding doors, folding doors, etc.). The advantage of grouping several objects into a family is that they can then share certain attributes with their siblings and inherit certain attributes from their parents. It is much more efficient to organize these shared attributes only once, in a parent object, than to have to customize all the attributes and values for each offspring.

Methods

In an object-oriented system, methods are functions and algorithms that act on an object by modifying its attributes. Rather than have a large set of centralized instructions that specify how to draw circles, squares and triangles, an object-oriented system delegates, encapsulating these instructions in the class or family of each object. How an object is to be constructed or modified is thus encoded as a method in the object itself. In the case of a circle, one such method could be to construct the circle by specifying the position of its centre and the value of its radius attribute. Another method could be to specify three points that circumscribe it.

The system can simply tell a circle to draw itself – or it can ask a door to reverse its opening. In a modern parametric system a typical object, even one as simple as a sphere, can have many parameters and methods **[fig. 6]**.

Parameters

At the heart of any modern parametric system is the term *parameter* and so it would be wise to define that term at this point. The word *parameter* derives from the Greek for *para* (besides, before or instead of) + *metron* (measure). If we look at the Greek origin of the word, it becomes clear that the word means a term that stands in for or determines another measure. The word *parameter* is often confused with *variable*, but it is more specific. In mathematics *parameter* is defined as a variable term in a function that 'determines the specific form of the function but not its general nature, as a in $f(x) = ax$, where a determines only the slope of the line described by $f(x)$'.[3]

In parametric CAD software, the term *parameter* usually signifies a variable term in equations that determine other values. A parameter, as opposed to a constant, is characterized by having a range of possible values. One of the most seductive powers of a parametric system is the ability to explore many design variations by modifying the value of a few controlling parameters **[fig. 7]**.

The remainder of this book presents a series of parametric design patterns of increasing complexity followed by exemplar case studies that reflect the potential of the associated patterns. The book ends with a discussion of the future of parametric design and its potential to form a language of design. The afterword by Brian Johnson closes the discussion with advice on how to craft new solutions, based on knowledge gleaned from this book.

3 From http://dictionary.com

fig. 6 The parameters and creation method options of a sphere in Autodesk's *3ds Max*.

fig. 7 In the *Matière à Rétro-projeter!* (Material Projects) exhibition at the Centre Pompidou, Paris, France, young visitors affect a regular field of light and shadow patterns as they move in front of it.

Case study Austrian Pavilion, Shanghai, China

Designer SPAN Architecture & Design
Client Austrian Government
Design 2008–09
Construction 2010

The Austrian Pavilion was designed and built for the Shanghai Expo 2010, a forum that has traditionally served as a scene for the trial and display of experimental forms and avant-garde architectural ideas. The pavilion was designed by SPAN (Matias del Campo & Sandra Manninger), in collaboration with Zeytonoglu, a Vienna-based architectural firm. SPAN brings a new approach, informed by contemporary issues, to an appreciation of the 'opulent repertoire of formations' that they find in nature. This approach derives from the firm's close attention to three 'desires', as they put it. First, they strive to explore architectural form and its corresponding underlying geometry in relation to animated matter and material. Second, they are inspired by the

Baroque formal tradition, which is characterized by a sensual, curvilinear iconography, and by a new ability to extend these forms to infinity. Finally, computer technology, with its ability to reveal dormant forms through algorithmic and generative processes, is the main method they use in order to generate and compose their design proposals.

The firm's general views, outlined above, have found an expression in the design of the Austrian Pavilion, a project for which it was commissioned after winning an architectural competition in 2008. 'The main driving force behind the design', the firm argues, 'can be described as acoustic forces or more accurately as music. Music as a concept that reflects continuity in terms of architectural articulation that seamlessly connects the various

Above
Night view of the pavilion from the southeast.

Opposite
Daytime view of the pavilion from the southwest.

Right
View of the staircase.

Below
The pavilion's red room.

Below
Ground, first-floor, and roof plan drawings.

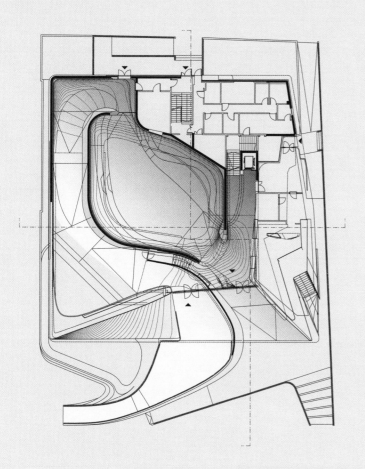

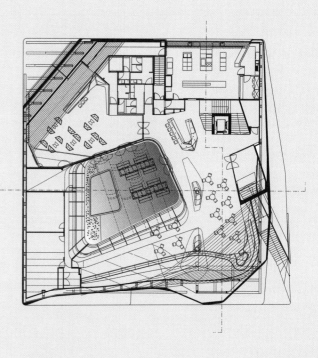

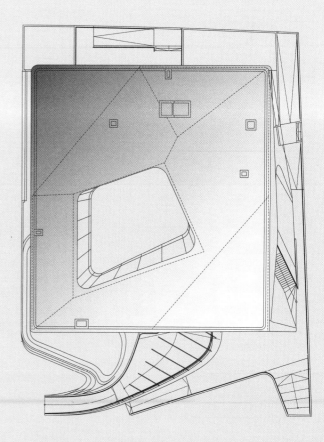

Right
Sectional drawings.

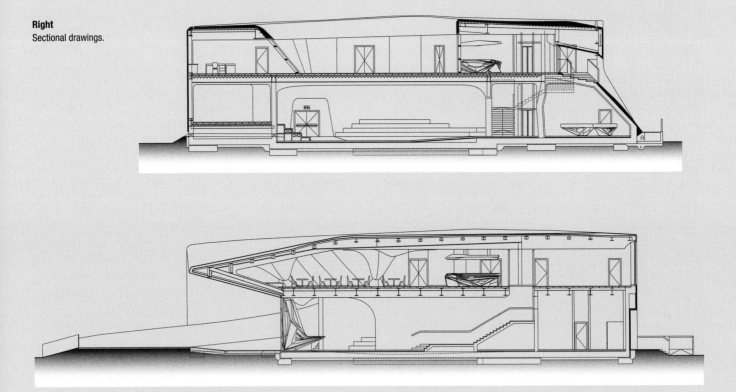

spaces within the programme.' Beginning with this thesis, and using TopMod software, the designers devised a topology: a computerized mathematical construct endowed with spatial properties (such as seamless circulation, a recessed entrance and roof garden, and a separate entrance for a restaurant) that could be maintained even while the topology underwent subtly varying transformations such as deformations, stretching or twisting. The software produced a number of alternatives that were evaluated according to functional, structural and aesthetic requirements. This process greatly reduced the number of acceptable solutions; the remaining designs were again run through a series of algorithms (various re-meshings, subdivisions, optimizing the size of spatial pockets) that led to the final layout of the pavilion.

The main aesthetic quality with which the designers sought to endow their project was fluidity. This is most clearly expressed in the spatial continuity of the interior and in the seamlessly flowing surface between the interior and the exterior. It is also present in the smooth functional transition between some of the interior spaces as well as in the arrangement of the core spaces, including the exhibition spaces of the ground floor and the restaurant facilities on the first floor.

Employing a comprehensive approach, the architects designed and produced the main pieces of furniture and other interior features (ceilings, openings, etc.) using CNC-milled polyurethane that was first coated with a synthetic resin and then highly polished. The process allowed a precise construction of highly complex curved objects that had been initially digitally designed and then visualized in 3D models.

The designers also employed an algorithmic approach to the treatment of the pavilion's skin. The organic fluid form of the building resulted in a continuous, curvilinear surface that is interrupted only at the points of entry. For the cladding of this surface, the designers applied a tessellation method. This led them to the adoption of very small, hexagonal porcelain tiles, and it also allowed them to manipulate the colour of the tiles across the surface. The final exterior comprised ten million tiles, transitioning from white to red over the building's surface, emphasizing both its stable placement on the ground and its biomorphic curvature.

Right
View of the main hall.

Below
View of the VIP bar.

Right
View of the gift shop.

Below
View of the restaurant.

Above
View of the exit space.

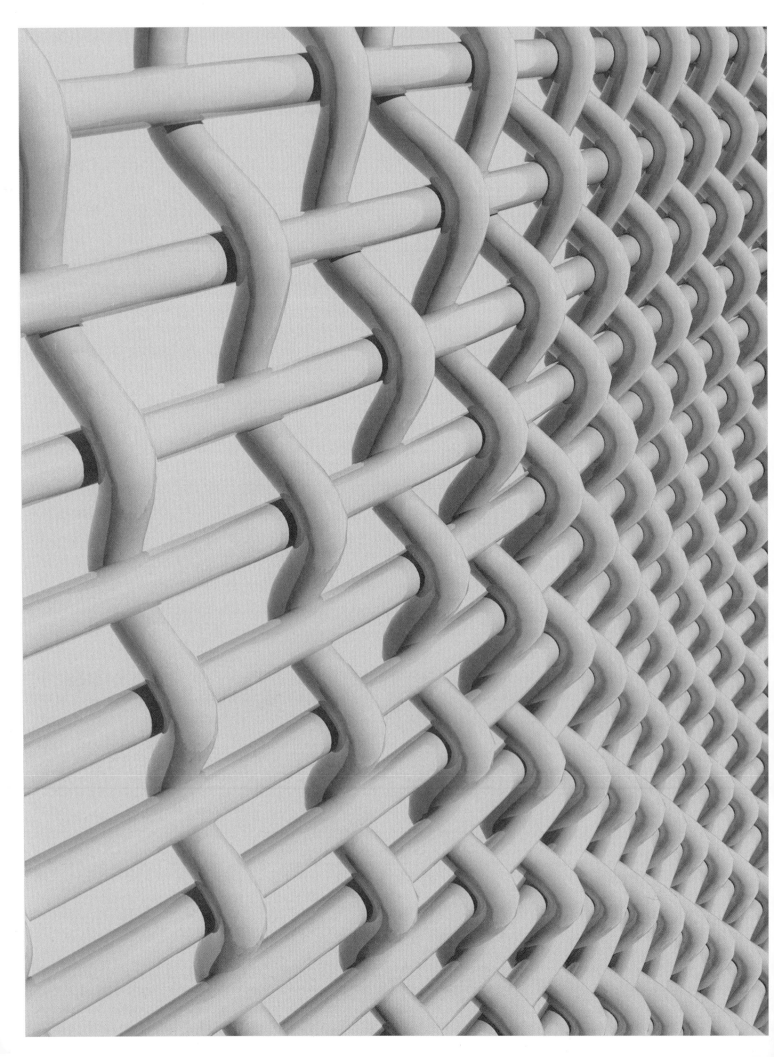

PART I ALGORITHMIC THINKING

Introduction

'From the time of ancient Vitruvian geometric ideals to modern Corbusian regulating lines and Miesian modular grids, architecture has always been bound to (if not by) a conscious use of numbers.'

Brett Steele ('Weapons of the Gods' in *The New Mathematics of Architecture* by Jane Burry and Mark Burry)

Rather than rely on an intuitive search for a solution, parametric design often involves precise, step-by-step techniques that yield a result according to rules and inputs. This way of thinking about the process of design as a rigorous rule-based system is referred to as *algorithmic thinking*. As Steele's quote above hints, mathematical knowledge and algorithmic thinking have always been the traits of an architect, certainly at least since the times of the ancient Egyptians and Greeks. Today, individuals who wish to use parametric design in architecture find themselves faced with the challenge of learning algorithmic concepts (as well as mathematics) that are more familiar to software programmers than to designers. Behind every piece of software is a set of precise instructions and techniques that interact with the user, respond to events, and read, manipulate and display data. Collectively, we call these instructions and techniques *algorithms*. Derived from the name of a Persian mathematician (Muhammad ibn Musa Al-Kwarizmi), an algorithm is defined as a set of precise instructions to calculate a function. An algorithm usually takes input (which can be empty or undefined), goes through a number of successive states, and ends with a final state and a set of outputs.

Learning programming concepts does not necessarily ensure that a designer will learn algorithmic thinking. The challenge is not dissimilar to learning cooking: one can learn the basics of mixing ingredients, heating, baking and so on, yet there is no guarantee of becoming an accomplished chef. As with most things, it takes a love for the craft, a methodical mind, some talent and, most importantly, practice. The metaphor also applies to the process itself: in the same way that cooking recipes vary in complexity, elegance and the taste of the final result, algorithms also vary in complexity, elegance, and the aesthetic and performative characteristics of the resulting design solution. While some recipes are invented from scratch, most are modifications of and variations on older recipes. The same applies in parametric design. The Internet is teeming with open-source algorithms that are offered for others to learn from, modify and expand. Beware, however, of the *microwave variety*: algorithms and definitions that are pre-packaged such that you cannot investigate and modify them. These types of algorithms are not always

clear and readable, and this is where a book such as this becomes useful. The elegance, modularity and readability of an algorithm usually have a direct relationship to its ability not only to produce elegant design solutions, but also to be understood and modified by others.

The good news, however, is that most designers wishing to use parametric techniques usually need to solve a relatively small and well-bounded design problem (unlike software developers, who create large and complex software products). For example, they might need to create a parametric building façade or a roof structure. They might need to mimic a natural phenomenon to create a design concept for their project. Algorithmic thinking allows designers to rationalize, control, iterate, analyze, and search for alternatives within a defined solution space. In the next section, we will explore the basics of algorithms. This brief introduction cannot replace a full discussion of algorithms and the inner workings of computer programming languages. For that information, there is a plethora of books on programming, online resources and university courses that are dedicated to this topic.

Overall structure

A traditional scripting environment is usually text-based. It provides an empty file to write out algorithms (steps) to perform a variety of operations. You type in the algorithm using very precise syntax. Any omissions, even something as small as a parenthesis or a semi-colon, can cause errors. The help files will instruct you in the syntax and peculiarities of the computer language you choose (e.g. *C, C++, Java, Python* or *MAXScript*). All computer languages will allow you to insert comments that are not interpreted as computer instructions. Comments are usually enclosed by the notation /* and */ (/* this is a comment */) or, for single lines, by the characters -- (-- *this is a comment*). Each language will have its own syntax for how to indicate that something is a comment. Comments allow you to explain to yourself and others what the code is doing at that point. I made the difficult decision to remove the comments in some of the provided code examples due to space limitations, but also because the code is explained in the main text of the book. Your code, however, should always be clearly documented with comments within the code itself. Computer languages differ in their readability and some lines of code may look very cryptic, so comments can explain what is going on.

Once complete, the scripting environment will provide you with a menu item or button to *execute* the script. When a script is executed, it is interpreted by a computer interpreter or compiler in order to produce *machine code* that runs and does all the things you have asked it to do (e.g. display buttons and checkboxes, accept user input, create and draw geometries). If the interpreter encounters an error, it usually will report that to the user and stop the interpretation process. Robust computing environments also give you debugging environments that allow you to pause and examine the code as it is running in order to find errors.

A script is usually made of standard parts: a declaration of what the script is and does, variables (think of variables as storage units to store information), functions (specialized and self-contained algorithms that accept input, act on it and produce output) and interfaces (declarations of what buttons, sliders and checkboxes to display and how to react to them). In more modern scripting environments the shift has been to what is called object-oriented programming (OOP). In OOP systems, instead of variables and functions you declare full objects that store in themselves their own variables and functions (called methods). For example, you can declare a door object that knows its own dimensions and what material it is made of. You can ask it to open and close itself using its publically declared methods and even enquire of it whether it is closed or open. In addition, objects that are similar are placed in families or classes, which share overall characteristics that can be inherited and, if needed, customized, by the individual object. This method of writing scripts has proven to be very powerful, elegant, modular and capable of being generalized.

Data types and variables

As we said above, a variable is a storage unit in which to place a value. When we store that value in a variable, we can recall it later in the code by using the name of the variable. The script will remember what we stored in it earlier. You can also change its value at any time. When writing scripts, we will need to store different types of information: numbers, words, lists of things, circles, rectangles, etc. Thus computer languages allow you to specify what type a variable is when you declare it. Different languages use different code words for specifying a variable's type, so you need to consult the user manual to find out what code word to use. The most common types of variable are:

Integer a whole number that does not have a decimal point. This is useful for counting objects.

Float (or real) a number that does have a decimal point. This is useful for measuring things.

String (or characters) a string of characters (e.g. words, sentences). This is useful for storing, manipulating and displaying textual information.

Array (or list) a special container that stores many variables and items. An array can be examined for how many items it has, what item exists in a certain row location, etc.

Boolean this is a special number that can have one of two values: true or false. This is useful to do logic operations, as we will see below.

Pointer think of a pointer as an address of something else. For example, if you create a box or a circle you can store a pointer to these objects in variables (e.g. *b = box()*, *c = circle()*). You can then access the attributes of the box and the circle by using the variables *b* and *c* respectively.

There are many other types of variable, as well as larger structures and objects that you may encounter, such as queues, stacks and sets, but the variables above are the most commonly used for storing and manipulating information.

Expressions

In programming languages, an expression is a contiguous series of tokens, variable, and constants that specifies how a value is to be computed. For example, if I stored the value 4 in a variable called *n* then the expression *2+n* will return 6 and the expression *2(n+1)* would return 10. In this book, you will encounter code that may look unintuitive, such as *a = a + 1*. That does not mean that *a* is equal to itself plus 1 (which is impossible), but that the interpreter should add 1 to *a* and then store the result back in *a* itself. This is very useful for counting numbers.

Logic and control

As we said earlier, algorithmic thinking is mainly about logic. When we use logic, we need to be able to assess a situation and, based on the presented conditions, choose from a menu of available decisions. In order for this to happen, the programming language needs to allow us to do two things: first, compare values to one another and report back the result (which we call the predicate) and, second, execute one of several groups of code based on these results. In order to compare values, computer languages allow you to use notation for equality (==), inequality (≠ or !=), greater than (>), less than (<), the logical opposite (*not(n)* or *!(n)*), and the Boolean set operations (*and()*, *or()*) that test whether both values are true, if at least one or the other is true, and so on. Notice that for testing equality we use two equal signs (==) in order to differentiate it from the assignment operation as discussed in the previous section. If you make a mistake and use one equal sign in a predicate, then the variable will be assigned the value and a true result would be returned regardless. This can lead to serious errors in the script.

Making a decision based on a predicate is usually done through what is called an *if-then* or an *if-then-else* statement. That is, *if* something is true, do *this*, *else* (i.e. otherwise) do *that*. Here is an example:

```
1    If (n < 4) then
2    (
3        do something here
4    )
5    else
6    (
7        do something else here
8    )
```

Functions

In order to keep the code manageable and readable, we often need to combine several coding steps in one group. If you find yourself repeating the same code multiple times, that is an indication that you should write it once as a function and call it on demand as many times as you need. A function is assigned a name, accepts input in the form of function arguments, and produces a result via return values as well as by storing values in global variables. For example, imagine that you repeatedly need to write a function that squares a number, adds another number to it and returns the result. You could write a function that you would give a name to such as squareAndAdd and define it as such:

```
1    fn squareAndAdd x y =
2    (
3        return (x*x) + y
4    )
```

Once the function is defined, we can call it and assign the result to a variable by writing *z = squareAndAdd x y*. The function would then take the value *x* and multiply it by itself, then add *y* to it and return a value that would then be stored in *z*. In *MAXScript* a function is defined using the built-in word *fn*. The actual syntax varies from one programming language to another, but the basic principle holds true: you can encapsulate any number of steps in one function, which can then be called with input arguments and evaluated for return values.

Iteration and recursion

In many situations, we would need to repeat the same block of code many times. Programming languages provide special notation for iteration usually called *for loops* or *while loops*. Imagine, for example, creating a row of squares. Each square is drawn with the same code but given a different location. In such a case, we can combine a *for loop* with the notation to increment the location variable. For example:

```
1    n = 4
2    for i = 1 to n by 1 do
3    (
4        drawASquare i*10
5    )
```

The above code would iterate the variable *i* from 1 to 4 and execute the code that exists between (and) four times – each time with the value of *i* automatically increased by 1. The imaginary function drawASquare would then draw a square at a location that is 10 multiplied by *i* (i.e. 10, 20, 30 and 40). Much as the moon orbits around the earth while the earth orbits around the sun, you can nest *for loops* inside one another to create multi-dimensional solutions (**fig. 8**).

Recursion is a special case of repetition and function calling where a function calls *itself* for the next iteration. Recursion can be difficult to grasp; it is somewhat akin to placing two mirrors opposite each other and creating a theoretically infinite number of reflections. Recursion, as you will see later in this book, is essential for fractal geometry and branching.

Objects, classes, attributes and methods

As mentioned above, modern scripting environments are object-oriented. They encapsulate attributes and methods in larger structures that are called *objects*. Objects that share similar features are grouped in *classes*. Rather than storing an attribute or a method in each object, these can be stored in the higher-level class and *inherited* by the member of the class when needed. Consider, for example, the *MAXScript* object *box*. Assume you have asked *MAXScript* to create a box and you stored a pointer to that box in a variable called *b*. We can then ask *b* for its width and height by evaluating the expression *b.width* and *b.height*. This dot notation allows us access to the pre-defined attributes of an object. We can use the same dot notation to change the value of the attribute (e.g. *b.width = 10*). Some objects also have methods associated with them, and these methods can be inherited. For example, in *MAXScript*, all objects belong to a class called *node*. A *node* knows how to move itself. So you could ask a box named *b* to move itself 10 units in the *x* direction, 5 units in the *y* direction and 20 units in the *z* direction, by issuing the command *move b [10,5,20]*. You could issue the same command to cylinders and spheres because they too belong to the *node* class of object.

Events and callback functions

A modern scripting environment that has a graphical user interface usually gives you the ability, in your own code, to react to user events or actions (e.g. the user has clicked a button or changed a value in the interface). In order to respond to these events, the scripting environment asks you to define a function that is given a pre-defined name. This is called a *callback function* because it gets called back from the system into your own code. For

example, if you have defined a button called *generate*, *MAXScript* allows you to react to the event of the button having been pressed, using the following syntax:

```
1    On generate_button pressed do
2    (
3        generate the geometry
4    )
```

This function, in your own code, would only be called and executed if the user presses the generate button.

As mentioned earlier, this chapter covers only the basics of algorithmic concepts at the simplest level. In no way does it substitute for a full study of programming languages, syntax, object-oriented methodology and the capabilities of the particular scripting environment. However, if pressed for time, you now know enough to read and understand the tutorials discussed in the next chapter.

fig. 8 Composed of two nested *for loops*, this algorithm creates an array of cubes that increasingly taper and twist along two dimensions.

```
1    for i = 0 to 4 by 1 do
2    (
3        for j = 0 to 4 by 1 do
4        (
5            b = box()
6            b.length = 10
7            b.width = 10
8            b.height = 10
9            b.lengthsegs = 10
10           b.widthsegs = 10
11           b.heightsegs = 10
12           addModifier b (taper amount:(-0.1*j))
13           addModifier b (twist angle:(10*i))
14           b.pos = [i*17, j*17, 0]
15       )
16   )
```

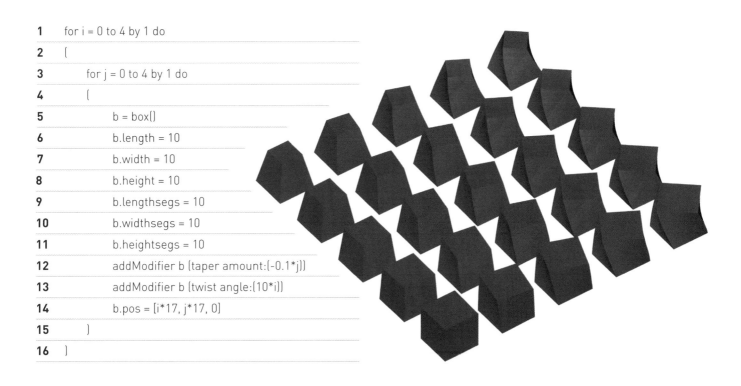

PART II PARAMETRIC PATTERNS

In his 1977 book, *A Pattern Language: Towns, Buildings, Construction*, Christopher Alexander pioneered the use of generative design patterns. He created an architectural system (or language) with the intention of creating practical and beautiful classical spaces and forms. (This built on his earlier work, including his doctoral dissertation in architecture, which was published in 1964 as *Notes on the Synthesis of Form*, a book which was widely read by students of computer science.) In 1994, inspired by his work, computer scientists Erich Gamma, Richard Helm, Ralph Johnson and John Vissides wrote a book titled *Design Patterns: Elements of Reusable Object-Oriented Software*. The book ushered in a new way of creating algorithms that focused, in particular, on the idea that one can recognize and thus more efficiently and quickly deploy repeating patterns that have a consistent logic and structure. For example, think of a queue at the local supermarket. The first person to enter the queue is the first person to be served at the till and to exit the queue. Now think of a librarian returning a stack of books piled vertically to their original location. The book that was placed last on top of the stack is the first one to be taken out of the stack. In order to reach a book in the middle of the stack, you would have to take out the ones that are stacked above it. Thus, a *stack* behaves in the opposite way to a *queue*. These patterns have exact counterparts in software programming. Once a pattern is defined and understood, it can be put to good and consistent use in developing an algorithm. Since parametric design relies heavily on algorithmic concepts, it is not surprising that it too has patterns. Parametric design patterns are still in development. Robert Woodbury and his team, for example, are collecting and systematically developing a comprehensive set of parametric patterns using a consistent template. You can see some of these patterns

published in his book, *Elements of Parametric Design*. Other authors have also attempted to describe reusable parametric and generative strategies for the derivation of form and organizational structures. Many other books, this one included, build on that kind of foundational work to develop higher-level patterns and algorithmic strategies for the derivation of form and the definition of topologies. Benjamin Aranda and Chris Lasch produced a concise and intriguing set of patterns in their book, *Tooling*, which provides succinct and high-level recipes for constructs such as *spirals*, *cracks* and *flocks*. Jane and Mark Burry, in their book, *The New Mathematics of Architecture*, also organize the chapters of their book around parametric themes such as *packing and tiling*, *optimization* and *topology*.

This book follows in the same long tradition started by Christopher Alexander and builds on the work of Woodbury, Aranda/Lasch and the Burrys. The selection of high-level parametric patterns in this book includes: controller, force field, repetition, tiling, recursion, subdivision, packing, weaving and branching. In trying to guide the reader from simpler patterns to more complex ones, I decided that a good progression might be one that starts with patterns that are mainly 2D and leads to ones that are mainly 3D. Many design problems are 2D in nature. Whether it is finding a planar organizational solution or modifying a field of elements based on perceived site forces, 2D parametric patterns can serve as excellent sources of interesting and rigorous solutions (fig. 9). Not surprisingly, a clear separation between 2D and 3D patterns is not as clear-cut as one might predict. Many 3D parametric solutions actually start with a 2D parametric technique that then gets developed (or folded or expanded) into a 3D parametric design. For example, the geometric basis for the 2002 Serpentine Gallery Pavilion in Hyde Park, London, by Toyo Ito and Arup was a simple recursive subdivision of the square plan, repeated seven times, resulting in a spiral of truncated squares that were then extended to create the overall planar pattern. The 2D pattern lines were then folded in the third dimension, draped over each side of the pavilion and thickened to create a structural system with the desired 3D spatial complexity (fig. 10). Alternatively, 3D form can yield interesting 2D patterns as illustrated by the elegant recursive features of the double helicoidal snail staircase at the Vatican Museum (fig 11). When this 3D structure is viewed from above, it compresses into a 2D fractal pattern. We seem to be intrinsically drawn to these types of fractal growth formations that result from the iterative application of rules at different scales. It is interesting

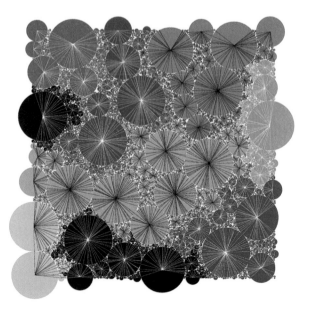

fig. 9 *Network Growth*, MATSYS
Design (Andrew Kudless).

Tea House by Yauatcha
& UniversalSHOPS in the
Serpentine Gallery Pavilion 2002
by Toyo Ito with Arup

Opening Times
8 October–5 November 2006
Thursday–Sunday
12pm–7pm

YAUATCHA
丘 轮茶苑

to note that this staircase, built in 1932, predates the discovery of the identical double helical structure of DNA. In this book, you will find discussions of patterns that blur the line between 2D and 3D. For example, the patterns for repetition and recursion both produce similar results in 2D and 3D. The discussion of subdivision includes the creation of a diagonal grid (a diagrid) as a 2D diamond-shaped pattern, as well as a 3D tessellation method for non-uniform rational b-spline surfaces (NURBS). As architects and designers, we continuously navigate between 2D and 3D representations, transforming one into the other as needed. CNC and laser cutting digital fabrication, for example, requires the flattening of 3D forms into unfolded or sectioned 2D cut patterns. These patterns, in turn, are re-assembled into physical 3D form. Therefore, I expect the reader will use the knowledge gleaned from this book to create and follow digital workflows that combine and alternate between 2D patterns and 3D constructs as needed.

fig. 10 2002 Serpentine Gallery Pavilion, Hyde Park, London, Toyo Ito and Arup.

fig. 11 Looking down the snail staircase, Vatican Museum, Rome, Italy, Giuseppe Momo.

Controller

In woodworking, one usually creates a rig that controls the construction of the desired object. For example, in order to create picture frames of different sizes, one might devise a modifiable picture frame rig (fig. 12). By modifying the parameters of the rig, different sizes of frames can be made. Parametric systems work in a very similar manner. Association allows us to create rigs that control the overall design by modifying a few of their controlling parameters. The basic concept behind the controller pattern is that it separates and clarifies the process by which the main model will change. In certain situations, a controller can be thought of as a *handle*: the main interface to the model in the same way that a door handle is the interface controller of a door. Similarly, the undulation of a NURBS surface could be changed by repositioning a few *controlling vertices* (CVs), which are interlinked with the model, but the undulation could also be controlled by changing the weight setting of those CVs. Think of the weight setting as the strength of the magnetic field of the CVs (fig. 13). In this example, the weight setting can be thought of as an independent controller that clarifies the rules by which the surface will change shape.

fig. 12 A woodworking rig that creates picture frames of different sizes.

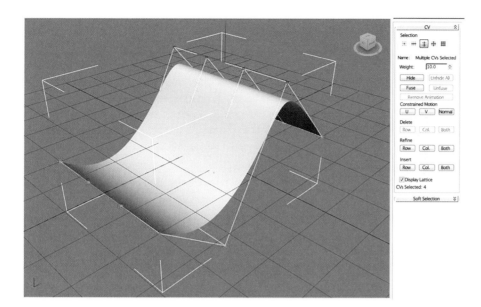

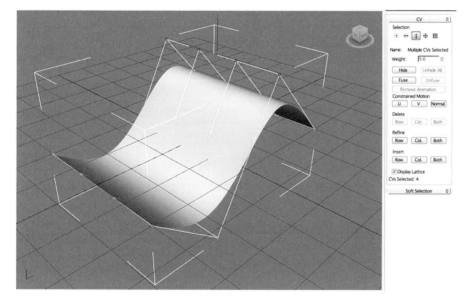

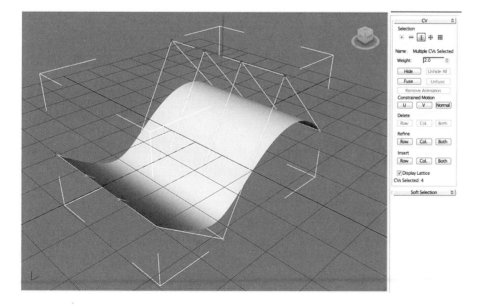

fig. 13 The effect of modifying the weight-setting controller of a set of NURBS *controlling vertices*.

TUTORIAL A PARAMETRIC CIRCLE

In this tutorial, you will create a very simple controller rig in which the location and radius of a circle is derived from the location of, and distance between, two points. (In another tutorial, we will use this whole construct of the two points and the circle as a rig that will define a radius of influence on an array of elements – but more on that later.)

Obviously, any simple CAD program can create a circle and allow you to define the location of its centre and specify the length of its radius. However, the objective of this tutorial is to introduce you to the concept of parametric association

and show you how you can build a rig to precisely control the parameters of one object through the attributes of another. The power of such rigs will become apparent later in the book. In this example, the task is to create two points, A and B, and a circle, C. The circle's centre will coincide with point A and its radius will be equal to the distance between point A and point B. The result will be a circle that will dynamically move when we move points A and B. Its centre will always follow point A while its circumference will always pass through point B.

STEP 1 CREATING THE MAIN OBJECTS

→ Start *3ds Max*. If the default configuration shows one viewport, press the **Maximize Viewport toggle** in the lower right corner to show the four viewports.

→ Press the **Create** tab, then **Helpers** and then **Point** (fig. 14).

→ Press inside the viewport titled **top** to create and locate the first point.

→ On the right side, rename the point to *Point A*.

→ Repeat the process to create a second point and name it *Point B*.

→ Press the **Create** tab, then **Shapes** and then **Circle** (fig. 15).

→ Hold the mouse button down and drag in the viewport titled **top** to create a circle.

→ On the right side, rename the circle to *Circle C*.

→ Now you should have two points and a circle in your viewport (fig. 16).

fig. 14 Creating a point.

fig. 15 Creating a circle.

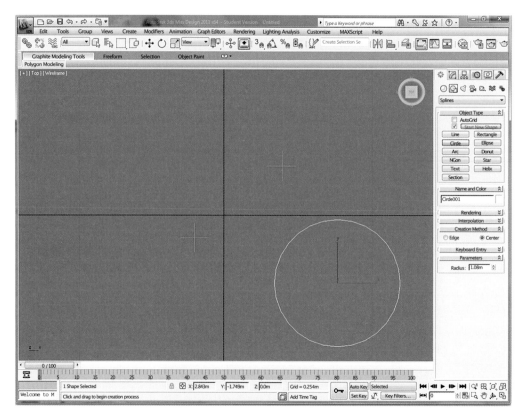

fig. 16 Two points and a circle in the viewport.

STEP 2 ASSOCIATING THE POSITION OF THE CIRCLE
WITH THE POSITION OF THE POINT

→ We now need to instruct *Circle C* to derive its position from the position of *Point A*. *3ds Max* uses the term **Parameter Wiring** for associating parameters. You can find the **Parameter Wiring** command under the **Animation** menu.

→ Press the **Select Object** button (a mouse arrow and a cube), then press on the circle in the viewport to select it.

→ Choose **Animation** → **Wire Parameters** → **Parameter Wire Dialog...** (fig. 17).

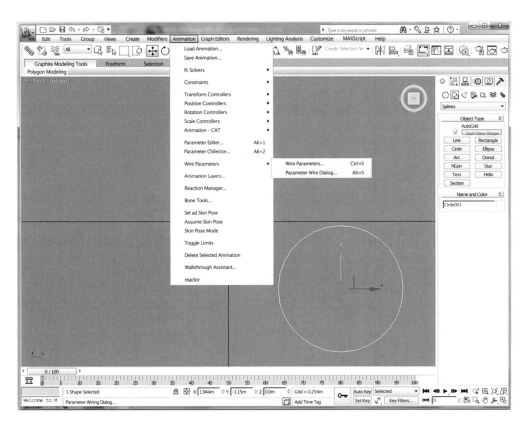

fig. 17 The Parameter Wire Dialog… menu item.

→ In the presented dialog box, in the left-hand window, locate and select the parameter titled **Position: Position XYZ** for *Circle C*. In the right-hand window locate and select the parameter titled **Position: Position XYZ** of the first of the two Points (*Point A*).

→ With both parameters selected, press on the arrow pointing from right to left (←). Then, press the button titled **Connect** (fig. 18).

→ You will now see that the circle has moved and centred itself on the first point. In order to test that this has worked, select *Point A* and move it around the screen. Verify that the circle moves along with it.

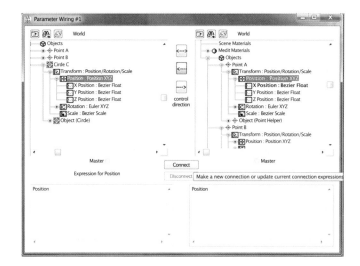

fig. 18 Wiring the parameters.

STEP 3 CREATING THE DISTANCE ATTRIBUTE

→ The next task is to compute and store the distance between the two points. *3ds Max* includes a modifier called **Attribute Holder** that can store and share custom attributes and their values. In this part of the tutorial, we will create a custom attribute called *distance* and store it in *Point B*.

→ Select *Point B* in the viewport and then press the **Modify** tab.

→ From the **Modifier List** drop down menu, under **Object-Space Modifiers**, select **Attribute Holder**.

→ Choose **Animation → Parameter Editor** (fig. 19).

→ Make sure the Parameter type is **Float**.

→ Change the name to *distance*.

→ Change the **Range To:** value to a large number (e.g. *5,000*). This will be the maximum value that this parameter can attain. Make sure it is larger than the expected maximum distance between the two points.

→ Press **Add** to add the distance attribute to *Point B*. You should see the custom attribute on the right-hand side of the interface.

→ The next step is to compute the actual value of this attribute as the distance between *Point A* and *Point B*.

→ Place your cursor inside the text field next to the word *distance* and right-click.

→ Choose **Show in Track View**.

→ In the Track View window choose **Controller → Assign** (fig. 20).

→ Choose **Float Expression** as the controller of this attribute and press **OK**. This will allow us to specify a mathematical expression (i.e. a function) that will define how this attribute is evaluated.

→ In the **Expression Controller** dialog box, next to **Name** type in *dist*, choose the **Scalar** type and press **Create**.

→ Repeat the process. Type in *posA*, choose the **Vector** type and press **Create**.

→ Type in *posB*, choose the **Vector** type and press **Create** (fig. 21).

→ From the list of vectors, select *posA* and press **Assign to Controller**.

→ From the next window find and select **Point A → Transform: Position/Rotation/Scale → Position: Position XYZ**. Press **OK**.

→ Repeat for *posB* by selecting the **Position** of *Point B* and assigning it as the controller for this variable.

→ Next, select the *dist* variable and type the following expression under the **Expression** text field:

$$\text{length(posA} - \text{posB)}$$

→ The **length** function finds the length of a vector, which in this case is the difference between *posA* and *posB*.

→ Press the **Evaluate** button. You should see on the right side of the interface that the **distance** attribute is no longer zero. It is actually the distance between *Point A* and *Point B* expressed in the default units. To experiment with this attribute, move *Point B* around the screen and verify that the distance changes accordingly.

fig. 19 Parameter Editor.

fig. 20 Track View Editor.

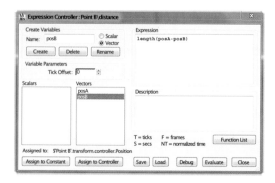

fig. 21 Expression Controller.

STEP 4 CONTROLLING THE RADIUS OF THE CIRCLE
USING THE DISTANCE ATTRIBUTE

The last step in this tutorial is to control the radius of the circle
using this **distance** attribute. To accomplish this, we will reuse the
same technique as in step 2 above, but will associate the radius of
the circle, rather than its position, to the **distance** attribute.

→ Select the circle.

→ Choose **Animation → Wire Parameters → Parameter Wire Dialog...**

→ In the presented dialog box, in the left-hand window, locate and select
the parameter titled **radius** for *Circle C*. In the right-hand window
locate and select the parameter titled **distance** of *Point B*.

→ With both parameters selected, press on the arrow pointing
from right to left (←). Then, press the **Connect** button.

→ You will now see that the circle has changed radius so that its
circumference passes through *Point B*. In order to test that this has
indeed worked, move *Point A* and *Point B* independently around the
screen and verify that the circle always stays centred on *Point A*
and its circumference always passes through *Point B* (fig. 22).

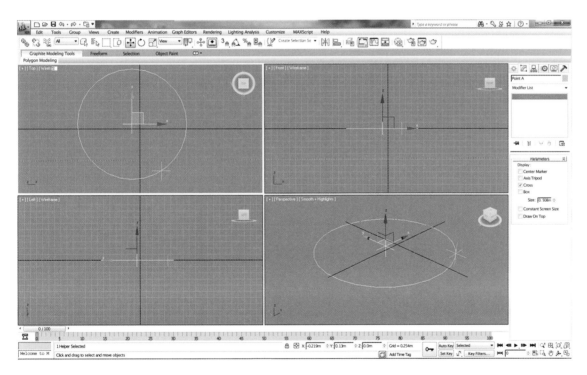

fig. 22 Parametric circle – final design.

→ Congratulations, you have created your first parametric object.
Symbolically, you have created a network of associated attributes using
direct controllers as well as computed expressions (fig. 23). Keep the
file you have created as you will need to use it for the next tutorial.

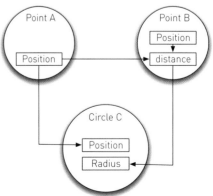

fig. 23 A symbolic view of the associated attributes.

Case study Aviva Stadium, Dublin, Ireland

Designer Populous (formerly HOK Sports Architecture)
Client LRSDC (Lansdowne Road Stadium Development Company)
Design 2005–2007
Construction 2007–2010

Aviva Stadium was designed to replace an earlier stadium located on the same site and to provide a modern facility that could accommodate 50,000 seated spectators and the home games of the Irish International Rugby and the Irish Football teams. A project requirement, from the outset, was to respect the historic site of Lansdowne Road by minimizing the impact of the new facility on surrounding buildings.

Populous (formerly HOK Sports Architecture) was commissioned for the project and it dedicated nearly two years to the planning and design of the new stadium. Their proposal consists of a flowing, organic, translucent form that they describe as 'both responsive and empathetic to the surrounding neighbourhood'. The designers did not attempt to produce a building that would formally blend in with its immediate surroundings. Instead, they sought to find a design with a contemporary geometry and language of expression that, through its transparency and flowing shape, still allowed maximum daylight to reach the surrounding built environment.

As the designers assert, the parametric design process constituted the most important aspect of the project. It allowed them to maximize the efficiency of the overall design and the refinement of the building's exterior skin, as well as ensuring a smooth collaboration between Populous and Buro Happold, the engineering firm for the project, helping to avoid errors and save time.

At the initial stages of the project's design, concepts and studies were explored through static 3D computer models implemented mainly in McNeel's *Rhinoceros* platform. The basic geometry of the building consisted of three elements: the footprint of the stadium, composed of eight tangential arcs; the plan of the inner roofline or drip line, also composed of eight tangential arcs; and a radial structural grid that eventually became the supporting system of the stadium's outer surface or skin, which functions as a façade as well as a roof.

The design of each section of the stadium's radial structural grid was particularly important

Above
General view of the stadium at night.

Opposite
View looking up at the mullion structure.

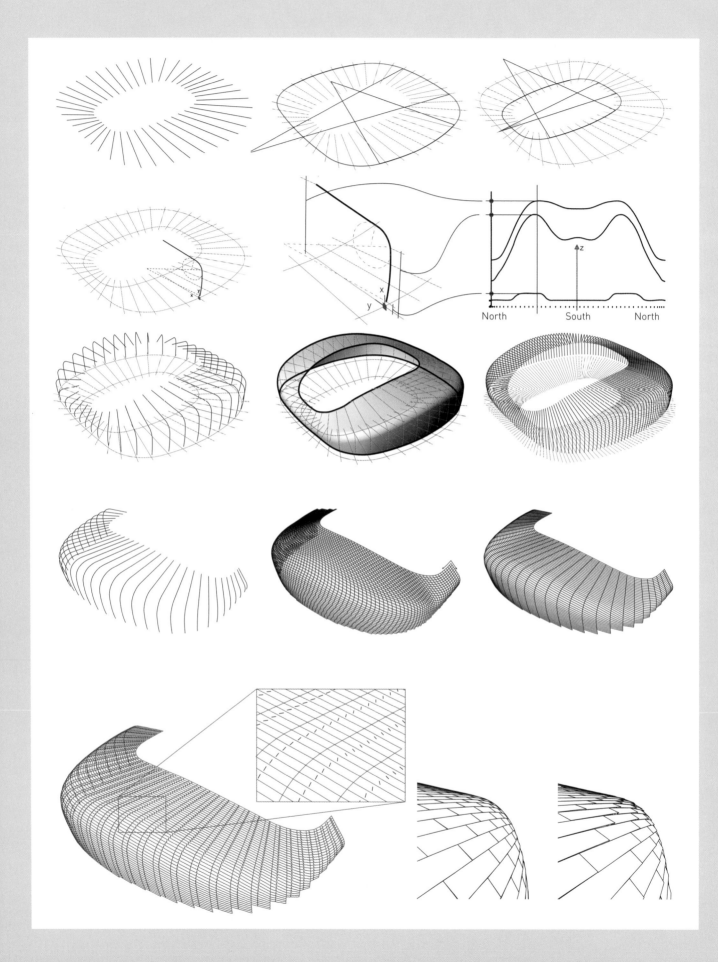

North   South   North

Opposite
Parametric development of the stadium's geometry,
structural elements and cladding system.

Right
The mullion and bracket system.

Below
The stadium under construction, showing the
attachment of the bracket to the underlying structure.

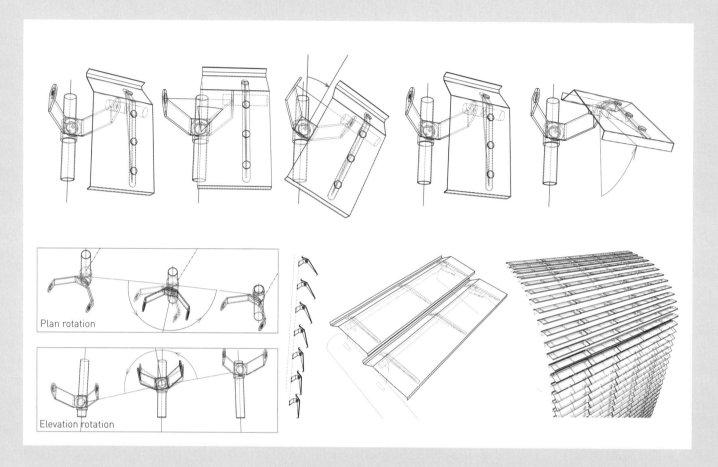

Plan rotation

Elevation rotation

because it needed to vary around the perimeter to create the overall flowing form. Each section consisted of a large, shallow arc beginning at the base of the building and composing its façade; a second, smaller and deeper arc, tangential to the first and making the transition between the façade and the roof; and, finally, a straight line also tangential to the smaller arc and functioning as the roof. The exact configuration of each of these tripartite sections had to be manipulated to correspond to the general plan of the stadium (footprint, drip line and seating bowl) and to accommodate the functional requirements of the interior.

After the initial static model was complete, the data from it were employed to build a second, parametric model using Bentley's *Generative Components* (*GC*) software. First, the coordinates of the initial *Rhinoceros* model were extracted and imported into a spreadsheet, so that they could be referenced in the *GC* model. Through this process, the form of each radial structural section could be manipulated and varied. The transfer to a parametric model was, according to the designers, 'the most critical single aspect of the … design'. It allowed the designers further aesthetic control over the overall shape of the

product and complete control over the design of the stadium's outer skin, and it also acted as the main controlling geometry for the many team members working on the project. Populous and Buro Happold agreed a common format for an *Excel* spreadsheet that would drive the solution of the structural system. Any changes to the parametric model were exported to a single spreadsheet and given to the structural engineers. The new data in the spreadsheet would then trigger automatic changes to the structural system solution, thus 'not allowing for any deviations from the base geometry to go unnoticed'.

The Aviva Stadium is an exemplary case study of a project executed during a transitional period in computer-aided design technology – one that saw a shift from static and bespoke 3D models to fully parametric and associative ones – and it demonstrates two important aspects of this shift. First, without the adoption of a fully parametric approach, Aviva Stadium and projects like it would have been more error-prone and more expensive to construct. Second, it demonstrates how parametric tools can allow designers to widen their exploration of architectural form while maintaining rigorous control over all aspects of their design proposal.

Above
A study of the mullions and brackets illustrating rotational flexibility, which accommodates various cladding conditions.

Above
The mullion and bracket system under construction.

Above right
A close-up view of the mullion and bracket system.

Below
A wide perspective view of the stadium's interior showing the undulating roofline.

Force field

A prevalent pattern in parametric design algorithms is that of the force field. When thinking about what affects the form of an object or building, it is natural to imagine the metaphor of various *forces* that are pushing and pulling on it. These vectors rhythmically change direction, shape or intensity based on their location in the force field and the presence or absence of various forces acting on them (fig. 24). As Nicholas Negroponte observed, 'Physical form is the resolution at one instant of time of many forces that are governed by rates of change.'[1] Gaudi's use of catenary curves is a prime example. A catenary curve is derived directly from the force of gravity applied to a chain when hanging under its own weight and suspended only at its ends. Linking hanging chains together creates a negotiation of forces and resulting structure that exhibits a graceful form constrained by internal topological connections and external forces acting upon it. Designers are drawn to these subtle but complex interpolations of form, which result from the application of competing force vectors. Examples can be found in rhythmic façade apertures as well as undulating surfaces.

For example, architect Jürgen Mayer-Hermann and Arup Engineering negotiated the extreme constraints of an archaeological site, an urban plaza and the need for shade in the design of their Metropol Parasol in the Plaza de la Encarnación, Seville, Spain (fig. 25). The glue-laminated structure appears as a malleable cloud-like form that has been moulded into and deformed by the forces of its surroundings. Fundamental to a successful application of forces in parametric design is the rigorous definition of the internal topological constraints of the object being acted on such that it deforms and adapts in a rich, graceful and consistent manner. Structures that have not been thus defined tend to create awkward moments and difficult and illogical details. In the next tutorial, we will create a field of circular panels that have internal constraints on their size, but are affected by an overall external force that yields a rhythmic pattern of circles with varying radii within a specified minimum and maximum dimension.

1 Negroponte, N. *The Architecture Machine*. MIT Press. 1970.

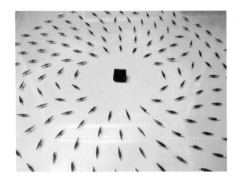

fig. 24 Magnetic field.

fig. 25 Metropol Parasol, Seville, Spain, Jürgen Mayer-Hermann and Arup Engineering.

TUTORIAL ATTRACTOR

In what has become a standard basic tutorial in parametric techniques, the attractor tutorial will show you how to build a field of circular panels that change in size based on their distance from, and the maximum radius of influence of, an attractor point. The net effect is akin to using a magnifying glass where objects near the centre of the magnifier are largest, tapering off to smaller objects at the periphery while not affecting objects that are outside the maximum radius

of influence (**fig. 26**). In order to accomplish this, we will have to define the location of the attractor point and a maximum radius of influence, and then connect that information to the size of the circle in question. The previous tutorial is a good starting point for this one, since we can reuse the parametric circle we have already created as our magnifying glass.

STEP 1 CREATING THE BASIC MODULE

→ Open your *3ds Max* file from the previous tutorial.

→ To start, we will create our basic module as a simple circle and specify its parameters. In this tutorial, we will create a circle with a radius that varies in size between 0.2 m and 1.0 m, and which has an initial default radius (*defR*) of 0.2 m. In order to change the size of the radius, we will create a multiplying factor (*mFactor*) that we will compute based on the distance between the circle and the centre of the magnifying glass. We will then multiply this factor by a specified default radius of the circle to arrive at its final radius size, *r*:

$$r = mFactor \times defR$$

→ Create a circle and define its custom attributes: a default radius, a minimum radius, a maximum radius and a multiplication factor.

→ Create a circle of radius size 1 m.

→ Add an **Attribute Holder** modifier.

→ Choose **Animation → Parameter Editor...** (or press **Alt+1**) (fig. 27)

→ Create a *minR* float attribute with a **minimum** of *0.2*, a **maximum** of *1.0* and a **default** value of *0.2*, then add it.

→ Create a *maxR* float attribute with a **minimum** of *0.2*, a **maximum** of *1.0* and a **default** value of *1.0*, then add it.

→ Create a *mFactor* float attribute with a **minimum** of *1.0*, a **maximum** of *5.0* and a **default** value of *1.0*, then add it.

→ Create a *defR* float attribute with a **minimum** of *0.2*, a **maximum** of *1.0* and a **default** value of *0.2*, then add it.

→ At this point, you should have four custom attributes stored in the **Attribute Holder** modifier of the circle object (fig. 28).

→ Click on the word **Circle** under the **Attribute Holder** modifier to examine the main parameters of the circle.

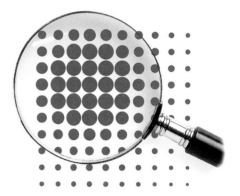

fig. 26 The concept of a magnifying glass affecting a field of circular panels.

fig. 27 Parameter Editor.

fig. 28 Attribute Holder modifier.

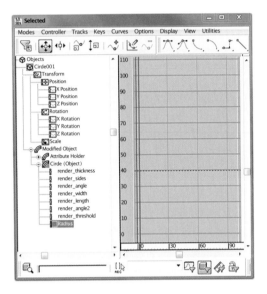

fig. 29 Track View.

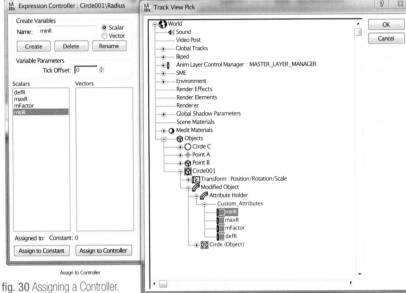

fig. 30 Assigning a Controller.

→ Right-click on the main radius value of the circle (not *defR*) and choose **Show in Track View** (fig. 29).

→ In the Track View window choose **Controller → Assign**.

→ As in the first tutorial, create four scalar variables named: *minR*, *maxR*, *mFactor* and *defR*.

→ Choose each variable in turn and press **Assign to Controller** to assign its controller. Choose from the circle object the corresponding custom attribute that you created above (e.g. assign the *minR* custom attribute to the *minR* scalar variable, etc.) (fig. 30).

We have now created four variables that derive their values from the custom attributes we had defined earlier, and which together can affect the size of the circular panel. Assuming that this panel would eventually be manufactured, we need to make sure that its size remains within a minimum and a maximum size regardless of the value of the multiplication factor. Thus we need to create a mathematical expression for the radius of the circular panel that multiplies *mFactor* by *defR* but maintains the final result between the *minR* and *maxR* values (fig. 31).

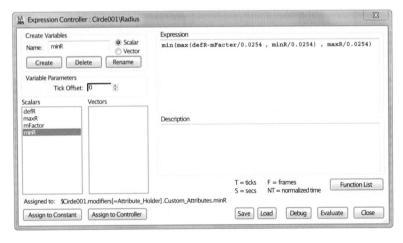

fig. 31 The Expression Controller.

TIP UNITS

Internally, *3ds Max* maps one unit of drawing measure to a known measuring unit (e.g. inch, centimetre, metre). This is different from how it handles drawing scale and input values and affects how it carries out its internal computations. In this tutorial, *3ds Max* was set to map 1 unit to 1 inch resulting in the need to divide by 0.0254 to convert to metres. If you wish to change the default unit system in *3ds Max*, choose **Customize → Units Setup** and then press the button titled **System Unit Setup**. You can then customize the system unit scale in the presented dialog box.

The mathematical expression in fig. 31 reads:

$$min(max(defR \times mFactor/0.0254 , minR/0.0254) , maxR/0.0254)$$

How was the above expression reached? Let us decode it step by step:

a. Compute an initial radius by multiplying *mFactor* by the default radius, *defR*:

$$defR \times mFactor$$

We could have stopped here and defined the radius as the result of multiplying a default value by a multiplication factor. However, the above expression has no minimum or maximum boundaries. If this were a real situation, where these are manufactured panels, we would need to limit their minimum and maximum sizes. We will do so next.

b. Compare the value of the above expression with the desired minimum radius and return the greater of the two values. This assures us that if the above expression yields a value less than the desired minimum, we then use the desired minimum value instead. The *max(arg1, arg2)* function computes the greater value of the two arguments passed to it.

$$max(defR \times mFactor , minR)$$

c. Compare the value of the above expression with the desired maximum radius and return the lesser of the two values. This assures us that if the above expression yields a value greater than the desired maximum, we then use the desired maximum value instead. The *min(arg1, arg2)* function computes the lesser value of the two arguments passed to it.

$$min(max(defR \times mFactor , minR) , maxR)$$

d. Finally, to convert the default internal *3ds Max* unit system, divide where appropriate by 0.0254.

$$min(max(defR \times mFactor/0.0254 , minR/0.0254) , maxR/0.0254)$$

At this stage, you should have your circular panel defined and appearing in the viewport next to the magnifying glass circle (fig. 32).

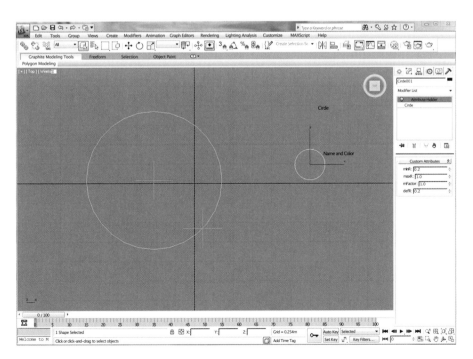

fig. 32 Magnifying glass and circular panel.

TIP CURVE EDITOR

If you want to re-examine the expression controller window of a variable and right-clicking on the value does not work, choose **Graph Editors → Track View – Curve Editor...**

STEP 2 WIRING THE CIRCULAR PANEL'S RADIUS TO ITS
DISTANCE FROM THE MAGNIFYING GLASS

The next step is to derive the radius of the circular panel, based on its distance
from the centre of the magnifying glass. The panel itself already limits how much
it can grow or shrink; we have assigned its *mFactor* attribute a minimum value
of 1 and a maximum value of 5 and, as a result, the maximum size of the panel
is 1 m (0.2 × 5.0). Therefore, we can write a mathematical expression that maps
the distance between the centre of the magnifying glass and the circular panel
to a number between 1 and 5, where 1 is the factor at the outer circumference
of the magnifying glass and 5 is the multiplication factor at its centre (fig. 33).

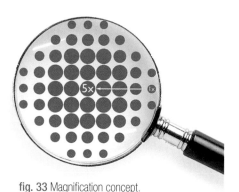

fig. 33 Magnification concept.

The mathematical expression to achieve this effect is:

$$((radius - length(posC-posMG))/radius) \times 5.0$$

$\rightarrow$ We calculate the distance from the circular panel to the centre of the magnifying
glass (*length(posC-posMG)*). We then subtract that value from the radius of the
magnifying glass and divide the result by the same radius. Finally, we multiply
the result by 5 to get us the 1x to 5x magnification that we are looking for.

$\rightarrow$ If you examine the above equation carefully, you find that, essentially, it yields
a fraction of the radius. If the circular panel is at the centre of the magnifying
glass we get a ratio of 1 (then multiplied by 5). If the distance is equal to
the radius (i.e. the circular panel is at the circumference of the magnifying
glass we get a ratio of zero. If the circular panel is outside the magnifying
glass (i.e. distance is larger than the radius) we get a negative number. We
obviously do not want a negative multiplication factor, but we are protected
from that by the fact that the *mFactor* attribute has a defined minimum value
of 1. However, you may want to pass the result of the above expression to a
max(arg1, arg2) function to limit explicitly the minimum value to 1 (fig. 34).

If you do this, the final mathematical expression then becomes:

$$max(1, ((radius - length(posC-posMG))/radius) \times 5.0)$$

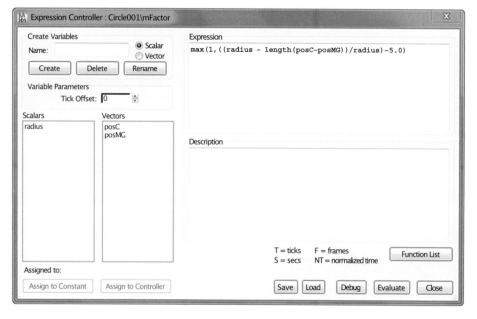

fig. 34 Expression Controller dialog box.

STEP 3 GENERATING A FIELD OF PARAMETRIC
CIRCULAR PANELS

⟶ You can now move the circular panel around and verify that it
indeed changes radius based on its distance from the centre of
the magnifying glass. You can also use the array command (**Tools
→ Array**) to create an array of circles that respond individually
and uniquely to the location of the magnifying glass (fig. 35).
Note, however, that in order for that effect to be successful you
need to create independent copies and not instances of the
original (choose the **Copy** option from the array dialog box).

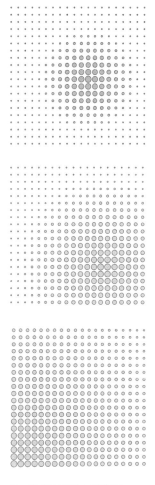

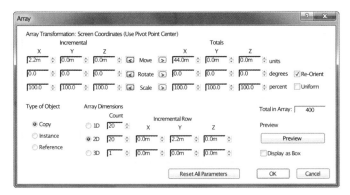

fig. 35 Array dialog box.

⟶ Once you have created an array of circular panels, you can now
move the magnifying glass around and change its radius to create
endless variations (fig. 36). Here, it is interesting to note that
although we have been creating 2D parametric patterns, the work
is readily applicable to 3D investigations and elaboration (fig. 37).

fig. 36 Parametric variations.

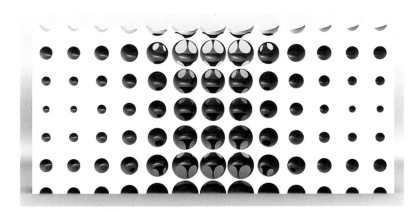

fig. 37 Boole's Lattice, Ronnie
Parsons and Gil Akos, Studio Mode,
Brooklyn, New York, USA. Boole's
Lattice is a research project with the
aim of producing a thickened screen
wall through subtractive processes that
take advantage of the movements of
a 6-axis articulated robot arm. The
geometric system utilizes multiple
series of circular volumes of different
scales within a regular box grid to
create opportunities for the penetration
of light and sight on the oblique.

Congratulations, you have created a field of modular objects that responds
dynamically to the location and size of a controlling object. You can
customize this tutorial by modifying the circular panel – try different
shapes and affect different attributes of that shape – or by investigating
how to affect the panels by more than one controlling object.

Repetition

Repetition can be thought of as the simple act of copying an element multiple times (**fig. 38**). In parametric systems, repetition can become more interesting, because a repeated element can maintain the basic topology of its predecessor without having to be exactly identical to it. Using a rule-based system, one can vary the repeated element according to any number of parameters (e.g. distance, time, location, etc.). In mathematical terms, a simple repetition could be in the form of 2, 2, 2, 2, 2 ... and so on. However, a repetition that uses the Fibonacci rule, which states that, given the first two numbers 0 and 1, any subsequent number is the sum of the two preceding numbers (0, 1, 1, 2, 3, 5, 8, 13, 21 ...), can become more interesting – and potentially more useful from a design perspective.

fig. 38 Clay tiles.

TUTORIAL FIBONACCI NUMBER GENERATOR

For this tutorial, we will use a piece of free open-source software called *Processing*. The *Processing* software is an environment for creating images, animations and interactive media. Before commencing this tutorial, you should download and install

Processing from Processing.org, and follow some of the basic examples on the Processing.org website. For this first simple tutorial, we will not draw any shapes. We will simply create an algorithm that prints out a Fibonacci sequence of numbers.

STEP 1 LISTING THE FIBONACCI SERIES

$\longrightarrow$ Start a new Sketch in *Processing* (**File $\longrightarrow$ New**)

$\longrightarrow$ Type the following text exactly in the sketch window. Any errors, misspellings or even a single missing semi-colon will make the script fail. So, be careful that you type it exactly as it is listed below (without the line numbers):

```
1    int a = 0;
2    int b = 0;
3    int fibonacci = 0;
4    int total = 14;
5    int i = 0;
6    for (i=0; i < total; i++) {
7        if (i == 0) {
8            fibonacci = 0;
9        }
10       else if(i == 1) {
11           fibonacci = 1;
12       }
13       else {
14           a = b;
15           b = fibonacci;
16           fibonacci = a + b;
17       }
18   print (fibonacci+" ");
19   }
```

$\longrightarrow$ Press the **Run** button in the top left corner of the sketch window to run this script. You should see, at the bottom of the window, the first 14 numbers of the Fibonacci series (0, 1, 1, 2, 3, 5, 8, 13, 21, 34, 55, 89, 144, 233).

Let's examine this script in detail. At the top of the script, we declare some variables that we will use in this script.

- *a* is an integer variable that will store the number prior to last in the Fibonacci series. It has an initial value of 0.

- *b* is an integer variable that will store the number prior to the current Fibonacci number. It has an initial value of 0.

- *fibonacci* is an integer variable that will store the current Fibonacci number that we are trying to compute. The first two occurrences of Fibonacci numbers are 0 and 1 respectively. After that we will compute it using the following formula: *fibonacci = a + b*.

- *total* is an integer variable that will store how many Fibonacci numbers we wish to compute.

- *i* is an integer variable that will store the current index of the Fibonacci number we are computing. Think of *i* as a counter that starts out as 0 and then increments by 1 every time we repeat the loop until it reaches *total*. Indices are useful because they tell us how many times we have repeated a loop, so we can customize the actions of the algorithm for that particular iteration.

→ Next, we create the actual loop that will repeat as long as *i* is less than *total*. In this loop *i* starts out at 0 and then is incremented by 1 at the start of each subsequent iteration through the loop.

STEP 2 DRAWING A GOLDEN RECTANGLE

If we apply the Fibonacci numbers to geometry, we can get complex shapes, such as the Fibonacci golden rectangle and the golden spiral, which is composed of circular arcs connecting the opposite corners of squares sized according to the Fibonacci numbers. The above algorithm can be easily modified to draw the golden rectangle and golden spiral. Let's start by drawing the golden rectangle. The changes are highlighted in bold below:

```
1    int a = 0;
2    int b = 0;
3    int fibonacci = 0;
4    int total = 14;
5    int i = 0;
6    size(600,400);
7    background(255,255,255);
8    fill(0,0,0,0);
9    smooth();
10   translate(384,148);
11   for (i=0; i < total; i++) {
12       if (i == 0) {
13           fibonacci = 0;
14       }
15       else if(i == 1) {
16           fibonacci = 1;
17       }
18       else {
19           a = b;
20           b = fibonacci;
21           fibonacci = a + b;
22       }
23       print (fibonacci+" ");
24       rotate(PI/2);
25       translate(b,-b);
26       rect(0,0,fibonacci, fibonacci);
27   }
```

Let's examine the script changes in detail. After the declaration of the variables as before, we specify the size of the window in which to draw the rectangle. In this case, we specified the size to be 600 pixels wide and 400 pixels high. We then specify the background to be white by specifying the maximum value (255) for the red, green and blue components of the background colour. We also specify the fill to be transparent and to draw using smooth lines and curves. Next, we shift the centre of the Cartesian coordinate system to the location (384, 148). These coordinates are specific to this example, and simply specify a good starting point for the 14 squares we are about to draw. At the bottom of the script, we actually set up the drawing. The first step is to define the rules by which we draw the next square in the Fibonacci series. The first rule is that for each square, we need to rotate the coordinate system. This is akin to manually rotating the whole piece of paper on which you are drawing. Then, we translate (i.e. move) the whole coordinate system by b in the horizontal direction and negative b in the vertical direction. If you recall, the variable b is the Fibonacci number just before the current one. Lastly, we draw a square starting at the origin of the newly rotated and translated coordinate system and with dimensions equal to those of the current Fibonacci number. The repetition of this basic procedure is what creates the golden rectangle (fig. 39).

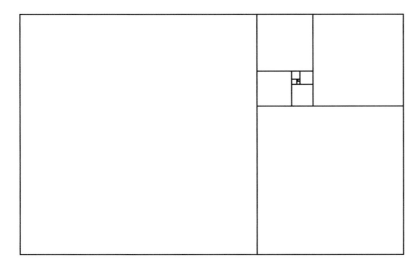

fig. 39 The golden rectangle.

STEP 3 DRAWING A GOLDEN SPIRAL

Adding the golden spiral is not difficult, but requires temporarily mirroring and moving the coordinate system before drawing the arc. The changes to the script are highlighted in bold below:

```
1    int a = 0;
2    int b = 0;
3    int fibonacci = 0;
4    int total = 14;
5    int i = 0;
6    size(600,400);
7    background(255,255,255);
8    fill(0,0,0,0);
9    smooth();
10   translate(384,148);
11   for (i=0; i < total; i++) {
12       if (i == 0) {
```

```
13        fibonacci = 0;
14    }
15    else if(i == 1) {
16        fibonacci = 1;
17    }
18    else {
19        a = b;
20        b = fibonacci;
21        fibonacci = a + b;
22    }
23    print (fibonacci+" ");
24    rotate(PI/2);
25    translate(b,-b);
26    rect(0,0,fibonacci, fibonacci);
27            scale(1,-1);
28            translate(0,-fibonacci);
29            arc(0, 0, fibonacci*2, fibonacci*2, 0, PI/2);
30            translate(0,fibonacci);
31            scale(1,-1);
32    }
```

After drawing the current square, the coordinate system is mirrored on the horizontal axis (thus the *scale(1,-1)* command), then moved by the amount *fibonacci* in the negative direction. Then a 90-degree arc is drawn at the origin of the new coordinate system, with dimensions *fibonacci**2 and from 0 to 90 degrees (90 degrees is equal to Π/2 in radians). After the arc is drawn, we need to reverse the operation we did on the coordinate system so we can continue to draw the squares at their proper location, thus we translate it back in the opposite direction and mirror it back again to get the original coordinate system before we drew the arc (**fig. 40**).

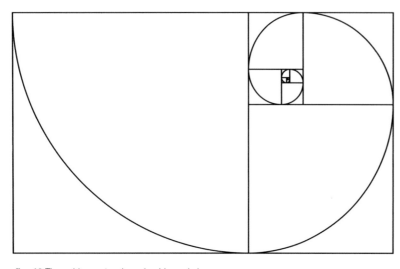

fig. 40 The golden rectangle and golden spiral.

TUTORIAL NESTED POLYGONS

For this next tutorial on repetition, we will continue to use the *Processing* software. We will create an algorithm that displays a set of 2D nested polygons using an iterative process. For each step of the iteration, the polygon to be drawn will be rotated and scaled down in size compared to the previous polygon. This will generate a spiral effect. Later in this book, we will create a similar construct, but we will use a recursive method rather than an iterative one. The defining parameters of this algorithm include the total number of polygons to draw, the number of vertices of the polygon (so we can choose to display triangles, squares, pentagons, etc.) and the degree of rotation for each iterative step, as well as the desired starting and end sizes of the polygons. It is important to note that while the basic installation of the *Processing* software does not include interactive sliders to allow the user to modify the parameters dynamically, there are several free third-party tools and libraries that can be added to *Processing* to allow that functionality. A complete version of this algorithm, which includes interactive sliders, is available from the publisher's website (fig. 41). That version uses a library called *ControlP5* that provides various user interface elements such as sliders, buttons and dials, which display within the *Processing* window and allow the user to affect the drawing interactively. Although it is beyond the scope of this

book, it is highly recommended that you install the *ControlP5* library and learn how to use it in conjunction with *Processing*. For the purposes of this simpler tutorial, any changes to the parameters will require you to modify the numbers in the code window itself and re-run the sketch to see the result.

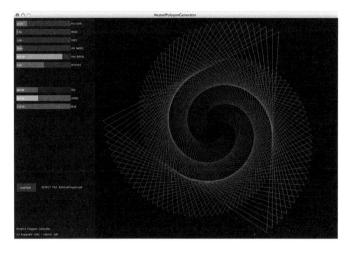

fig. 41 The full interface of the algorithm with interactive sliders for parametric variation.

⟶ Start a new Sketch in *Processing* (**File → New**)

⟶ Type the following text exactly in the sketch window. Any errors, misspellings or even a single missing semi-colon will make the script fail. So, be careful that you type it exactly as it is listed below:

```
1    int windowWidth = 950;
2    int windowHeight = 600;
3
4    int polygons;
5    float angle;
6    int vertices;
7    float minRadius;
8    float maxRadius;
9
10   void setup() {
11       size(windowWidth, windowHeight);
12       polygons = 40;
13       angle = 3.50;
14       vertices = 3;
15       minRadius = 100.0;
16       maxRadius = 300.0;
17   }
18
```

```
19      void draw () {
20          translate (width/2,height/2);
21          for(int i = 0; i<polygons; i++)
22          {
23              rotate(PI*angle/180.0);
24              drawPolygon (vertices, (float) minRadius + i*(maxRadius-minRadius)/polygons);
25          }
26      }
27
28      void drawPolygon(int numVerts, float radius) {
29          float vxorig = 0.0;
30          float vyorig = 0.0;
31          float vxa = 0.0;
32          float vya = 0.0;
33          float vxb = 0.0;
34          float vyb = 0.0;
35
36          vxorig = cos(0.0 * TWO_PI) * radius;
37          vyorig = sin(0.0 * TWO_PI) * radius;
38
39          for(int i = 0; i < (numVerts-1); i++) {
40              vxa = cos((float)i / numVerts * TWO_PI) * radius;
41              vya = sin((float)i / numVerts * TWO_PI) * radius;
42              vxb = cos((float)(i+1) / numVerts * TWO_PI) * radius;
43              vyb = sin((float)(i+1) / numVerts * TWO_PI) * radius;
44              line(vxa, vya, vxb, vyb);
45          }
46          line(vxb,vyb,vxorig, vyorig);
47      }
```

→ Press the **Run** button in the top left corner of the sketch window to run this script. A new window will open and in it you will see an image of the nested polygons (fig. 42).

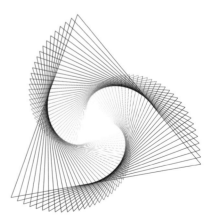

fig. 42 A series of nested triangles produced by the algorithm.

Let's examine this script in detail:

```
1        int windowWidth = 950;
2        int windowHeight = 600;
3
4        int polygons;
5        float angle;
6        int vertices;
7        float minRadius;
8        float maxRadius;
```

At the top of the script, we declare some variables that we will use in this script. These are the width and height of the display window, the number of polygons we wish to display, the angle of rotation for each polygon, the number of vertices of the polygons, and the minimum and maximum sizes (or radius) of the polygons.

```
10       void setup() {
11           size(windowWidth, windowHeight);
12           polygons = 40;
13           angle = 3.50;
14           vertices = 3;
15           minRadius = 100.0;
16           maxRadius = 300.0;
17       }
```

The setup function does exactly what the name implies. It is called by the software at the start of the execution of the code to set up the drawing window and store initial amounts in any variables we wish to use later. In this case, we have initialized the values of the various parameters for our geometric construction.

```
19       void draw () {
20           translate (width/2,height/2);
21           for(int i = 0; i<polygons; i++)
22           {
23               rotate(PI*angle/180.0);
24               drawPolygon (vertices, (float) minRadius + i*(maxRadius-minRadius)/polygons);
25           }
26       }
```

The draw function gets called repeatedly to redraw the contents of the screen. Although the image will look static (because the contents do not change), it is actually being redrawn several times a second. The draw function starts by shifting the origin of the drawing to the centre of the window (*width/2* and *height/2*). This allows us to display the polygons neatly in the centre of the window regardless of its actual width and height. The function then starts a repetitive *for loop* that repeats for exactly the number of polygons we have set. At the start of each iteration in this loop, we rotate the canvas of the drawing (imagine rotating the paper you are drawing on, rather than rotating your hand in order to draw a rotated shape more easily). Since the *rotate* function in *Processing* expects the value in radians and not in degrees, we multiply the increment by the constant *PI* (π). We then call a function, called *drawPolygon* (which we will write next), to draw a single polygon. We will examine the *drawPolygon* function in detail, but for now just assume that it draws a polygon at the specified size and rotation. At the end of this loop we would have drawn all the needed polygons, each time rotating the canvas by an angular increment just before drawing the polygon on it. We pass two values to this function: first, the number of vertices that the polygon will possess and second, the size of the polygon, calculated as the radius of an imaginary circle that circumscribes the polygon. We calculate this radius through a simple mathematical formula that incrementally increases the size with each iteration through this loop.

28	void drawPolygon(int numVerts, float radius) {
29	float vxorig = 0.0;
30	float vyorig = 0.0;
31	float vxa = 0.0;
32	float vya = 0.0;
33	float vxb = 0.0;
34	float vyb = 0.0;

The *drawPolygon* function expects to receive the number of vertices and the radius of the polygon to draw. Since the background canvas has already been rotated, *drawPolygon* only needs to draw the polygon, without worrying about rotating it. This function draws the polygon by deciding on the location of its vertices and then connecting a line between them. Since it will repeat this process for each side, we can limit the number of vertices we need to two, plus an additional two for the first vertex so that we can return to it in order to close the polygon. We start the function by assigning initial (0.0) values to all variables.

36	vxorig = cos(0.0 * TWO_PI) * radius;
37	vyorig = sin(0.0 * TWO_PI) * radius;

Using trigonometry, we can derive the *x*-coordinate of the first vertex by multiplying the cosine of the angle connecting the centre of the polygon to this first vertex by the length of the side. In this case, the result is the same as the radius, because the cosine of 0 is 1. Similarly, the sine of 0 is 0 and thus the *y*-coordinate of the first vertex is 0. Therefore, a distance of *radius* horizontally distances the first vertex from the origin along the positive *x* direction.

39	for(int i = 0; i < (numVerts-1); i++) {
40	vxa = cos((float)i / numVerts * TWO_PI) * radius;
41	vya = sin((float)i / numVerts * TWO_PI) * radius;
42	vxb = cos((float)(i+1) / numVerts * TWO_PI) * radius;
43	vyb = sin((float)(i+1) / numVerts * TWO_PI) * radius;
44	line(vxa, vya, vxb, vyb);
45	}

Next, we create another *for loop* to iterate through the number of vertices. We calculate the x-coordinate and the y-coordinate of the endpoints of the current line, using the same trigonometric formula that is explained above. We then draw a line that connects these points.

46   line(vxb,vyb,vxorig, vyorig);

47   }

The last instruction in this function, before returning to the parent algorithm, is to draw the last line back to the first vertex of the polygon in order to close it.

By modifying the parameters at the top of this algorithm you can achieve almost endless parametric variations (fig. 43).

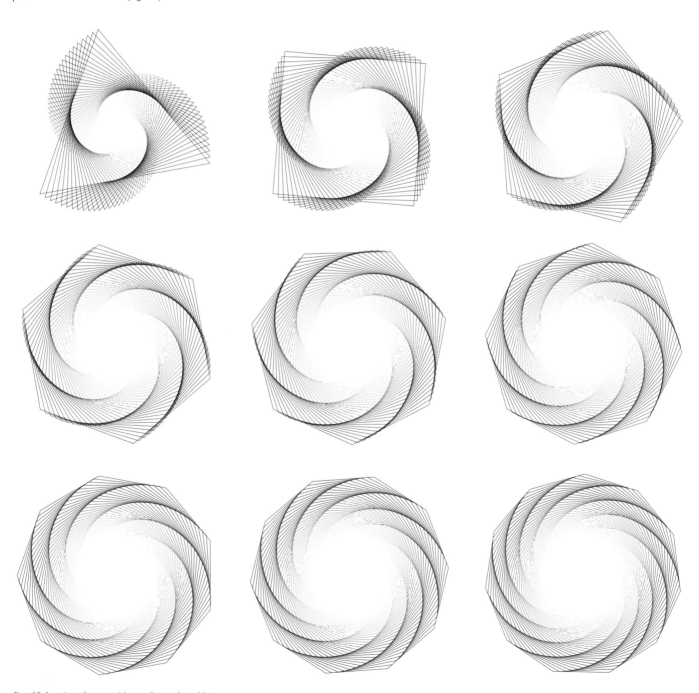

fig. 43 A series of parametric results produced by varying only the number of sides of the polygon.

Tiling

In mathematics, tiling is defined as the arrangement of identical planar shapes to completely cover a given area without overlapping (fig. 44). Thus, one can think of tiling as a natural extension of the concept of repetition, but in 2D. Often, the tiling pattern relies on an underlying grid of rows and columns. As we have seen previously, we can use loops to create repetition. In order to create a tiling pattern, we can take advantage of a nested loop (or a loop within a loop) to repeat a script that creates a single tile unit over the required number of rows but that also, within each row-creating repetition, iterates the tile unit over the required number of columns. This will result in a 2D plane of tiling units. Parametrically, any aspects of the tile can be varied as it repeats. For this introductory tutorial, however, we will specify only a few standard parameters: the size of the individual tile, the number of rows and columns, and the spacing between the tiles. In order to create a more interesting and challenging pattern, we will use a hexagonal tile as our module. The geometry of the hexagon creates a mild challenge in that as the tiles are aggregated, they need to be offset in order to match one edge of the hexagon to the other.

fig. 44 Mosaic dome interior, Nasir al-Mulk mosque, Shiraz, Iran.

TUTORIAL HEXAGONAL TILING PATTERN

In order to write a parametric script that creates a hexagonal tiling pattern, we need to understand the geometric relationship between the various elements of a hexagon (fig. 45). If you inscribe a regular hexagon in a circle with radius *r* then the length of each side of the hexagon is also equal to *r*. The interior angle of each vertex of any polygon is given by the formula: $a = ((180° \times n - 360°) / n)$ where *a* is the interior angle and *n* is the number of sides of the polygon. Thus, the interior angle of a regular hexagon is $(180° \times 6 - 360°) / 6 = 120°$. The distance *d* of the line drawn from the centre of the hexagon to the midpoint of one of its chords can be derived, using trigonometry, as $d = \cos(30°) \times r$. These simple geometric relationships will help us compute the location of hexagonal tiles as we loop through the rows and columns of the tiling pattern.

Horizontally, the distance between each tile is $r + r/2 = 1\frac{1}{2}\,r$. Vertically, the distance between each tile is $2d$, but additionally, the algorithm to generate the hexagonal tiles will need to offset the tiles vertically by *d* on alternating columns (fig. 46). We can test if the column we are drawing is an even or odd-numbered one to either include or exclude this additional offset.

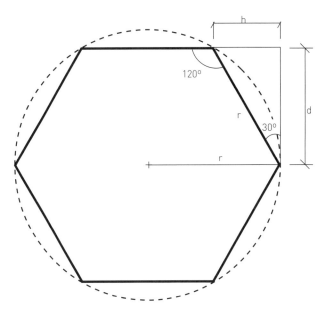

fig. 45 The geometry of a regular hexagon inscribed in a circle.

STEP 1 CREATING A BASIC HEXAGONAL GRID

We now have all the information we need to write the script to generate the basic hexagonal tiling pattern. Open *3ds Max*, save and close prior scenes, create a new empty scene and choose **MAXScript** → **New Script** from the top menu. In the script window that opens, type the following basic algorithm:

```
1   radius = 20.0
2   columns = 5
3   rows = 5
4   offset = (cos 30)*radius
5   for i = 0 to (columns - 1) do
6   (
7        for j = 0 to (rows - 1) do
8        (
9             hex = Ngon radius:radius nsides:6 scribe:1 pos:[0,0,0]
10            case of
11            (
12                 (mod i 2 == 0) : move hex[(i*1.5*radius), ((j*2*offset) + offset), 0]
13                 (mod i 2 != 0) : move hex[(i*1.5*radius), (j*2*offset), 0]
14            )
15        )
16  )
```

→ Save your script and then choose **Tools** → **Evaluate All** to run the script. You should see a hexagonal grid made out of 25 hexagons. Let's take a closer look at the script:

HEXAGONAL TILING PATTERN/CONTINUED

The first few lines define the variables we will use to construct the grid: radius, columns, rows and the offset, as discussed earlier. Next, we create two nested loops. The outer loop generates the columns while the inner loop generates the rows for each column. A hexagon, stored in the variable called *hex*, is created using the *Ngon* command with 6 specified as the number of sides (*nsides*), inscribed in a circle by specifying 1 as the value of the *scribe* parameter and positioned initially at [0,0,0]. Next, we test if the variable *i* (i.e. the current column) is even or odd. The modulo operation, *mod*, computes the remainder after a number is divided by another number. In this case, if the remainder after division by 2 is not 0 then that means that the number is odd. If the remainder is 0 then the number is even. Based on this test (using the *case of* syntax) one of the two move operations is carried out. If you look closely at the *x* (horizontal) and *y* (vertical) coordinates for the move operation, they are the same as those depicted in the hexagonal tiling figure below (fig. 46), with the additional offset amount applied to alternating columns. For each tile, we have to multiply the *x* and *y* offset distance by the number of the current row and current column to get the correct overall offset distance (i.e. if the *x* and *y* spacing between tiles should be 10 mm, then the tile at the fifth column and second row should be positioned at *x* = 50 mm and *y* = 20 mm.

While the above algorithm achieves the basic functionality, it is cumbersome to use: to generate a new hexagonal grid, one has to change the values manually, erase the current geometries and re-evaluate the script. One main advantage of parametric systems is their ability to generate alternatives quickly and fluidly. Another advantage is that once you set the parameters, some of the generated alternatives could be unanticipated and positively surprise you. If you can predict all the possible iterations, then the parametric system is hardly informative. In this particular case, adding an additional spacing amount to further separate the hexagons, or overlapping them by using a negative spacing amount, could yield some interesting results. The spacing factor needs a bit of attention, as it is easy to assume that it should be the perpendicular distance between the edges of the hexagons, rather than the horizontal and vertical offset the algorithm actually requires. Using the Pythagorean theorem regarding the relationship between the three sides of a right-angled triangle, we can derive the desired horizontal offset as follows: $a^2 + (s/2)^2 = s^2$; thus $a = s\sqrt{0.75}$ (fig. 47). You will find this applied in the expanded algorithm in the following script.

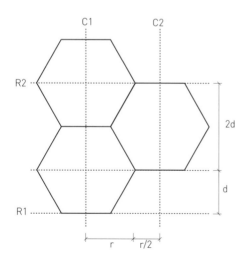

fig. 46 The tiling distances for creating edge-to-edge hexagonal tiling.

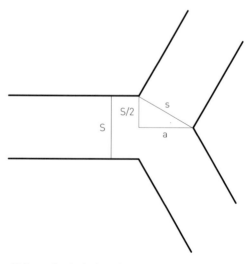

fig. 47 Computing the horizontal and vertical offsets for additional spacing between the tiles.

STEP 2 CREATING A PARAMETRIC HEXAGONAL GRID

→ To make our hexagonal grid parametric, we need to enhance the above script.
First, we need to add an additional parameter (to be called *spacing*). Then, we
need to create an interface that presents the desired parameters to the user,
who can then view different alternatives in real time by changing the values of the
parameters. This can be achieved simply in *3ds Max* by creating a utility script
with a rollout user interface. We can encapsulate the above basic algorithm
in a function that is called upon when the interface reports back that the user
has changed the value of a certain parameter. In order to update the hexagonal
grid fluidly, the function should erase the grid and redraw it with the new
parameters. On modern computers, this happens so quickly that the resulting
effect is that of instantaneous change. The expanded script is found below:

```
1    utility Hexagons "Hexagons"
2    (
3        global radius = 20.0
4        global spacing = 0
5        global rows = 5
6        global columns = 5
7        global myHexagons = #() -- an array of hexagons
8
9        -- This function erases the previous grid and creates a new one.
10       fn generateHexagons =
11           (
12               -- Empty the myHexagons array and delete all the hexagons in it.
13               hexCount = myHexagons.count
14               for i = 1 to hexCount by 1 do
15                   (
16                       tobedeleted = myHexagons[1]
17                       deleteItem myHexagons 1
18                       if(isDeleted tobedeleted != true) then
19                           (
20                               delete tobedeleted
21                           )
22                   )
23               myHexagons.count = 0
24
25               offset = (cos 30)*(radius) + (spacing / 2.0)
26
27               for i = 0 to (columns - 1) by 1 do
28                   (
29                       for j = 0 to (rows - 1) by 1 do
30                           (
31                               hex = Ngon radius:radius nsides:6 scribe:1 pos:[0,0,0]
32                               hex.wirecolor = white
33                               case of
34                                   (
```

```
35              (mod i 2 == 0) : move hex [(i*((radius*1.5) + (spacing * (sqrt 0.75)))), ((j*2*offset) + offset), 0]

36              (mod i 2 != 0) : move hex [(i*((radius*1.5) + (spacing * (sqrt 0.75)))), (j*2*offset), 0]

37                    )

38              append myHexagons hex

39                 )

40              )

41           )

42

43     -- Create the User Interface

44

45     spinner radius_spinner "Radius: " range:[1,5000,radius]  type:#WorldUnits

46     spinner spacing_spinner "Spacing: " range:[-5000,5000,spacing] type:#WorldUnits

47     spinner rows_spinner "Rows: " range:[0,5000, rows] type:#integer

48     spinner columns_spinner "Columns: " range:[0,5000, columns] type:#integer

49     button generate_button "Generate" enabled:true

50

51     on radius_spinner changed amt do -- when spinner value changes...

52        (

53           radius = amt

54           generateHexagons()

55        )

56

57     on spacing_spinner changed amt do -- when spinner value changes...

58        (

59           spacing = amt

60           generateHexagons()

61        )

62

63     on rows_spinner changed amt do -- when spinner value changes...

64        (

65           rows = amt

66           generateHexagons()

67        )

68

69     on columns_spinner changed amt do -- when spinner value changes...

70        (

71           columns = amt

72           generateHexagons()

73        )

74

75     on generate_button pressed do
```

76	(
77	generateHexagons()
78	)
79	)
80	-- end of utility

$\longrightarrow$ Save your script and then choose **Tools → Evaluate All** to run the script. The actual interface can be found by clicking on the utilities icon (the hammer), then by clicking on the **MAXScript** button and choosing the **Hexagons** utility from the Utilities menu in the **MAXScript** rollout that appears. You can experiment with various values to the parameters to generate interesting hexagonal tiling patterns (fig. 48).

fig. 48 Different parametric hexagonal tiling patterns generated by the same script using positive and negative spacing.

Case study RK4 Tiles, New York, USA

Designer Studio Mode (Ronnie Parsons and Gil Akos)
Client Private Commission
Design and Construction 2010

Left
A single RK4 tile made of highly reflective polyurethane.

Opposite
Close-up view of the RK4 tile showing its flowing plasticity.

Studio Mode, a Brooklyn, New York research and design studio, is actively engaged in the employment of digital technologies in order to investigate form-making. The studio defines its main focus as 'material and the processes by which it is formed and informed'. Their projects constitute formal explorations of broader, long-standing issues in architectural theory, which are now enhanced by the new potentials of the computer. In their diPloids project, for example, they used a single, flexible shape as a stitching or weaving unit to produce multiple iterations of a new architectural skin iconography. In their ParaGrove installation, the studio investigated the technique of stitching as both a design tool and a methodology for creating a contemporary interpretation of the relationship between structure, surface and enclosure. Here we will make a more detailed reference to their RK4 Tiles. In this project, the studio focused on the implementation of a new surface

iconography based on the digital manipulation of a traditional tiling pattern, called Cairo tessellation. The tiles designed by the studio were used to compose a relief panel for a residential entry foyer, in which the original pattern of the Cairo tiling is also maintained, but only as a geometric background.

For the design of the tiles, the firm began with a 30-degree tilted square grid that underwent four stages of tessellation. The result was a grid of irregular pentagons that maintained the topology of the original tiles. The studio identified five focal points on each pentagon, inspired by the pattern of the Cairo tiling, and applied a network of curvilinear streamlines – a visualization of flows – between those points. The pattern that was produced in this manner visually suggested a 3D interpretation of the original 2D floral pattern of the Cairo tiles. The designers took advantage of this quality to produce tiles with a surface that embodied both the flowing plasticity and

Above
Segmentation of the pattern into pentagonal tiles.

Below
Derivation of the curvilinear streamlines based
on an underlying Cairo tessellation pattern.

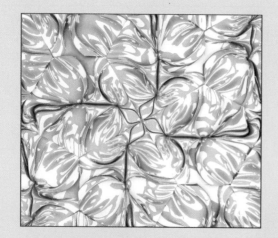

the sculptural quality of the streamlines. The
choice of the focal points was instrumental in
making possible the surface continuity across
the edge of the tiles and thus turning the 2D
pattern of the streamlines into a fluid, 3D relief
that moves seamlessly across the tiles.

Using a computer model that was built
according to the process described above, they
were able to accurately calculate the cross-
section profile of the designed tiles and therefore
the exact form of their 3D surface. Based on
this model, a positive milled mould was made
using CNC equipment and was then employed
to produce a silicon negative mould. In the final
stage of the process, the silicon negative mould
facilitated the production of the final tiles. These

final tiles are made from polyurethane and they
possess a highly reflective, undulating surface that
lacks any classical geometric clarity or symmetry,
but which echoes the repetitive geometry of
the traditional Cairo tile. In the final product,
the geometric essence of the Cairo tile pattern
has been morphed into a freer, more seductive
form, which extends into the third dimension.

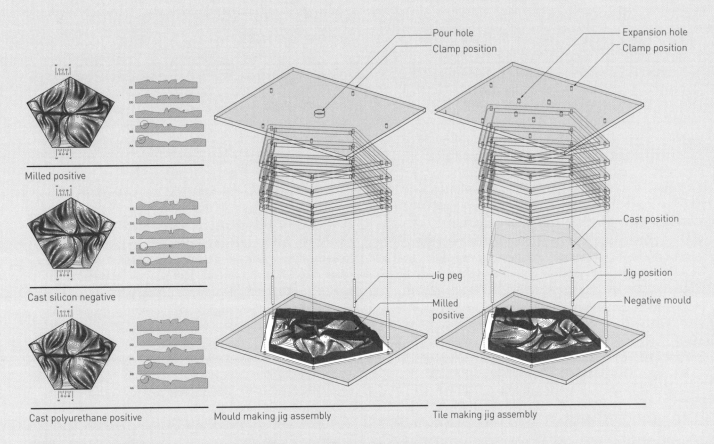

Milled positive

Cast silicon negative

Cast polyurethane positive

Mould making jig assembly

Tile making jig assembly

Pour hole
Clamp position

Expansion hole
Clamp position

Cast position

Jig peg

Jig position

Milled positive

Negative mould

Above
A set of drawings illustrating the process of digitally fabricating and assembling the mould for pouring the polyurethane tiles.

Below
Measured elevation drawing of the full panel of tiles.

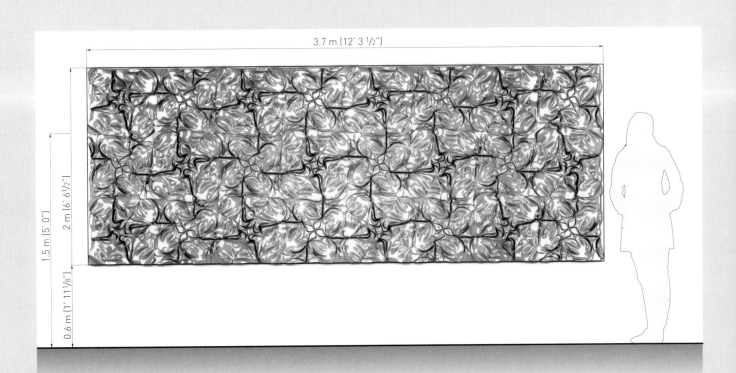

3.7 m (12' 3 ¹/₂")

2 m (6' 6¹/₂")

1.5 m (5' 0")

0.6 m (1' 11¹/₈")

Recursion

Recursion is a special case of repetition in which the repetition is achieved by having a process call upon *itself* to generate the next iteration. Formally, recursion is defined as the process of repeating items in self-similar ways. A Menger sponge is a classic example of a mathematical construct that exhibits clear recursion. A Menger sponge, named after Karl Menger who described it in 1926, is said to have an infinitely large surface area while simultaneously and paradoxically enveloping a null volume. To create a Menger sponge, you start with a cube. You then subdivide this cube into 27 identical smaller cubes (9 squares on each side). You then delete the cube at the very centre of its parent cube as well as the six cubes that occupy the centre of each of the faces of the parent cube. This creates a hollow 3D cross shape in the centre of the parent cube. Then, you recursively apply the above steps to each of the remaining 20 smaller cubes as many times as you wish. This recursive operation results in the characteristic self-similar pattern of a Menger sponge (fig. 49). Fractals are another classic example of recursion; the propagation of this kind of pattern depends on the same action being performed on the root pattern, on all its descendants, on all their descendants and so on (fig. 50). For example, if a pattern calls for creating a second

square that is half the size of the original square, then at the next iteration, the newly generated square would be half of the size of the one that preceded it and thus one quarter of the size of its *grandparent* square. In nature, the recursive pattern is usually distorted and limited by the environment in which it is taking place. As the pattern repeats, it parametrically takes into consideration the conditions of the parent pattern as well as the forces of nature operating on it, as seen in the Brassica Romanesco plant (fig. 51). However, in an ideal situation where the recursive function can continue unhindered, we can imagine infinitely small or infinitely large self-similar patterns. Thinking of the metaphor of the branching hierarchy of a family tree or the nesting of Russian *matryoshka* dolls is useful in understanding how recursion works algorithmically (fig. 52). One important step in writing a recursive algorithm is to always specify a limiting factor lest the function recursively repeat itself an infinite amount of times. The algorithm would thus never stop and never yield a result and would have to be interrupted. This limiting factor could be in the form of testing the size of the pattern to be generated (i.e. defining a minimum size), the total number of generated elements or the level of recursion that has taken place thus far (i.e. defining a maximum number of recursive iterations).

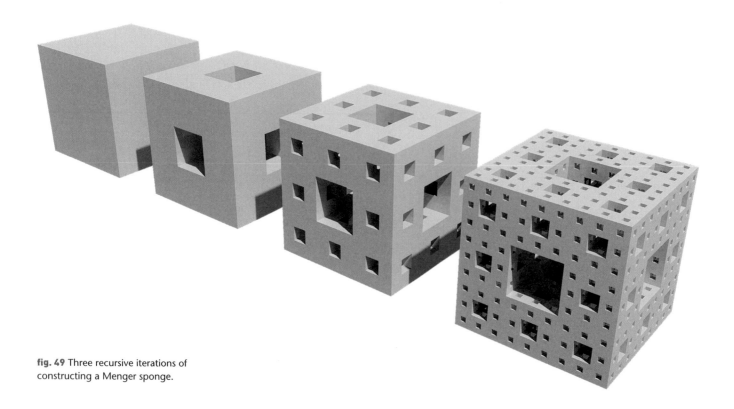

fig. 49 Three recursive iterations of constructing a Menger sponge.

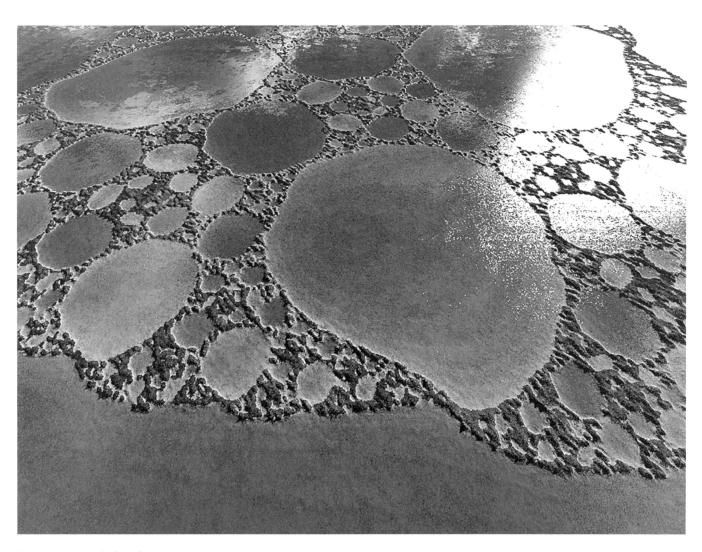

fig. 50 A Magnet Julia fractal
set rendered as a landscape.

fig. 51 The Brassica
Romanesco plant.

fig. 52 Russian *matryoshka* dolls.

TUTORIAL NESTED GEOMETRY

In this introductory tutorial, we will create a simple recursive function that starts with an initial geometry – in this case a box – which is then copied, rotated and scaled. This process is recursively repeated to build a helical form. This algorithm can be easily converted into an interactive and parametric *3ds Max* utility, following the same procedure as step 2 of the tutorial to create a hexagonal tiling pattern (see page 61).

→ To start, open *3ds Max*, save and close any prior scenes, create a new empty scene and choose **MAXScript** → **New Script** from the top menu. In the script window that opens, type the following basic algorithm:

```
1   resetMaxFile #noPrompt
2   level = 1
3   parentBox = box width:100 length:100 height:10
4   fn createChild arg currentLevel =
5   (
6       if currentLevel < 50 then
7       (
8           child = copy arg
9           child.width = (arg.width)*0.95
10          child.length = (arg.length)*0.95
11          child.height = (arg.height)*0.95
12          child.pos.z = arg.pos.z + arg.height
13          rot = eulerangles 0 0 3.5
14          rotate child rot
15          currentLevel = currentLevel + 1
16          child.parent = arg
17          createChild child currentLevel
18      )
19  )
20  createChild parentBox level
```

→ Save your script and then choose **Tools** → **Evaluate All** to run the script. You should see a helical form made of 50 boxes (fig. 53).

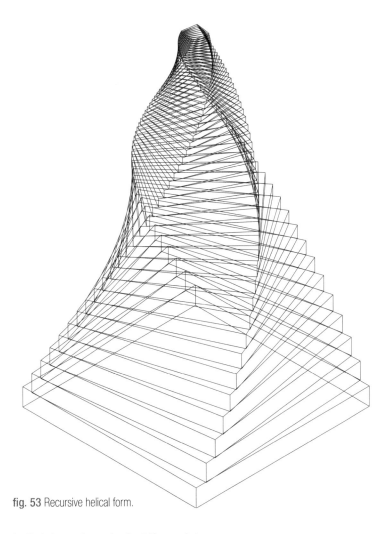

fig. 53 Recursive helical form.

Let's take a closer look at the script:

The first step is to reset *3ds Max*. This step erases all existing objects and resets *3ds Max*, so be careful not to have any prior scene objects that you wish to keep. Next, we create a variable called *level* to store the current level of recursion. We will use this variable as the limiting factor for our recursion. At the start of each recursive iteration, we will add 1 to this variable and then test whether it has reached a pre-defined maximum. If it has, then we will stop the algorithm at that level. Then we create the initial geometry that will be copied. In this case, it is a simple box of dimensions 100 x 100 x 10. Next, the recursive function, *createChild*, is defined. This function accepts two arguments: the first, called *arg*, is the geometry to be copied. This geometry will be updated for each consequent iteration. The second argument is the current recursion level. We will use that variable to stop the recursion. In this function, we have chosen to execute it only if the recursion level is less than 50. The actual function is simple: it copies *arg* into a new geometry, scales it down by 5%, lifts it up to sit on top of the prior geometry and rotates it by 3.5°. The recursion level is then incremented by 1. The next (optional) step is to link the child object to its parent by setting the parent attribute of the new geometry to be *arg*. This step makes it easy to drag the final result in *3ds Max* as if it is a single geometry. It creates a chain link from the topmost box of the helical form to the lowest one at its base. The actual recursion happens at the last step, where the function calls itself, but with the newly created child object and the new recursion level. The whole procedure is kick-started at the last line of the code, by calling *createChild* with the original parent object and a level of 1.

TUTORIAL SIMPLE FRACTALS

In this slightly more advanced tutorial, we will write a recursive function that creates square-shaped fractal geometry. It starts with an initial geometry – in this case a box – that is then propagated into four smaller *children* boxes to be placed at the four corners of the parent box (**fig. 54**). The operation is then recursively repeated on each of these four boxes.

However, the second and subsequent iterations pose a slight problem. If not modified, the rule would result in one of the three boxes being embedded inside its *grandparent* box (**fig. 55**). Thus, for each of the four boxes, we need to test for intersection with the grandparent box and, if true, we need to delete the intersecting grandchild box.

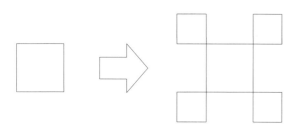

fig. 54 Initial propagation rule.

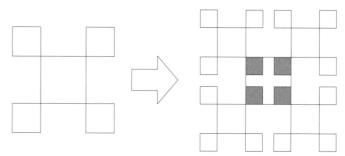

fig. 55 Second recursive iteration rule.

→ Open *3ds Max*, save and close any prior scenes, create a new empty scene and choose **MAXScript → New Script** from the top menu. In the script window that opens, type the following algorithm:

```
1    resetMaxFile #noPrompt
2    myLevel = 1
3    global rootBox = box width:20 length:20 height:10
4
5    fn intersect newBox rBox =
6    (
7        result = false
8
9        if(rBox == undefined) then
10       (
11           return false
12       )
13
14       if(newBox == undefined) then
15       (
16           return false
17       )
18       d1 = distance newBox.pos rBox.pos
19       d2 = (newBox.width)*0.5 + (rBox.width)*0.5
20       if(d1 < d2) then
21       (
22           result = true
23       )
24       return result
```

```
25   )
26
27   fn createChildren arg currentLevel =
28   (
29       if currentLevel < 6 then
30       (
31           child01 = copy arg
32           child01.width = (arg.width)*0.5
33           child01.length = (arg.length)*0.5
34           child01.height = (arg.height)*0.75
35           child01.pos.x = arg.pos.x + (arg.width)*0.75
36           child01.pos.y = arg.pos.y + (arg.length)*0.75
37
38           result01 = intersect child01 arg.parent
39           if (result01 == false) then
40           (
41               child01.parent = arg
42           )
43           else
44           (
45               delete child01
46           )
47
48           child02 = copy arg
49           child02.width = (arg.width)*0.5
50           child02.length = (arg.length)*0.5
51           child02.height = (arg.height)*0.75
52           child02.pos.x = arg.pos.x - (arg.width)*0.75
53           child02.pos.y = arg.pos.y + (arg.length)*0.75
54
55           result02 = intersect child02 arg.parent
56           if (result02 == false) then
57           (
58               child02.parent = arg
59           )
60           else
61           (
62               delete child02
63           )
64
65           child03 = copy arg
66           child03.width = (arg.width)*0.5
67           child03.length = (arg.length)*0.5
```

```
68          child03.height = (arg.height)*0.75
69          child03.pos.x = arg.pos.x + (arg.width)*0.75
70          child03.pos.y = arg.pos.y - (arg.length)*0.75
71
72          result03 = intersect child03 arg.parent
73          if (result03 == false) then
74          (
75                  child03.parent = arg
76          )
77          else
78          (
79                  delete child03
80          )
81
82          child04 = copy arg
83          child04.width = (arg.width)*0.5
84          child04.length = (arg.length)*0.5
85          child04.height = (arg.height)*0.75
86          child04.pos.x = arg.pos.x - (arg.width)*0.75
87          child04.pos.y = arg.pos.y - (arg.length)*0.75
88
89          result04 = intersect child04 arg.parent
90          if (result04 == false) then
91          (
92                  child04.parent = arg
93          )
94          else
95          (
96                  delete child04
97          )
98
99          currentLevel = currentLevel + 1
100         for i = 1  to arg.children.count by 1 do
101         (
102                 createChildren arg.children[i] currentLevel
103         )
104     )
105 )
106
107 createChildren rootBox myLevel
```

$\rightarrow$ Save your script and then choose **Tools** $\rightarrow$ **Evaluate All** to run the
script. You should see a fractal form made of many boxes (fig. 56).

 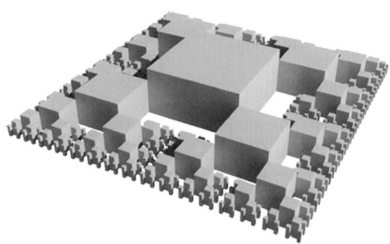

fig. 56 The recursion script is used to create an imaginary fractal city.

Let's take a closer look at the script:

1	resetMaxFile #noPrompt
2	myLevel = 1
3	global rootBox = box width:20 length:20 height:10

The first step is to reset *3ds Max*. This step erases all existing objects and resets *3ds Max* so be careful not to have any prior scene objects that you wish to keep. Next, we create a variable called *myLevel* to store the current level of recursion. We will use this variable as a limiting factor for our recursion. At the start of each recursive iteration, we will add 1 to this variable and then test if it has reached a pre-defined maximum. If it has, then we will stop the algorithm at that level. Then, we create the initial geometry that will be copied. In this case, it is a simple box of dimensions 20 x 20 x 10.

5	fn intersect newBox rBox =
6	(
7	result = false
8	
9	if(rBox == undefined) then
10	(
11	return false
12	)
13	
14	if(newBox == undefined) then
15	(
16	return false
17	)
18	d1 = distance newBox.pos rBox.pos

19	d2 = (newBox.width)*0.5 + (rBox.width)*0.5
20	if(d1 < d2) then
21	(
22	result = true
23	)
24	return result
25	)

The *intersect* function accepts two arguments (*newBox* and *rBox*). The function returns *true* if the two boxes intersect and *false* if they do not. If either of the two boxes is undefined for any reason, it also returns *false*. Next, it carries out a simplified intersection test that compares the distance between the centroids of the boxes (*d*) to the sum of half of their widths (*(w1 + w2) /2*). While not a true intersection test, we can use this simplified method to determine if the box lies inside its grandparent box, because in this case, *d* will always be less than *(w1 + w2) /2* (fig. 57).

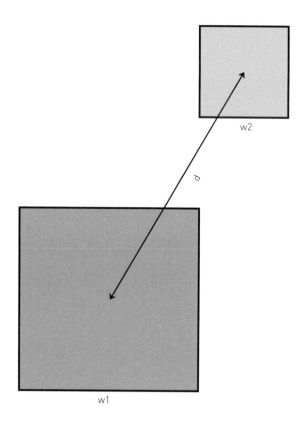

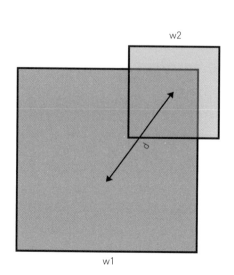

d > (w1 + w2) / 2 => Boxes do not intersect

d < (w1 + w2) / 2 => Boxes do intersect

fig. 57 A simplified intersection test.

```
27   fn createChildren arg currentLevel =
28   (
29        if currentLevel < 6 then
30        (
31            child01 = copy arg
32            child01.width = (arg.width)*0.5
33            child01.length = (arg.length)*0.5
34            child01.height = (arg.height)*0.75
35            child01.pos.x = arg.pos.x + (arg.width)*0.75
36            child01.pos.y = arg.pos.y + (arg.length)*0.75
37
38            result01 = intersect child01 arg.parent
39            if (result01 == false) then
40            (
41                child01.parent = arg
42            )
43        else
44            (
45                delete child01
46            )
```

The *createChildren* function is the recursive function that creates four children boxes at each corner of the box it receives through the *arg* argument. It will only execute its code if the current recursion level (*currentLevel*) is less than 6. Thus, it will create a maximum of 5 levels of recursion. A child (*child01*) is created as a copy of the current *arg* box, reduced in size, and placed at a corner vertex. Once it is created, the simplified intersection test is called in order to determine whether the child box intersects its grandparent (i.e. the parent of the *arg* box). If the intersection test returns *false*, then the *arg* box is defined as the parent of the child. Otherwise, the child is deleted. This process is repeated for the other three boxes.

```
99            currentLevel = currentLevel + 1
100           for i = 1  to arg.children.count by 1 do
101           (
102               createChildren arg.children[i] currentLevel
103           )
```

After the four children have been created (one always having been deleted because it intersected its grandparent, leaving three new boxes), the current recursion level is incremented by 1. Next, we loop through the newly created children of *arg* and, for each of them, we recursively call the *createChildren* function to create three more children, and so on.

```
107   createChildren rootBox myLevel
```

The recursive cycle is actually started at the very last line of code where the *createChildren* is called with the initial central box (*rootBox*) and a level of 1 (*myLevel*).

Case study Genetic Stair, Upper West Side, New York, USA

Designer Caliper Studio, Brooklyn, New York, USA
Client Private Commission
Design and Construction 2009

The Genetic Stair was designed to be the centrepiece of a renovated apartment and art gallery in New York's Upper West Side. The goal was to create a slender stair that would only be supported at the bottom and top, and that would turn three times to climb 4.6 m. The design required a rethinking of both the design process and the role of the architect.

At the beginning of the process, agreed design details and their limiting factors became the driving geometric constraints for the stair's overall parametric model. Custom software was created and integrated with McNeel's *Rhinoceros 3D* software to generate potential arrangements

for the stainless-steel hollow pipes and solid rods that formed the structural latticework under the stair. The candidate solution was then passed, as a series of centrelines, to a structural finite elements analysis (FEA) system. The customized software used the FEA results within a genetic algorithm to 'breed' strong members and remove weaker ones. The final form of the stair was reached after several iterations of this analysis of the structural performance of members, which selected strong ones and eliminated weaker ones while adhering to strict fabrication constraints.

With this process, the architectural team was able to remove the design and fabrication

Above
Genetic Stair within the space.
Photograph © Ty Cole.

Opposite
Approach from below.
Photograph © Ty Cole.

makeFirstGeneration Creates one generation of completely random stair configurations.

RHINO 4.0 + RhinoScript

- **DO** until number of individuals reached
  - **DO** until allowable number of rods reached
    - **addRandomRod**
      Adds random diaganol element that meets predetermined fabrication constraints and does not intersect previously created elements.
  - **LOOP** until allowable number of rods reached

  - **exportTextFile**
    Converts software-specific 3D information into nodes, connections and material identities. Writes data to a newly created text file.
- **LOOP** until number of individuals reached

TEXT FILES DESCRIBING GEOMETRIC AND MATERIAL INFO FOR EACH INDIVIDUAL IN GENERATION

---

evaluateStairConfigurations Imports text files and evaluates configurations for structural performance.

CADRE Lite 3.2 + VBscript

- **FOR EACH** stair configuration in generation
  - **importStairConfiguration**
    Converts text-based node and connection data to 3D geometry.
  - **applyMaterials**
    Assigns material properties (strength, stiffness, etc.) to 3D members.
  - **FOR EACH** node in structural model
    - **constrainNode**
      Assigns degrees of freedom, including completely fixed connections at the top and bottom.
    - **applyLoads**
      Assigns units of force acting on node due to dead weight and live load.
  - **NEXT** node in structural model

  - **solveModel**
    Performs finite element analysis on fully constrained and loaded 3D model.
  - **exportResults**
    Writes results of finite element analysis to separate text files.
- **NEXT** stair configuration in generation

TEXT FILES DESCRIBING STRUCTURAL PERFORMANCE OF EACH INDIVIDUAL IN GENERATION

---

makeNextGeneration Creates a new generation based on weighted selection of genetic material.

RHINO 4.0 + RhinoScript

- **DO** until number of individuals reached
  - **importStair_1**
    Selects and imports text file of configuration from previous generation. Probability of selection is determined based on structural performance.
  - **importStair_2**
    Selects and imports text file of configuration from previous generation. Probability of selection is determined based on structural performance.
  - **assignCrossoverPoint**
    Location chosen at random between top and bottom of stair layout.
  - **removeRodsFromStair_1**
    Rods above Crossover Point are removed from the Stair_1 configuration.
  - **removeRodsFromStair_2**
    Rods below Crossover Point are removed from the Stair_2 configuration.
  - **removeIntersectingRods**
    Conflicts in the new configuration that would have a negative impact on constructability are resolved with an eye towards minimal disruption to the new arrangement.
  - **mutationFunction**
    Occasionally adds, removes or alters one or more rods in random fashion.
  - **exportTextFile**
    Converts software-specific 3D information into nodes, connections and material identities. Writes data to a newly created text file.
- **UNTIL** number of individuals reached

TEXT FILES DESCRIBING GEOMETRIC AND MATERIAL INFO FOR EACH INDIVIDUAL IN GENERATION

Left
Flowchart of the algorithm that generates and analyzes the structural members of the staircase.

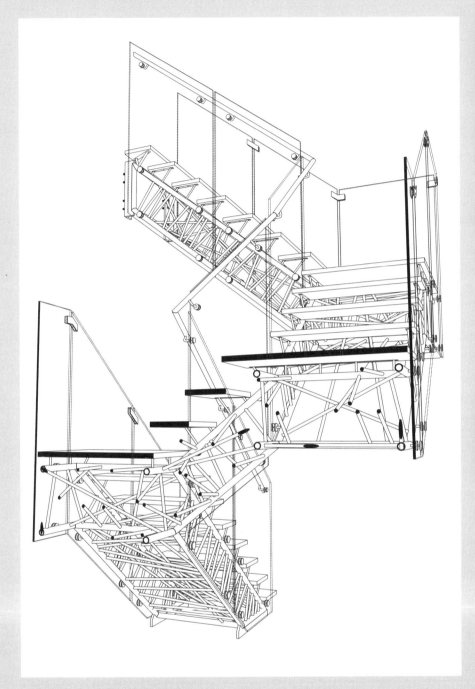

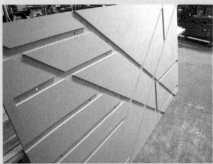

Left
Section-perspective drawing of stair.

Top
CNC-milled guide for tubes placement.

Above
Tubes placed in guide and ready for welding.

of the stair from the purview of the contractor – a rarity in traditional architectural projects. More importantly, however, and in a reversal of a traditional design process, the fabrication team collaborated on the details of the stair from the outset of the project, and the designers were active throughout the fabrication phase. In order to build the complex intersecting latticework with sufficent accuracy, formwork panels were digitally derived and fabricated to guide the placement of pipes and rods. Intricate intersections between pipes and rods were unfolded from the 3D model and printed on paper

templates, which were then wrapped around the steel members to act as guidelines for hole and edge cutting. This resulted in very accurate and clean joinery of the structural elements.

The result is a beautiful, free-standing structure, which integrates parametric, material, structural and aesthetic concerns. As Caliper Studio's Nicholas Desbiens explains, the Genetic Stair is made of '48 unique stainless-steel pipes with 1,400 angled holes, 253 connecting steel rods cut to length, 22 translucent Corian treads, 18 plates of glass and over 250 miscellaneous connecting components. The tubular-steel

frame is punctuated by varying densities of diagonal struts as it turns its way unsupported through 270 degrees in a visual language that speaks to a controlled complexity inherent to the process by which it was designed.'

Subdivision

In many cases, designers working with smooth surfaces and forms need to subdivide them in order to unfold them into planar components that can be digitally fabricated on CNC machines or laser cutters. Subdivision of a surface is something like the cracks found in deserts (fig. 58). It is a process of separating an otherwise continuous surface into smaller components by tracing, scoring or cutting lines through the surface. Most modern 3D modelling software can render smooth surfaces and allow for their automatic subdivision and approximation (fig. 59). However, without the power of scripting, one would have little control over the method of subdivision and would have to accept what the software offers. For example, converting a NURBS surface in *3ds Max* using one of the standard surface approximation techniques could yield several interesting topological subdivisions, but can also create undesirable ones (fig. 60). If precise control over topological subdivision is desired and, in particular, if the desired solution is one that is not easily achievable by manipulating the user interface of the modelling environment, then a custom script needs to be written (fig. 61).

fig. 58 Desert cracks.

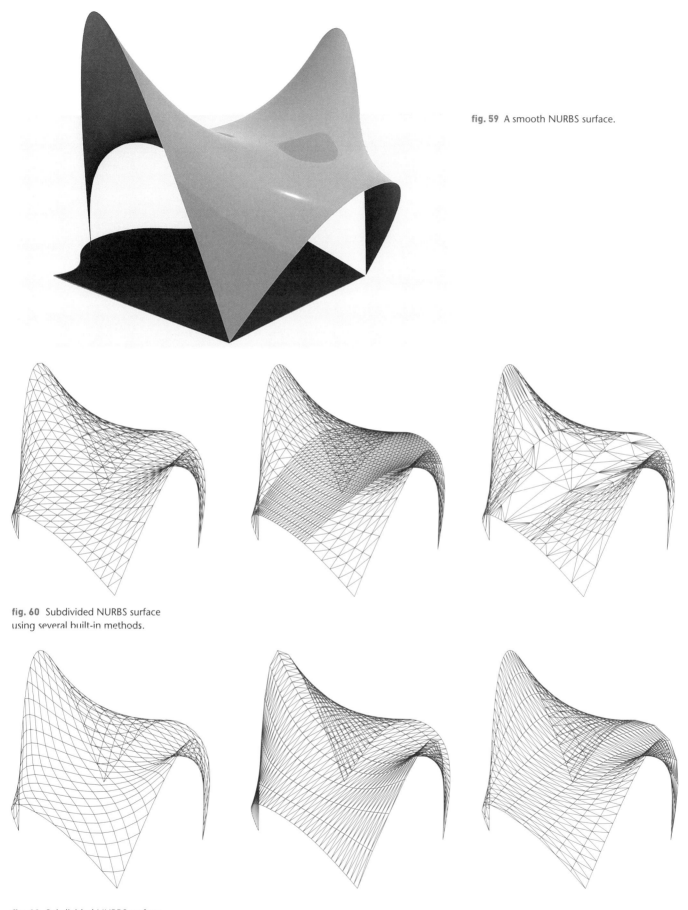

fig. 59 A smooth NURBS surface.

fig. 60 Subdivided NURBS surface using several built-in methods.

fig. 61 Subdivided NURBS surface using a custom diagrid script.

TUTORIAL SIMPLE DIAGRID MESH

In this introductory tutorial, we will create a flat mesh surface that is subdivided using a diagonal grid (diagrid). While this may seem an easy task, creating a properly formed mesh surface in *3ds Max MAXScript* requires careful planning. To start, we need to understand how *3ds Max* creates and stores a mesh data structure. A mesh surface in *3ds Max* is made of two lists, or, more precisely, two arrays: a *vertices* array and a *faces* array. The *vertices* array contains all the vertices of the surface, stored as 3D points. That is, each row contains a 3D point with *X*, *Y* and *Z* coordinates. (One requirement for a well-formed mesh surface is that vertices should not coincide. That is, if a vertex exists at a certain location, no other vertex should exist at that same location.) Each row in the *faces* array contains three integers, which are the indices of three 3D points in the *vertices* array that, together, make up one triangle. For example, if one wishes to create a triangular face that connects the fifth, second and fourth points in the *vertices* array, then one would store [5, 2, 4] in one row of the *faces* array (fig. 62).

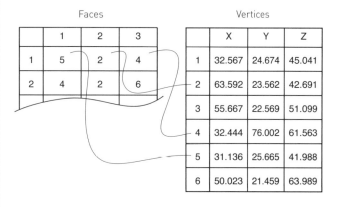

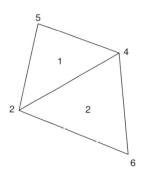

fig. 62 Mesh data structure.

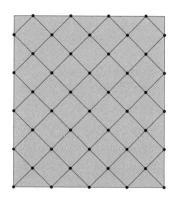

fig. 63 Vertex organization in a diagrid mesh.

Now that we understand the internal data structure of meshes, we can start building our own mesh. If we look closely at the vertices of a diagrid mesh, we notice that every other row has one less vertex than the one before it. Moreover, the vertices are also shifted by half the unit grid size (fig. 63).

We are now ready to create the script. In this case, we are going to create a true parametric geometry that can be modified at will in exactly the same manner as other geometries in *3ds Max*.

→ Open *3ds Max*, save and close any prior scenes, create a new empty scene and choose **MAXScript** → **New Script** from the top menu. In the script window that opens, type the following algorithm:

```
1    plugin simpleObject diagridmesh_plugin_def
2        name:"Diagrid Mesh"
3        classID:#(0x43771d8e, 0x561950f2)
4        category:"Scripted Primitives"
5    (
6        parameters main rollout:params
7        (
8            u type:#integer ui:u_spinner default:5
9            v type:#integer ui: v_spinner default:5
10           meshLength type:#worldunits ui:meshLength_spinner default:50
11           meshWidth type:#worldunits ui:meshWidth_spinner default:50
12           rotated type:#boolean ui:rotated_checkbox default:false
13       )
```

```
14
15        rollout params "Parameters"
16        (
17              spinner u_spinner "U:" type:#integer range:[1,10000,10]
18              spinner v_spinner "V:" type:#integer range:[1,10000,10]
19              spinner meshLength_spinner "Length" type:#worldunits range:[-10000,10000,0]
20    spinner meshWidth_spinner "Width" type:#worldunits range:[-10000,10000,0]
21    checkbox rotated_checkbox "Rotated" checked:rotated
22        )
23
24        on buildMesh do
25        (
26              vertices = #()
27              faces = #()
28              nc = u
29              nr = v*2
30
31              case of(
32                    (rotated == true) : (unitLength = meshWidth/ nr; unitWidth = meshLength/ nc)
33                    (rotated == false) : (unitLength = meshLength/ nr; unitWidth = meshWidth/ nc)
34              )
35
36        -- Create Vertices.
37        for i = 0 to nr by 1 do
38        (
39              case of(
40                    (mod i 2 != 0) : (hoffset = 0.5; deduct = 1)
41                    (mod i 2 == 0) :  (hoffset = 0.0; deduct = 0)
42              )
43              for j = 0 to (nc - deduct) by 1 do
44              (
45                    vx = (j + hoffset)*unitWidth
46                    vy = i*unitLength
47                    case of(
48                          (rotated == true) : append vertices  [vy, vx, 0]
49                          (rotated == false) : append vertices  [vx, vy, 0]
50                    )
51              )
52        )
53
54              -- Create first set of triangles.
55              for i = 1 to nr by 2 do
56              (
```

```
57          for j = 1 to nc by 1 do
58          (
59                  v1 = (i - 1)*(nc + 1) - ((i - 1)/2) + j
60                  v2 = (i - 1)*(nc + 1) - ((i - 1)/2) + j + 1
61                  v3 = (i - 1)*(nc + 1) - ((i - 1)/2) + j + (nc + 1)
62                  append faces [v1, v2, v3]
63
64                  if (j < nc) then
65                  (
66                          v1 = (i - 1)*(nc + 1) - ((i - 1)/2) + j + (nc + 1)
67                          v2 = (i - 1)*(nc + 1) - ((i - 1)/2) + j + 1
68                          v3 = (i - 1)*(nc + 1) - ((i - 1)/2) + j + (nc + 2)
69                          append faces [v1, v2, v3]
70                  )
71              )
72          )
73
74      -- Create second set of triangles.
75      for i = 3 to (nr+1) by 2 do
76      (
77          for j = 1 to nc by 1 do
78          (
79                  v1 = (i - 1)*(nc + 1) - ((i - 1)/2) + j + 1
80                  v2 = (i - 1)*(nc + 1) - ((i - 1)/2) + j
81                  v3 = (i - 3)*(nc + 1) - ((i - 3)/2) + j + (nc + 1)
82                  append faces [v1, v2, v3]
83
84                  if (j < nc) then
85                  (
86                          v1 = (i - 3)*(nc + 1) - ((i - 3)/2) + j + (nc + 1)
87                          v2 = (i - 3)*(nc + 1) - ((i - 3)/2) + j + 1 + (nc + 1)
88                          v3 = (i - 1)*(nc + 1) - ((i - 1)/2) + j + 1
89                          append faces [v1, v2, v3]
90                  )
91              )
92          )
93
94      -- Create left and right triangular edges
95      for i = 1 to nr by 2 do
96      (
97          v1 = (i - 1)*(nc + 1) - ((i - 1)/2) + 1
```

```
98         v2 = (i - 1)*(nc + 1) - ((i - 1)/2) + 1 + (nc + 1)
99         v3 = (i + 1)*(nc + 1) - ((i + 1)/2) + 1
100        append faces [v1, v2, v3]
101
102        v1 = (i + 1)*(nc + 1) - ((i + 1)/2) + nc + 1
103        v2 = (i - 1)*(nc + 1) - ((i - 1)/2) + nc + (nc + 1)
104        v3 = (i - 1)*(nc + 1) - ((i - 1)/2) + nc + 1
105        append faces [v1, v2, v3]
106      )
107
108      -- Create the mesh
109      setMesh mesh verts:vertices faces:faces
110    )
111
112    -- Respond to user interaction events
113    tool create
114    (
115      on mousePoint click do
116      (
117        case click of
118        (
119          1: nodeTM.translation = gridPoint
120          2: #stop
121        )
122      )
123
124      on mouseMove click do
125      (
126        case click of
127        (
128          2: (meshWidth = gridDist.x; meshLength = gridDist.y)
129          3: #stop
130        )
131      )
132    )
133  )
```

→ Save your script and then choose **Tools → Evaluate All** to run the script. Set the viewport to display face edges by clicking on the display mode (e.g. *Realistic* or *Smooth+Highlights* in the upper left corner of the viewport) and choosing that option. This will enable you to see the diagrid lines as you create the surface. Since we created an actual scripted geometry you will find the button to create the diagrid mesh under **Create → Geometry → Scripted Primitives**. This option is available at the bottom of the pull-down geometry categories menu. Next, click on the **Diagrid Mesh** button and drag a rectangle in the viewport. Press the *Escape* key to end the creation process. You should see a rectangle in the viewport subdivided using a diagrid.

Let's take a closer look at the script:

1	plugin simpleObject diagridmesh_plugin_def
2	name:"Diagrid Mesh"
3	classID:#(0x43771d8e, 0x561950f2)
4	category:"Scripted Primitives"
5	(

This creates a simple object plugin that we are naming *diagridmesh_plugin*. We then define the actual button title that is displayed in the user interface as 'Diagrid Mesh'. Each plugin in *3ds Max* requires a unique class ID. This ID can be generated at any time. Choose **MAXScript → MAXScript Listener...** then type *genClassID()* into the lower portion of the window. A number similar to :#(0x43771d8e, 0x561950f2) will be displayed. Copy and paste that number in your script to create your own unique ID for your plugin. Alternatively, you can also keep the above ID as it is. Next, we create a new class of geometries called 'Scripted Primitives', in order to distinguish it from other categories such as 'Standard Primitives', 'Extended Primitives', etc.

6	parameters main rollout:params
7	(
8	u type:#integer ui:u_spinner default:5
9	v type:#integer ui: v_spinner default:5
10	meshLength type:#worldunits ui:meshLength_spinner default:50
11	meshWidth type:#worldunits ui:meshWidth_spinner default:50
12	rotated type:#boolean ui:rotated_checkbox default:false
13	)

In the next section of the script we create the parameters for our scripted geometry. In this case, we specify *u* and *v* values (think of *u* and *v* as rows and columns), the overall mesh length and width, and whether we wish to rotate the diagrid 90 degrees. This last parameter is a true/false option that will be represented using a checkbox. Each parameter specifies a user interface (*ui*) element from which it derives its value.

15	rollout params "Parameters"
16	(
17	spinner u_spinner "U:" type:#integer range:[1,10000,10]
18	spinner v_spinner "V:" type:#integer range:[1,10000,10]
19	spinner meshLength_spinner "Length" type:#worldunits range:[-10000,10000,0]
20	spinner meshWidth_spinner "Width" type:#worldunits range:[-10000,10000,0]
21	checkbox rotated_checkbox "Rotated" checked:rotated
22	)

The next section, titled *rollout*, specifies and connects each parameter to its user interface element. We are careful to use the same name for the user interface elements that we specified in the prior section. The *u* and *v* parameters are integers (no decimal point). The mesh length and width are of type *#worldunits* (so they will display measurement units per the user preference). And lastly, the *rotated_checkbox* user interface is simply a checkbox. When it is checked, the diagrid is rotated 90 degrees.

```
24      on buildMesh do
25      (
26          vertices = #()
27          faces = #()
28          nc = u
29          nr = v*2
30
31          case of(
32              (rotated == true) : (unitLength = meshWidth/ nr; unitWidth = meshLength/ nc)
33              (rotated == false) : (unitLength = meshLength/ nr; unitWidth = meshWidth/ nc)
34          )
```

The next section is a *callback function*. It needs to be named *buildMesh* because it gets automatically called by *3ds Max* whenever it needs to re-build and display the mesh (e.g. if the user changed the parameters or hid and then re-displayed the mesh). The code in this section includes full instructions on how to create the resulting mesh. At the start of this function we specify two arrays called *vertices* and *faces* to store the data for the diagrid mesh. We also define two variables for the number of columns (*nc*) and number of rows (*nr*) that are derived from the specified *u* and *v* values. In order to create a well-formed diagrid, we restrict the number of rows to an even number by multiplying the given *v* value by 2. What remains to be done is to derive the unit length and unit width by dividing the overall length by the number of rows and the overall width by the number of columns. We swap these values if the user has chosen to rotate the grid.

As you will see later, at the end of this function, you will store the mesh in a specific variable called, unsurprisingly, *mesh*. It is this data structure that *3ds Max* will use to display the mesh.

```
36      -- Create Vertices
37      for i = 0 to nr by 1 do
38      (
39          case of(
40              (mod i 2 != 0) : (hoffset = 0.5; deduct = 1)
41              (mod i 2 == 0) :  (hoffset = 0.0; deduct = 0)
42          )
43          for j = 0 to (nc - deduct) by 1 do
44          (
45              vx = (j + hoffset)*unitWidth
46              vy = i*unitLength
47              case of(
48                  (rotated == true) : append vertices  [vy, vx, 0]
49                  (rotated == false) : append vertices  [vx, vy, 0]
50              )
51          )
52      )
```

SIMPLE DIAGRID MESH/CONTINUED

In this section we create two nested *for loops* in order to specify the location of the rows and columns of vertices. We use the *mod* function, as we have done previously in step 1 of the tutorial to create a hexagonal tiling pattern (see page 59) to determine if we are on an odd or even numbered iteration. For an odd-numbered iteration (which translates into an even-numbered row, since we are counting from 0), we shift the vertices by half the original unit distance and deduct one vertex from the total number of columns to create. If the user has chosen to rotate the grid, we also swap the values for *x* and *y*. Finally, we append the calculated *x* and *y* coordinates to the *vertices* array. Since this is a flat surface, the *z* coordinate is zero. It is important to map the index of the vertices in the array to their spatial location in order to correctly create triangles that connect them (fig. 64).

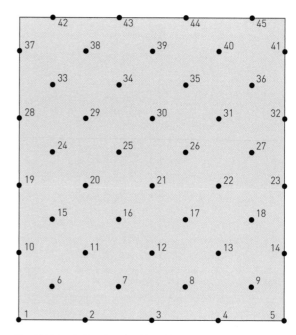

fig. 64 Vertex indices in a diagrid mesh.

54	-- Create first set of triangles.
55	for i = 1 to nr by 2 do
56	{
57	for j = 1 to nc by 1 do
58	{
59	v1 = (i - 1)*(nc + 1) - ((i - 1)/2) + j
60	v2 = (i - 1)*(nc + 1) - ((i - 1)/2) + j + 1
61	v3 = (i - 1)*(nc + 1) - ((i - 1)/2) + j + (nc + 1)
62	append faces [v1, v2, v3]
63	
64	if (j < nc) then
65	{
66	v1 = (i - 1)*(nc + 1) - ((i - 1)/2) + j + (nc + 1)
67	v2 = (i - 1)*(nc + 1) - ((i - 1)/2) + j + 1
68	v3 = (i - 1)*(nc + 1) - ((i - 1)/2) + j + (nc + 2)
69	append faces [v1, v2, v3]
70	}
71	}
72	}

In this section we create two nested *for loops*, in order to specify triangles that connect sets of three vertices (fig. 65). In this section we actually create only half the necessary triangles, by skipping a row. Three vertices, *v1*, *v2* and *v3*, are calculated based on where we are in the iteration of rows and columns. As long as we are not at the last column ($j < nc$) then we also create another, upside-down triangle that fits with the one before it. A similar approach is used to create the second set of rows, as well as the left and right triangles to finish off the surface.

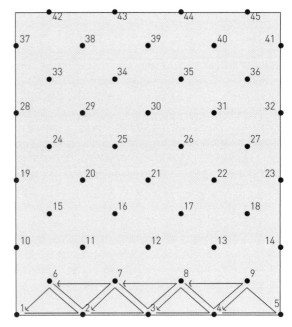

fig. 65 Connecting vertex indices in a diagrid mesh.

| 108 | -- Create the mesh |
| 109 | setMesh mesh verts:vertices faces:faces |

The last step in the *buildMesh* function is to set the mesh using the *vertices* and *faces* arrays. This will allow *3ds Max* to display it on-demand.

112	-- Respond to user interaction events
113	tool create
114	(
115	on mousePoint click do
116	(
117	case click of
118	(
119	1: nodeTM.translation = gridPoint
120	2: #stop
121	)
122	)
123	
124	on mouseMove click do
125	(
126	case click of
127	(
128	2: (meshWidth = gridDist.x; meshLength = gridDist.y)
129	3: #stop
130	)
131	)
132	)
133	)

The last section of the code specifies how a user creates the diagrid and how the software should react to mouse clicks and drags. When a user clicks the mouse, the location of the click (*gridPoint*) is considered the origin of the mesh. When the user moves the mouse, the second click is used to derive the width and the length of the mesh. This is identical to how a user creates a 2D rectangle. Pressing the *escape* key stops the creation of the diagrid.

Since the diagrid mesh is created as a scripted plugin, it behaves exactly like other geometries. Its parameters can be modified in the **modify** panel as well as animated using the timeline. Finally, the mesh surface can be manipulated by adding modifiers such as *Edit Mesh* or *FFD 3x3x3* (fig. 66). A complex organic form can be similarly achieved (fig. 67). In this case, a hollowed out diagrid mesh was distorted using the *bend* and *spherify* built-in modifiers. To achieve the final organic form, the geometry was then thickened and smoothed using the built-in *shell* and *turbosmooth* modifiers.

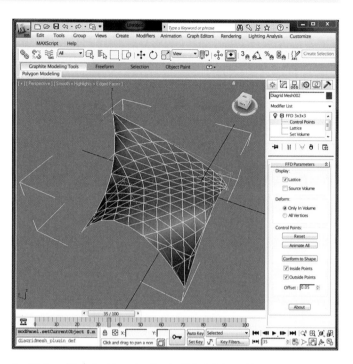

fig. 66 A modified diagrid mesh using the FFD 3x3x3 modifier.

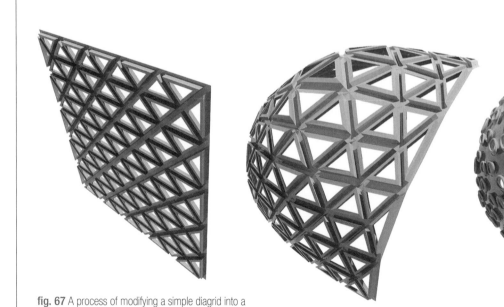

fig. 67 A process of modifying a simple diagrid into a curvilinear, organic form, using geometry modifiers.

TUTORIAL DERIVING A DIAGRID MESH FROM A NURBS SURFACE

In this second tutorial on subdivision, we will derive a diagrid mesh from any NURBS surface. The *MAXScript* environment allows procedural access to its built-in NURBS representations, facilitating the construction of new geometries that can subdivide the surface according to any desired topology. As we have seen above, *3ds Max* provides some built-in topologies, but in this case we would like to create our own.

NURBS surfaces contain formulas for surface and curve interpolation and approximation based on a derivation of points in the *u* and *v* directions of the surface. While you can think of *u* and *v* as horizontal and vertical increments in the case of a simple flat rectangular plane, in reality, they are normalized (i.e. 0 to 1) parametric offsets along two directions on any undulating surface. We can iterate through the *u* and *v* parameters of a NURBS surface and request the 3D coordinates of a point on the surface that exists at that particular *u* and *v* parametric coordinate. This allows us to create a pattern of vertices of our choosing and a set of triangular faces that connect them.

Unlike the previous tutorial, we will create a scripted utility called *DiagridMesh* rather than a scripted plugin.

$\rightarrow$ Open *3ds Max*, save and close any prior scenes, create a new empty scene and choose **MAXScript →
New Script** from the top menu. In the script window that opens, type the following algorithm:

```
1    utility DiagridMesh "Diagrid Mesh"
2    (
3        global u = 10 -- the number of u steps.
4        global v = 10 -- the number of v steps.
5        global vertices = #() -- the array of vertices.
6        global faces = #() -- the array of faces.
7        global nc  -- the number of columns.
8        global nr  -- the number of rows.
9        global selectedObject  = undefined -- the selected object.
10       global ns  -- the NURBS set (derived from the selected object).
11       global minu, maxu -- the minimum and maximum u values for the surface.
12       global minv, maxv  -- the minimum and maximum v values for the surface.
13       global udist, vdist -- the unit u and unit v distances.
14       global resultingMesh
15
16       global globalCounter = 1 -- a counter we will use to generate a unique name.
17
18       -- A function to select only NURBS surfaces.
19       fn nurbs_filt obj = (classOf obj == NURBSSurf)
20
21       pickbutton selectNURBS "Select NURBS" width:140 filter:nurbs_filt
22       edittext selectedObject_tf "NURBS: " text:"NONE" readonly:true width:138
23
24       group "Parameters"
25       (
26           spinner u_spinner "U:" type:#integer range:[1,10000,u]
27           spinner v_spinner "V:" type:#integer range:[1,10000,v]
28       )
```

```
29
30        button generate_button "Generate Diagrid" enabled:true
31
32        on selectNURBS picked obj do
33            (
34                    --see if the user did not cancel the picking.
35                    if obj != undefined do
36                        (
37                            selectedObject = obj
38                            -- display the name of the object on the button.
39                            selectedObject_tf.text = obj.name
40                        )
41            )
42
43        on u_spinner changed amt do
44            (
45                u = amt
46            )
47
48        on v_spinner changed amt do
49            (
50                v = amt
51            )
52
53        on generate_button pressed do
54        (
55            resultingMesh = undefined
56            nc = u*2
57            nr = v
58
59            if (selectedObject == undefined) then
60            (
61                return false
62            )
63
64            if (isDeleted selectedObject) then
65            (
66                return false
67            )
68
69            -- Get the NURBS set from the selected object.
```

```
70        ns = getnurbsset selectedObject #relational

71

72        for k = 1 to ns.count by 1 do

73            (

74

75                if ((superClassOf ns[k]) == NURBSSurface) then

76                (

77

78                    -- Delete any pre-existing vertices.

79                    for i = 1 to vertices.count by 1 do

80                    (

81                        deleteItem vertices 1

82                    )

83

84                    -- Delete any pre-existing faces.

85                    for i = 1 to faces.count by 1 do

86                    (

87                        deleteItem faces 1

88                    )

89

90                    minu = ns[k].uParameterRangeMin

91                    maxu = ns[k].uParameterRangeMax

92

93                    minv = ns[k].vParameterRangeMin

94                    maxv = ns[k].vParameterRangeMax

95

96                    udist = 1.0 / (float) nc

97                    vdist = 1.0 / (float) nr

98                    oddeven = 2

99

100                    -- Create Vertices.

101                    for i = 0 to nc by 1 do

102                    (

103                        case of(

104                            (mod oddeven 2 != 0) : (offset = 0.5; deduct = 1)

105                            (mod oddeven 2 == 0) :  (offset = 0.0; deduct = 0)

106                        )

107                        for j = 0 to (nr - deduct) by 1 do

108                        (

109                            vx = i/(float) nc

110                            vy = (j+offset)/(float) nr

111                            append vertices  (evalpos ns[k] (minu + (maxu-minu)*vx) (minv + (maxv-minv)*vy))

112                        )
```

113	oddeven = oddeven + 1
114	}
115	
116	if(ns[k].closedInV == false) then
117	{
118	-- Create left and right triangular edges for open NURBS surfaces.
119	for i = 1 to nc by 2 do
120	{
121	v1 = (i - 1)*(nr + 1) - ((i - 1)/2) + 1
122	v2 = (i - 1)*(nr + 1) - ((i - 1)/2) + 1 + (nr + 1)
123	v3 = (i + 1)*(nr + 1) - ((i + 1)/2) + 1
124	append faces [v1, v2, v3]
125	
126	v1 = (i + 1)*(nr + 1) - ((i + 1)/2) + nr + 1
127	v2 = (i - 1)*(nr + 1) - ((i - 1)/2) + nr + (nr + 1)
128	v3 = (i - 1)*(nr + 1) - ((i - 1)/2) + nr + 1
129	append faces [v1, v2, v3]
130	}
131	}
132	else
133	{
134	-- Create triangles for closed NURBS surfaces.
135	for i = 1 to nc by 2 do
136	{
137	v1 = (i - 1)*(nr + 1) - ((i - 1)/2) + 1
138	v2 = (i - 1)*(nr + 1) - ((i - 1)/2) + 1 + (nr + 1)
139	v3 = (i - 1)*(nr + 1) - ((i - 1)/2) + nr + (nr + 1)
140	append faces [v1, v2, v3]
141	
142	v1 = (i - 1)*(nr + 1) - ((i - 1)/2) + nr + (nr + 1)
143	v2 = (i - 1)*(nr + 1) - ((i - 1)/2) + 1 + (nr + 1)
144	v3 = (i + 1)*(nr + 1) - ((i + 1)/2) + nr + 1
145	append faces [v1, v2, v3]
146	}
147	}
148	
149	-- Create first set of triangles.
150	for i = 1 to nc by 2 do
151	{
152	for j = 1 to nr by 1 do
153	{

154	v1 = (i - 1)*(nr + 1) - ((i - 1)/2) + j
155	v2 = (i - 1)*(nr + 1) - ((i - 1)/2) + j + 1
156	v3 = (i - 1)*(nr + 1) - ((i - 1)/2) + j + (nr + 1)
157	append faces [v1, v2, v3]
158	
159	if (j < nr) then
160	(
161	v1 = (i - 1)*(nr + 1) - ((i - 1)/2) + j + (nr + 1)
162	v2 = (i - 1)*(nr + 1) - ((i - 1)/2) + j + 1
163	v3 = (i - 1)*(nr + 1) - ((i - 1)/2) + j + (nr + 2)
164	append faces [v1, v2, v3]
165	)
166	)
167	)
168	
169	-- Create second set of triangles.
170	for i = 3 to (nc+1) by 2 do
171	(
172	for j = 1 to nr by 1 do
173	(
174	v1 = (i - 1)*(nr + 1) - ((i - 1)/2) + j + 1
175	v2 = (i - 1)*(nr + 1) - ((i - 1)/2) + j
176	v3 = (i - 3)*(nr + 1) - ((i - 3)/2) + j + (nr + 1)
177	append faces [v1, v2, v3]
178	
179	if (j < nr) then
180	(
181	v1 = (i - 3)*(nr + 1) - ((i - 3)/2) + j + (nr + 1)
182	v2 = (i - 3)*(nr + 1) - ((i - 3)/2) + j + 1 + (nr + 1)
183	v3 = (i - 1)*(nr + 1) - ((i - 1)/2) + j + 1
184	append faces [v1, v2, v3]
185	)
186	)
187	)
188	
189	-- Create the mesh.
190	m = mesh vertices:vertices faces:faces
191	
192	-- Weld any congruent vertices.
193	allVerts = #{1..(m.numVerts)} -- get all verts list.
194	meshop.weldVertsByThreshold m allVerts 0.001
195	
196	-- Set the mesh properties and position at same location as original surface.

197	m.name = selectedObject.name+"-"+(k as string)+"-diagrid"
198	m.rotation = selectedObject.rotation
199	m.scale = selectedObject.scale
200	m.pos = selectedObject.pos
201	
202	if((resultingMesh == undefined) or (isDeleted resultingMesh)) then
203	(
204	resultingMesh = copy m
205	)
206	else
207	(
208	resultingMesh += m
209	)
210	delete m
211	
212	-- Make the mesh the current selection.
213	resultingMesh.name = selectedObject.name+"-Diagrid"+(formattedPrint globalCounter format:"03d")+"-"+(u as string)+"X"+(v as string)
214	select resultingMesh
215	)
216	)
217	globalCounter = globalCounter + 1
218	)
219	)

→ Save your script and then choose **Tools** → **Evaluate All** to run the script. Set the viewport display to display face edges by clicking on the display mode (e.g. *Realistic* or *Smooth+Highlights* in the upper left corner of the viewport) and choosing that option. This will enable you to see the diagrid lines when you derive the surface. Next, create a NURBS surface.

→ To run the actual script utility, go to **Utilities** (hammer icon) → **MAXScript** → **Utilities** (Pull-down menu) → **Diagrid Mesh**. Use the pick button, titled **Select NURBS**, to select the NURBS surface from the scene. You can choose any number of *u* and *v* sections (rows and columns). Once you have selected the desired parameters, press the **Generate Diagrid** button. This will generate an editable mesh diagrid at the same location as the original NURBS surface. Select the **move** command and move the diagrid so you can view it (fig. 68). The diagrid will have the same name as the original NURBS surface followed by the suffix "-Diagrid" and additional identifying numbers.

TIP CREATING A NURBS SURFACE

To create a NURBS surface, select **Create** → **Geometry** → **NURBS Surfaces** → **CV Surf** and drag a rectangle in the viewport. If you wish to undulate the surface, select it, go to the modify panel, click on the **+** sign next to the word 'NURBS Surfaces' to open the sub-objects list and then choose **Surface CV**. You can then select one or more of the yellow control vertices in the viewport and move them in any direction to undulate the surface. Once done, deselect **Surface CV** and select the whole NURBS surface.

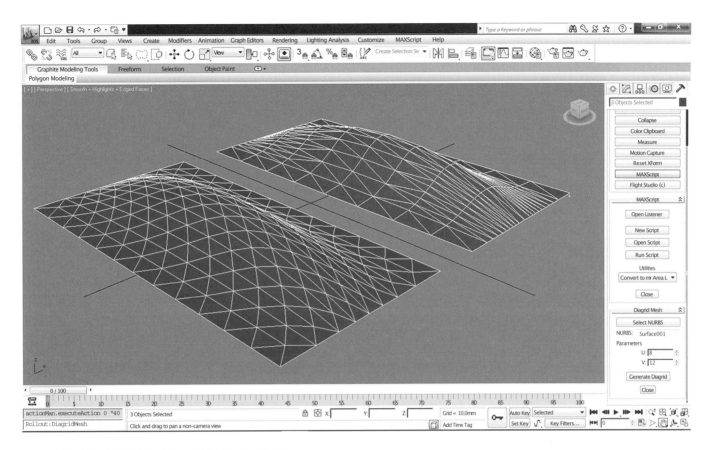

fig. 68 A diagrid mesh (left) derived from a NURBS surface (right).

Let's take a closer look at the script:

1	utility DiagridMesh "Diagrid Mesh"
2	(
3	global u = 10 -- the number of U steps
4	global v = 10 -- the number of V steps
5	global vertices = #() -- the array of vertices
6	global faces = #() -- the array of faces
7	global nc -- the number of columns
8	global nr -- the number of rows
9	global selectedObject = undefined -- the selected object
10	global ns -- the NURBS set (derived from the selected object)
11	global minu, maxu -- the minimum and maximum U values for the surface
12	global minv, maxv -- the minimum and maximum V values for the surface
13	global udist, vdist -- the unit U and unit V distance
14	global resultingMesh
15	
16	global globalCounter = 1 -- a counter we will use to generate a unique name

We declare a scripted utility that we name *DiagridMesh*. We give it the title 'Diagrid Mesh'. This scripted utility will be stored under the **Utilities** (hammer icon) tab under the **MAXScript** category of utilities. We declare four main global variables. The *u* and *v* values are the number of rows and columns we wish to divide the surface into. The *vertices* and *faces* arrays will store the resulting mesh information. Last, we declare the global variable *resultingMesh* to store the resulting diagrid mesh.

```
19      fn nurbs_filt obj = (classOf obj == NURBSSurf)
```

The above function returns a value of *true* only if the selected object belongs to the *NURBSSurf* class.

```
21      pickbutton selectNURBS "Select NURBS" width:140 filter:nurbs_filt
22      edittext selectedObject_tf "NURBS: " text:"NONE" readonly:true width:138
23
24      group "Parameters"
25      (
26          spinner u_spinner "U:" type:#integer range:[1,10000,u]
27          spinner v_spinner "V:" type:#integer range:[1,10000,v]
28      )
29
30      button generate_button "Generate Diagrid" enabled:true
```

We then define the rollout interface with a pick button to select the NURBS surface from the scene, two spinners for defining the *u* and *v* subdivisions, and a button to generate the mesh when pressed.

```
43      on u_spinner changed amt do
44          (
45              u = amt
46          )
47
48      on v_spinner changed amt do
49          (
50              v = amt
51          )
```

This section specifies what happens when the user changes the amount in the spinner field (i.e. changes the amount of the *u* and *v*). The code simply updates the amount saved in the variables with the new amount from the user interface.

```
53      on generate_button pressed do
54          (
55              resultingMesh = undefined
56              nc = u*2
57              nr = v
```

The remainder of the script executes only when the **Generate Diagrad** button is pressed. The script starts by setting the resulting mesh to the value *undefined* and specifying two new variables: *nc* (number of columns) and *nr* (number of rows). To ensure a proper result for the diagrid, we ensure an even number of columns by multiplying the specified *u* value by 2.

59	if (selectedObject == undefined) then
60	(
61	return false
62	)
63	
64	if (isDeleted selectedObject) then
65	(
66	return false
67	)

The above code ensures that we continue to generate a diagrid only if the selected object is defined and has not been deleted. If these conditions are not met, the code returns the value *false* and stops executing.

70	ns = getnurbsset selectedObject #relational

The built-in *getnurbset* function returns an idealized version of the selected NURBS object that can be queried for its components (vertices, curves, surfaces, etc.). We store this set in the *ns* variable.

72	for k = 1 to ns.count by 1 do
73	(
74	
75	if ((superClassOf ns[k]) == NURBSSurface) then
76	(

We then create a large loop to iterate through all the elements of the *ns* NURBS construct. We consider a sub-object only if it is a *NURBSSurface*.

90	minu = ns[k].uParameterRangeMin
91	maxu = ns[k].uParameterRangeMax
92	
93	minv = ns[k].vParameterRangeMin
94	maxv = ns[k].vParameterRangeMax
95	
96	udist = 1.0 / (float) nc
97	vdist = 1.0 / (float) nr

We then compute the minimum and maximum extents of the surface. Since *u* and *v* are normalized (i.e. span between 0 and 1), we define the unit *udist* and *vdist* distance as 1 divided by the number of rows and columns. The remainder of the script is almost identical to the previous tutorial, so we will cover only the differences between the two scripts.

DERIVING A DIAGRID MESH FROM A NURBS SURFACE /CONTINUED

109	vx = i/(float) nc
110	vy = (j+offset)/(float) nr
111	append vertices (evalpos ns[k] (minu + (maxu-minu)*vx) (minv + (maxv-minv)*vy))

In the above snippet of code, we call the *evalpos* function with an offset in the *u* and *v* parametric space of the surface to obtain an actual 3D point at that location. This is computed by adding a factor of the *u* and *v* dimension (e.g. *maxu – minu*) to the minimum value of each dimension (e.g. *minu*). However, we first adjust for any horizontal offsets due to the shifting of the vertices on odd-numbered rows. After we obtain that point, we append it to the *vertices* array (this is done in one step in the code, using nesting of functions). The faces are created in exactly the same way as in the previous tutorial: finding the index of the relevant vertices in the *vertices* array, connecting them and adding the resulting three-point array to the *faces* array.

116	if(ns[k].closedInV == false) then

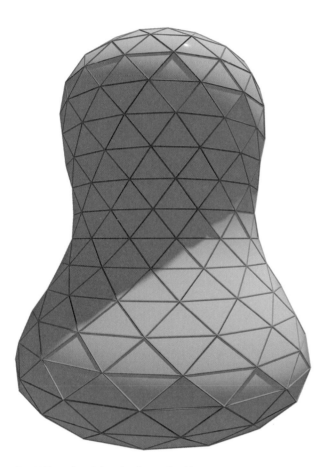 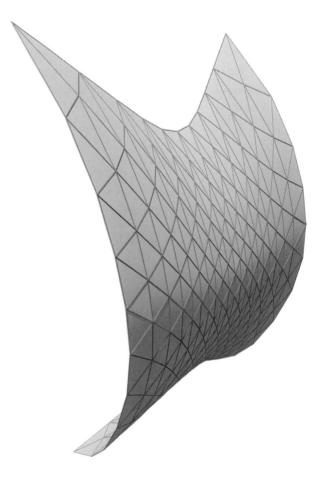

fig. 69 Examples of closed and open diagrids.

A NURBS surface in *3ds Max* can tell us if it is closed or open in either of its *u* or *v* directions (fig. 69). The built-in method/attribute *closedInV* reports back if the surface is closed in the *v* direction, information that we need in order to make sure that we do not replicate the edges of our diagrid. Imagine a ribbon that is closed into a circle. At the seam, where the ribbon meets itself, we need to ensure that only one edge exists. In our case, the triangles at the seam need to be constructed from one set of edges rather than two to ensure a properly configured mesh.

190	m = mesh vertices:vertices faces:faces
191	
192	-- Weld any congruent vertices.
193	allVerts = #{1..(m.numVerts)} -- get all verts list
194	meshop.weldVertsByThreshold m allVerts 0.001
195	

In this section of the code, the mesh is created from the two arrays of vertices and faces. Its vertices are then welded to make sure there are no redundancies.

The remainder of the code involves setting the properties of the mesh and completing some housekeeping operations. It should be self-explanatory. The resulting mesh can be modified in *3ds Max* to extract its vertices, edges and surfaces to create a skin and a structure (fig. 70).

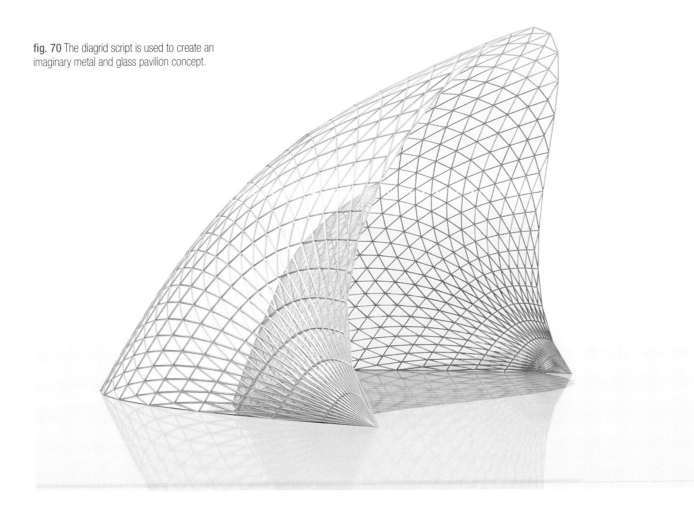

fig. 70 The diagrid script is used to create an imaginary metal and glass pavilion concept.

Case study Screen for Eurocont Headquarters, Badalona, Spain

Designer HYBRIDa scp
Client Eurocomercial de Neuvas Tecnología (Eurocont), Spain
Design and Construction 2010

Eurocont is a Barcelona-based company specializing in innovative technological products for the building industry. Their headquarters is an industrial building that combines extensive workshop areas with the company's offices. The project under consideration here is a partition screen intended to separate the company's ground-level workshop space from the office areas, which are mostly located on a mezzanine level. The functional requirements for this project were rather mundane: the completed screen had to provide a controlled visual connection between the two areas, to insulate the office area acoustically, and to ensure proper lighting and temperature conditions. For the designers, however, the project was an opportunity to create an iterative geometric process that satisfied these requirements while creating an 'apparent chaos'.

Beginning with a study of the texture of an eggshell, the designers, J. Truco and S. Felipe,

defined three methods for the subdivision of the screen surface. The resulting geometries, arranged in separate layers, were then selectively collapsed to produce a variety of patterns, which varied depending on the layers that had been juxtaposed to produce them. This led to an overwhelming proliferation of geometry, which needed to be subjected to a selection process. The designers chose several criteria (including the number of sides of the polygons, the area of perforation and the number of connections between vertices) and treated them as parameters to include in a script. The script calculated and drafted panels with varying degrees of opacity (0% to 100%), which could then be positioned on the partition screen according to acoustic and visual connection requirements. Multiple iterations were run, and the emerging patterns were then evaluated and adjusted according to the functions taking place behind different sections

Above
View from lower level.

Opposite
Light filtration qualities of the screen.

Below
Establishing the main generative rules of
the design.

Bottom
Juxtaposition of geometric lines to
achieve varying degrees of opacity.

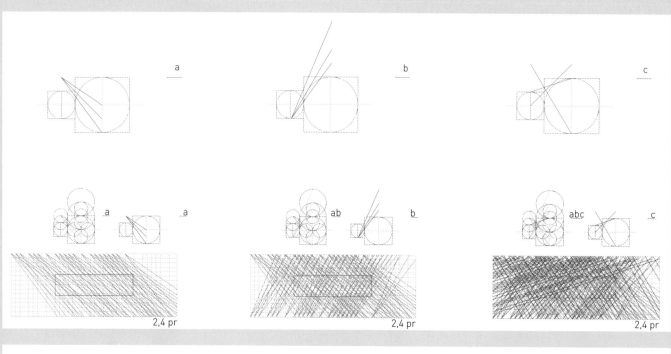

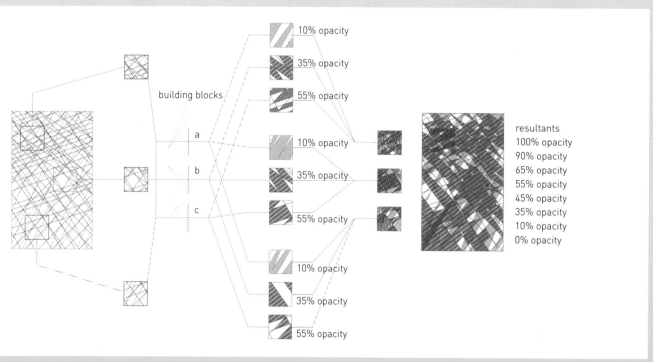

of the partition screen. The designers stopped the iterative process once they were satisfied with the effect and the function of the emergent pattern. This method eventually determined the algorithm that produced the final design.

The completed screen measured 27 m wide. It was digitally fabricated by a CNC machine and consisted of 70 methacrylate panels, 12 mm thick, with varying porosities. Each of these panels was encased between two insulation glass panes and mounted within a metal frame. Running across these panels are unique polygons that are the result of a common geometric manipulation. This process, as the designers argue, 'links them all and makes them understandable as a whole'. It is important to note that the language of expression that characterizes the Eurocont screen does not depend on formal manipulation by the designers. Instead, it is a direct result of the process by which it was designed. The end result reflects the employment of geometric patterns, formalistic criteria and the determination of a specific algorithm – all of which, however, have been placed in the service of the very pragmatic functional requirements prescribed by the brief.

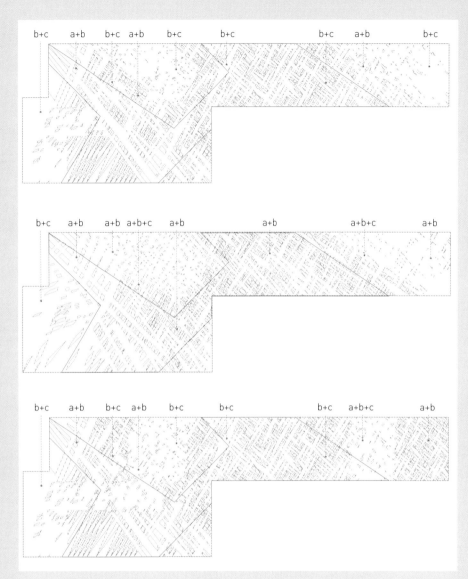

Above right
Pattern analysis based on occupancy and space functions.

Right
Segmentation of pattern into individual panels.

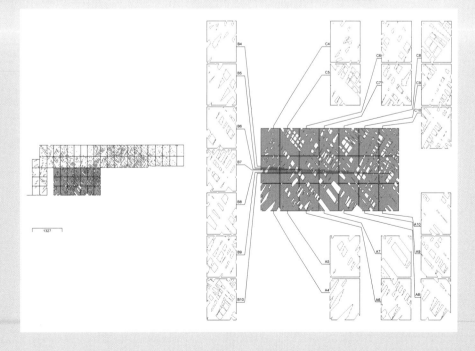

Above
Digital fabrication of methacrylate panels.

Above right
Installation of panels.

Below left and right
Close-up views of completed panels.

Below
Varying degrees of visual separation.

Packing

Closely related to the concepts of tiling and subdivision is the concept of packing: the placement of many objects in a space, such that little or nothing of it is left over. Packing in nature happens at many different scales. The natural force of growth within a constrained space leads to packing in both the cellular structure of charcoal (**fig. 71**) and the seeds of a pomegranate (**fig. 72**). Weathering and erosion can be viewed as the inverse of packing — one can think of void pockets as the packed material, as seen at a molecular level in Biochar (**fig. 73**) and at a much larger scale in Tafoni structures (**fig. 74**). Humans have long been interested in packing techniques to ensure an economy of means and the efficient use of resources. The pivot point irrigation system is a good example of how

humans employ packing techniques on a geographical scale, given constraints in the terrain, climate and production technology (**fig. 75**). In architecture, we have seen an interest in packing for both spatial organization as well as structural strength (**fig. 76**). However, unlike tiling and subdivision, both of which are likely to have a global ordering system that governs their form, packing is often an opportunistic process. That is, components in a packing system seek empty space to occupy, and a first-come, first-served process governs the growth pattern. Thus, the results of packing are not always regularly tiled or fully optimized. Packing algorithms also vary in their efficiency as they contain trade-offs between the number of objects to pack and the time needed to generate a solution.

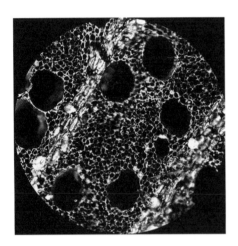

fig. 71 Microscope photo of charcoal at high magnification.

fig. 72 An open pomegranate showing packed seeds.

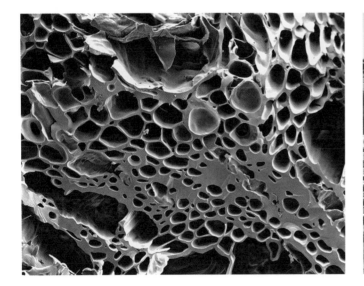

fig. 73 Microscope photo of Biochar at high magnification.

fig. 74 Tafoni structure at Pebble Beach, San Mateo Coast, California.

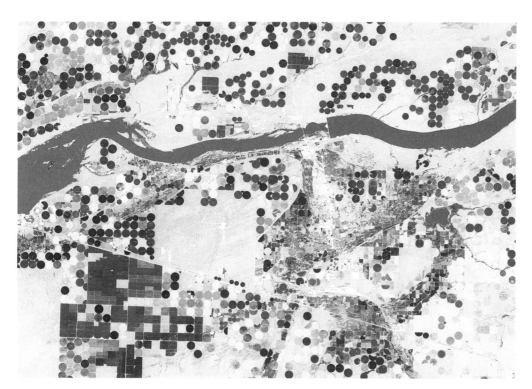

fig. 75 Irrigation and land surface temperature in Oregon.

fig. 76 Packed Pavilion, Shanghai, China (2010). Project designed by Michele Leidi, Min-Chieh Chen and Dominik Zausinger with the help of Jeannette Kuo and the supervision of Tom Pawlofsky.

TUTORIAL CIRCLE PACKING

In this tutorial on packing we will create a generative algorithm that takes any 2D shape as input and packs into it as many circles as it can (up to a specified maximum, and within the specified time limit and other parameters).

$\longrightarrow$ Open *3ds Max*, save and close any prior scenes, create a new empty scene. Choose **MAXScript → New Script** from the top menu. In the script window that opens, type the following algorithm:

```
1    utility circlePacking "Circle Packing"
2    (
3        global selectedShape
4        global maxCircles = 600
5        global minRadius = 1
6        global maxRadius = 5
7        global maxAttempts = 10000
8        global minX = 0
9        global maxX = 100
10       global minY = 0
11       global maxY = 100
12       global circles = #()
13       global radius = 10
14       global accuracy = 32
15
16       fn shape_filt obj = ((superClassOf obj) == Shape)
17
18       pickbutton selectShape "Select Shape" width:140 filter:shape_filt
19       edittext selectedShape_tf "Shape: " text:"NONE" readonly:true width:138
20
21       spinner maxCircles_spinner "Circles: " range:[1,10000,maxCircles] type:#integer
22       spinner minRadius_spinner "Min. Radius: " range:[0.1,10000,minRadius]  type:#worldunits
23       spinner maxRadius_spinner "Max. Radius: " range:[0.1,10000,maxRadius]  type:#worldunits
24       spinner maxAttempts_spinner "Attempts: " range:[1,100000,maxAttempts]  type:#integer
25       spinner accuracy_spinner "Accuracy: " range:[4,64,accuracy]  type:#integer
26       button generate_button "Generate" enabled:false width: 140 height:20
27       progressbar Attempts_prog color:red
28       progressbar generate_prog color:green
29       edittext packedCircles " Packed: " text:"0 Circles" readonly:true width:138
30       edittext coverage " Coverage: " text:"0 %" readonly:true width:138
31
32       on selectShape picked obj do
33           (
34               --see if the user did not cancel the picking.
35               if obj != undefined do
36                   (
```

```
37                          -- display the name of the object on the button:
38                          selectedShape_tf.text = obj.name
39                          selectedShape = obj
40                          generate_button.enabled = true
41                  )
42          )
43
44      fn overlaps aCircle circles =
45      (
46          if(circles.count < 1) then
47          (
48                  return false
49          )
50          for i=1 to i=circles.count do
51          (
52                  result = (distance aCircle.pos circles[i].pos) < = (aCircle.radius + circles[i].radius)
53                  if result then return result
54          )
55          return false
56      )
57
58      fn outside_mesh aCircle aMesh =
59      (
60
61          for i = 0 to accuracy by 1 do
62          (
63                  ang = (i/accuracy as float)*360
64                  vx = aCircle.pos.x + cos(ang) * aCircle.radius
65                  vy = aCircle.pos.y + sin(ang) * aCircle.radius
66                  testRay = ray [vx, vy, 1] [0, 0, -10]
67                  if (intersectRay aMesh testRay == undefined) then
68                  (
69                          return true
70                  )
71          )
72          return false
73      )
74
75      fn createCircle minRadius maxRadius ratio =
76      (
77              radius = random minRadius (maxRadius - ((maxRadius*ratio/maxAttempts) as float))
78          x = random (minX + radius) (maxX - radius)
79          y = random (minY + radius) (maxY - radius)
```

```
80          newCircle = circle radius:radius
81          newCircle.pos = [x,y,0]
82          return newCircle
83      )
84
85      on generate_button pressed do
86      (
87          if (selectedShape == undefined) then return false
88          if (isDeleted selectedShape) then
89          (
90              selectedShape_tf.text = "NONE"
91              return false
92          )
93
94          coverageArea = 0
95
96          ep_mod = edit_poly()
97          addModifier selectedShape ep_mod
98
99          totalArea=0
100         for i=1 to selectedShape.numfaces do totalArea+=(polyop.getfacearea selectedShape i)
101
102         bb = nodeGetBoundingBox selectedShape (matrix3 1)
103         minX = bb[1].x
104         maxX = bb[2].x
105         minY = bb[1].y
106         maxY = bb[2].y
107
108         -- Empty the circles array and delete all the circles in it.
109         circlesCount = circles.count
110         for i = 1 to circlesCount by 1 do
111         (
112             tobedeleted = circles[1]
113             deleteItem circles 1
114             if(isDeleted tobedeleted != true) then
115             (
116                 delete tobedeleted
117             )
118         )
119         circles.count = 0
120         packedCircles.text = "0/"+(maxCircles as string)+" Circles"
```

```
121        coverage.text = "0 %"
122        redrawViews()
123
124        j = 1
125        attempts = 0
126        while (circles.count < maxCircles) and (attempts < maxAttempts) do
127        (
128            aCircle = createCircle minRadius maxRadius j
129            if ((overlaps aCircle circles) or (outside_mesh aCircle selectedShape)) then
130            (
131                delete aCircle
132            )
133            else
134            (
135                append circles aCircle
136                j = j + 1
137                coverageArea = coverageArea + pi*radius*radius
138            )
139            attempts = attempts + 1
140            attempts_prog.value = 100.*attempts/maxAttempts
141            generate_prog.value = 100.*j/maxCircles
142        ) --end of the for loop.
143
144        for m in selectedShape.modifiers do
145            (
146                if classOf m==Edit_Poly do deleteModifier selectedShape m
147            )
148
149        packedCircles.text = (circles.count as string)+"/"+(maxCircles as string)+" Circles"
150        coverage.text = ((coverageArea/totalArea*100) as string)+" %"
151    )
152
153    on maxCircles_spinner changed amt do
154    (
155        maxCircles = amt
156    )
157    on maxAttempts_spinner changed amt do
158    (
159        maxAttempts = amt
160    )
161    on minRadius_spinner changed amt do
162    (
163        minRadius = amt
```

164	if(maxRadius < minRadius) then
165	(
166	maxRadius = minRadius
167	maxRadius_spinner.value = minRadius
168	)
169	)
170	on maxRadius_spinner changed amt do
171	(
172	maxRadius = amt
173	if(minRadius > maxRadius) then
174	(
175	minRadius = maxRadius
176	minRadius_spinner.value = maxRadius
177	)
178	)
179	on accuracy_spinner changed amt do
180	(
181	accuracy = amt
182	)
183	)

$\rightarrow$ Save your script and then choose **Tools** $\rightarrow$ **Evaluate All** to run the script. You will find the script utility under **Utilities** (hammer icon). Click on the **MAXScript** button and then choose **Circle Packing** from the **Utilities** pull down menu (fig. 77).

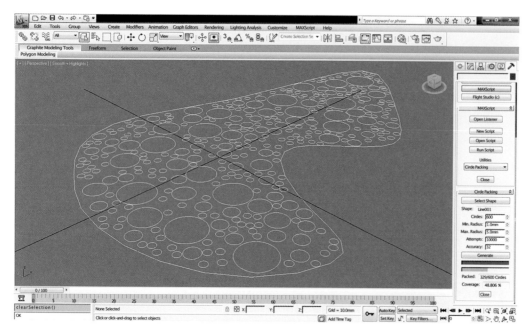

fig. 77 Circle Packing Utility Script.

$\longrightarrow$ To run the script, create any 2D closed spline in the **TOP** view. Then click on the **Select Shape** button and select the spline. Specify the parameters for the maximum number of circles, the minimum and maximum radii for the generated circles, the maximum allowed number of attempts, and the accuracy of the intersection test. The latter equates to the number of points on the circle to intersect with the surface to test if it lies within it. For simpler shapes (such as a rectangle) testing only 4 points on a circle may be sufficient and would speed up the algorithm. Once all the parameters are set, click on the **Generate** button to generate the circles. The 2D spline will be filled with a solid colour and two progress bars will appear. The top, red progress bar is an indication of the number of attempts tried thus far. The lower, green progress bar is an indication of the number of circles successfully packed into the selected shape. The two progress bars will appear to be in a race against each other. Ideally, you would want the green bar to be farther ahead. If you find that it isn't, then the total amount of allowed attempts needs to be increased. Once the algorithm is done packing the circles, it reports the total number of circles it could successfully pack as well as the coverage area percentage of the original 2D surface.

Let's take a closer look at the script:

1	utility circlePacking "Circle Packing"
2	(
3	global selectedShape
4	global maxCircles = 600
5	global minRadius = 1
6	global maxRadius = 5
7	global maxAttempts = 10000
8	global minX = 0
9	global maxX = 100
10	global minY = 0
11	global maxY = 100
12	global circles = #()
13	global radius = 10
14	global accuracy = 32

We define a utility script called *circlePacking* and titled with the same name. We define several global variables to store the selected shape, the desired maximum number of circles to pack, the minimum and maximum radius for a generated circle (the script will randomly choose a number in this range), the maximum allowed number of attempts to generate and pack a circle, and an accuracy setting for the intersection test that determines if a circle is inside or outside a shape. Other variables are also needed for various other functions, as we will see below.

16	fn shape_filt obj = ((superClassOf obj) == Shape)

This function acts as a selection filter so that the user is restricted only to selecting a 2D shape.

18	pickbutton selectShape "Select Shape" width:140 filter:shape_filt
19	edittext selectedShape_tf "Shape: " text:"NONE" readonly:true width:138
20	
21	spinner maxCircles_spinner "Circles: " range:[1,10000,maxCircles] type:#integer
22	spinner minRadius_spinner "Min. Radius: " range:[0.1,10000,minRadius] type:#worldunits

```
23    spinner maxRadius_spinner "Max. Radius: " range:[0.1,10000,maxRadius] type:#worldunits
24    spinner maxAttempts_spinner "Attempts: " range:[1,100000,maxAttempts] type:#integer
25    spinner accuracy_spinner "Accuracy: " range:[4,64,accuracy] type:#integer
26    button generate_button "Generate" enabled:false width: 140 height:20
27    progressbar Attempts_prog color:red
28    progressbar generate_prog color:green
29    edittext packedCircles " Packed: " text:"0 Circles" readonly:true width:138
30    edittext coverage " Coverage: " text:"0 %" readonly:true width:138
```

This block of code defines a user interface rollout with the necessary spinners, buttons, text fields and progress bars.

```
32    on selectShape picked obj do
33        (
34            --see if the user did not cancel the picking...
35            if obj != undefined do
36                (
37                    -- display the name of the object on the button:
38                    selectedShape_tf.text = obj.name
39                    selectedShape = obj
40                    generate_button.enabled = true
41                )
42        )
```

Once a shape is selected, this callback function is executed. If the selected object is defined it places its name in the rollout user interface, copies its address into another variable for later use and enables the generate button, so that it can be clicked by the user to generate the circles.

```
44    fn overlaps aCircle circles =
45    (
46        if(circles.count < 1) then
47        (
48            return false
49        )
50        for i=1 to i=circles.count do
51        (
52            result = (distance aCircle.pos circles[i].pos) < = (aCircle.radius + circles[i].radius)
53            if result then return result
54        )
55        return false
56    )
```

This function tests if a circle overlaps any of the previous circles that have already been generated (and stored in the *circles* array). The test is simple: if the distance between the two centres of the circles is less than the sum of their radii, then the two circles overlap (fig. 78).

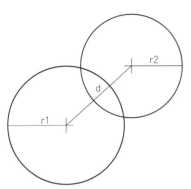 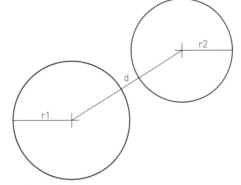

d < (r1 + r2) => Circles overlap   d > (r1 + r2) => Circles do not overlap

fig. 78 Circle intersection test.

```
58        fn outside_mesh aCircle aMesh =
59        (
60
61            for i = 0 to accuracy by 1 do
62            (
63                ang = (i/accuracy as float)*360
64                vx = aCircle.pos.x + cos(ang) * aCircle.radius
65                vy = aCircle.pos.y + sin(ang) * aCircle.radius
66                testRay = ray [vx, vy, 1] [0, 0, -10]
67                if (intersectRay aMesh testRay == undefined) then
68                (
69                    return true
70                )
71            )
72            return false
73        )
```

This function tests whether the circle is inside or outside the selected shape. In order to do so, the script actually temporarily applies an *Edit Poly* modifier to the shape to turn it into a meshed surface that can be tested for intersections. The method of intersection is simple. Several rays (i.e. vectors) are drawn from the circle down to the surface. *3ds Max* has a built-in function, called *intersectRay*, to test if a ray intersects a surface. The ray vectors we construct trace the circumference of the circle (but start 1 unit above) and have a z-length of -10 so that they are guaranteed to cross the XY ground plane. Any positive z coordinate for the start of the ray and a negative z coordinate for its end would suffice to test the intersection with a flat surface on the XY plane **(fig. 79)**.

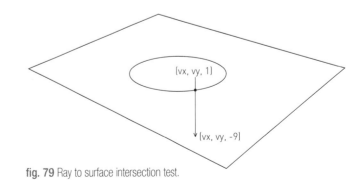

fig. 79 Ray to surface intersection test.

75	fn createCircle minRadius maxRadius ratio =
76	(
77	radius = random minRadius (maxRadius - ((maxRadius*ratio/maxAttempts) as float))
78	x = random (minX + radius) (maxX - radius)
79	y = random (minY + radius) (maxY - radius)
80	newCircle = circle radius:radius
81	newCircle.pos = [x,y,0]
82	return newCircle
83	)

This function simply creates a circle within the minimum and maximum ranges for radius and position. It uses the built-in random function to create a circle within the specified radius range and the specified position boundary. The position boundary is determined as the bounding box of the surface, because anything beyond that would obviously result in a circle outside the shape. Once a circle is created inside the bounding box of the shape, it is tested more accurately for overlap with other circles and for location within the shape itself, using the above functions. The *ratio* parameter incrementally decreases the maximum radius of a circle as more circles are generated. As the shape gets filled up with circles it becomes more and more unlikely that large circles would fit. Thus, with every circle that is successfully generated, we decrease the maximum allowed radius to force the algorithm to generate smaller and smaller circles as it progresses.

85	on generate_button pressed do
86	(

This is the main callback function to generate the circles once the **Generate** button is pressed.

87	if (selectedShape == undefined) then return false
88	if (isDeleted selectedShape) then
89	(
90	selectedShape_tf.text = "NONE"
91	return false
92	)

If the selected shape is undefined or has been deleted before the button is pressed, we stop the script, update the interface text field with 'NONE' as the name of the selected shape and return *false*.

94	coverageArea = 0
95	
96	ep_mod = edit_poly()
97	addModifier selectedShape ep_mod
98	
99	totalArea=0
100	for i=1 to selectedShape.numfaces do totalArea+=(polyop.getfacearea selectedShape i)

We then set the coverage area variable to 0 and apply the *Edit Poly* modifier to the shape to transform it into a polygon. This allows us to test for intersections as well as to compute its total area.

102	bb = nodeGetBoundingBox selectedShape (matrix3 1)
103	minX = bb[1].x
104	maxX = bb[2].x
105	minY = bb[1].y
106	maxY = bb[2].y

Next, we compute the shape's bounding box in order to restrict the zone within which we create circles. This helps us increase the likelihood that a generated circle will fall within the boundaries of the selected shape.

109	circlesCount = circles.count
110	for i = 1 to circlesCount by 1 do
111	(
112	tobedeleted = circles[1]
113	deleteItem circles 1
114	if(isDeleted tobedeleted != true) then
115	(
116	delete tobedeleted
117	)
118	)
119	circles.count = 0
120	packedCircles.text = "0/"+(maxCircles as string)+" Circles"
121	coverage.text = "0 %"
122	redrawViews()

Next, we empty the current array of circles to start anew. If the user has not manually deleted any circle, we delete it ourselves. At the end of this block of code, we set the count of the *circles* array to 0, update the user interface and redraw the scene.

124	j = 1
125	attempts = 0
126	while (circles.count < maxCircles) and (attempts < maxAttempts) do
127	(
128	aCircle = createCircle minRadius maxRadius j
129	if ((overlaps aCircle circles) or (outside_mesh aCircle selectedShape)) then
130	(
131	delete aCircle
132	)
133	else
134	(
135	append circles aCircle
136	j = j + 1
137	coverageArea = coverageArea + pi*radius*radius

138	}
139	attempts = attempts + 1
140	attempts_prog.value = 100.*attempts/maxAttempts
141	generate_prog.value = 100.*j/maxCircles
142	} --end of the for loop

We then start the main loop of this script. While we have not reached the maximum number of circles and the maximum number of attempts, we continue to generate a circle and test its intersection with prior circles and with the selected shape. If it does overlap with other circles or is fully or partially outside the shape, we delete it. Otherwise, we append it to the array of circles and increment the coverage area. Next, we increment the number of attempts and update both progress bars in the user interface.

144	for m in selectedShape.modifiers do
145	(
146	if classOf m==Edit_Poly do deleteModifier selectedShape m
147	)

At the end of the algorithm we remove the temporary *Edit Poly* modifier by searching for it in the list of modifiers that have been applied to the selected shape and deleting it.

149	packedCircles.text = (circles.count as string)+"/"+(maxCircles as string)+" Circles"
150	coverage.text = ((coverageArea/totalArea*100) as string)+" %"
151	)

Finally, we update the interface to inform the user of the number of circles that have been successfully packed and the total percentage of area coverage.

The last section of the script contains the usual callback functions for the user interface elements that we use to update the various parameters. Make note of how the minimum and maximum radius parameters are linked to each other such that the maximum radius can never be smaller than the minimum radius and the minimum radius can never be larger than the maximum radius.

This packing algorithm is one of the simplest, as it does not optimize the generation of the circles (fig. 80). You could enhance it by, for instance, making sure that any generated circle touches another circle, or by ensuring a minimum separation distance from all other circles. Once the script has generated a 2D pattern, we can easily use *3ds Max*'s built-in functionality to apply the circles to 3D constructs (fig. 81).

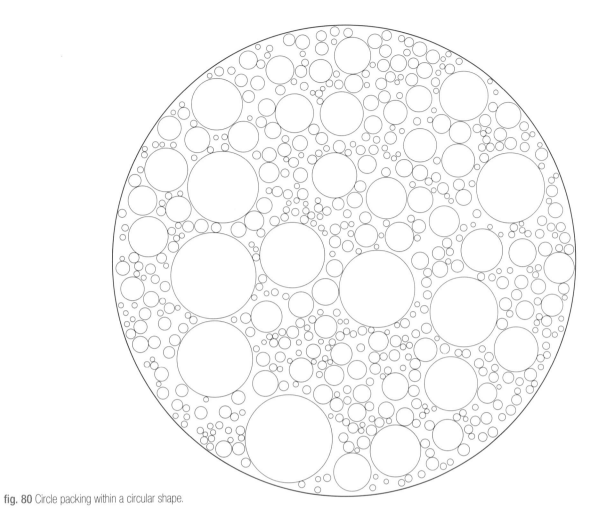

fig. 80 Circle packing within a circular shape.

fig. 81 The Circle Packing script is used to create an imaginary pavilion structure.

Case study The Beast, Museum of Science, Boston, USA

Designer Neri Oxman in collaboration with Craig Carter
Client Museum of Science, Boston, USA
Design 2009
Construction 2010

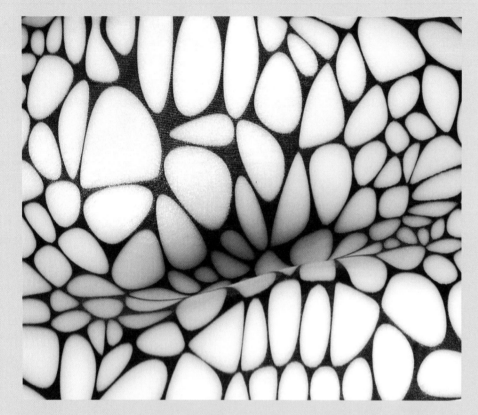

Left
Monocoque 1.

Neri Oxman is a researcher and designer whose work focuses on the exploration of a new language of architecture that emerges from the usage of modern digital tools, a project that she calls 'material ecology'. In her work, computing is an integral part of the design process, from conception to fabrication. The form of a designed artefact is determined by the digital methodology that produced it, but that methodology itself may draw on natural processes: Oxman advocates 'a synergetic approach to design whereby material organization and behaviour, as they appear in the physical world, may be integrated into digital tools for design exploration'. This intimate connection between digital tool and designed artefact must be maintained through the production phase of design. 'The tool, technique or technology has as much value and meaning as the artefact itself, inherently promoting explicit effects', she states. To this end, she uses digital

tools not just to create forms using existing materials but also to help create new materials with new formal expressions and behaviour.

For Oxman, nature constitutes a source not only of formal inspiration, but also of technical solutions. Oxman has focused in particular on the fibre composition of biological materials and their ability to map the performance requirements of material structuring and allocation. In order to emulate this attribute of natural materials, she has created what she calls the variable property design (VPD) method, which allows her to model, simulate and fabricate material assemblies with varying properties. This allows her to avoid default material choices and fabrication methods. Instead, she combines well-known materials, such as latex and resin, and manipulates them in order to produce responsive surfaces. These new assemblies exhibit anisotropic qualities that can be used to design responsive surfaces and entities

with customized performance and behaviour.

One such assembly is a resin-impregnated latex membrane. Oxman has investigated the behaviour of this new material in both physical and digital models, and has designed and fabricated a number of innovative projects with it. Monocoque 1 and 2 (2007) constitute explorations of the structural behaviour of a material in relation to its geometric configuration. Employing a Voronoi algorithm (which also supplied the iconography of the surface), the designer produced vein-like networks made of a stiff material. Both the distribution and density of the cellular entities in between these networks and the variation of the surfaces' overall thickness became means of expressing the structure of the final project. In Monocoque 1, for instance, the stiff, black resin composite networks become denser and thicker in vertical areas that perform under compression, while the soft, white, acrylic-

Above
Close-up of black resin composite and
white acrylic-based cellular elements.

Below
When The Beast is positioned vertically, the
kneeling female figure becomes clearly visible.

based photopolymer cellular elements take more
space in the horizontal parts, providing greater
flexibility in areas working under tension. The
arrangement is similar in Monocoque 2. In this
case, however, the cellular elements remain
empty, resulting in an open, 3D framework.

In The Beast, which is the prototype for a
chaise longue, the designer expanded on the
ideas of the Monocoque projects. Resembling a
kneeling female figure, The Beast again uses the
Voronoi pattern, and the single undulating surface
has the appearance of a stiff, dark, vein-like
network. In order to determine the composition
of this surface, a digital analysis of its structural
function identified the requirements of strain,
stress and comfort in each area, and an algorithm
assigned one of five materials for its construction.
The materials vary in softness and flexibility, as
well as in translucency and colour, resulting in
a chair that seems to respond to the needs of

the user, and which attains a greater material
sophistication than the Monocoque projects.
However, the main objective of the project was
to apply a tiling algorithm, using Voronoi cell
tessellation, which implemented the results of a
quantitative categorization and analysis. Through
this project, Oxman points to a new direction for
future architecture that tightly couples material
research with digital form-finding processes.
This approach, which we might understand to
be *material-as-parameter*, combines innovative
parametric design and digital fabrication
techniques with new, synthetically engineered and
fabricated materials, resulting in an increase in
structural and environmental performance and the
optimization of material efficiency and distribution.

Weaving

Weaving was known in the Palaeolithic era and continues to this day. In its simplest form, weaving creates a fabric from the interlacing of two threads at right angles to each other. The lateral threads do not undulate and are called the *weft* while the longitudinal threads interlace the weft and are called the *warp*. This basic method of giving a surface structural strength is still used today for basket weaving (**fig. 82**), and it is also employed metaphorically in architectural screens (**fig. 83**) and façades (**fig. 84**). In his seminal book, *The Four Elements of Architecture*, the nineteenth-century German architectural theorist and philosopher Gottfried Semper dedicates a chapter to the textile arts (at the beginning of which he laments not having an entire book to devote to the discussion). At the start of the chapter, he explains the architectural reason for his keen interest: 'All operations in the textile arts seek to transform raw materials with the appropriate properties into products, whose common features are great pliancy and considerable strength … used as pliant surfaces to cover, to hold, to dress, to enclose and so forth.' In the section on weaving, Semper makes an important point, which still fascinates designers today.

He writes: 'Style, as far as it is dependent on the purpose of a thing, can be more easily formulated into principles than can the speculative theory of form be deduced in those areas where the form must be considered as a function of the technical means that come into play.' In this passage, he is advocating the idea that the form of an object or building should reflect the process of its creation; if it does so, this will give rise to theories of form and ultimately the principles of a style. It is exactly this notion of encoding the process of design in its final result that attracts designers to parametric processes. Parametric digital weaving is an excellent example; the form is not created intuitively, but rather it results from an intelligent understanding and encoding of its process of creation. However, digitally creating a weave is a challenge, as it must fulfil several conditions. First, the weave should

fig. 82 A basket weave with weft and warp threads.

fig. 83 *Design 3* continuous interwoven screen for the church in Leising, Vienna, Austria, Erwin Hauer.

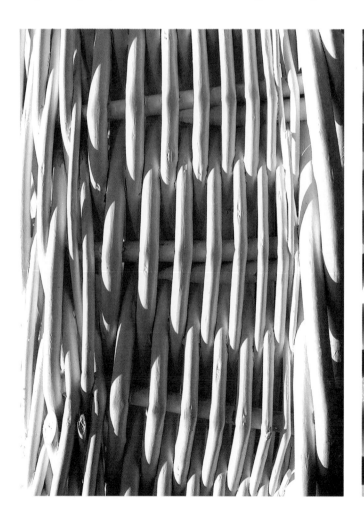

be able to populate any curved or undulating surface and not just simple flat planes. Second, the threads of a weave need to maintain their continuity along the surface. Unlike tiling and subdivision, a weave – especially the warp component – cannot segment the surface into repeatable, identical modular units. Instead, it has to simultaneously take into consideration the global and local conditions of the surface (curvature, orientation) in order to continually thread the entire surface in a smooth manner. To add even more to the complexity, a warp reverses its orientation with every row. Finally, the weave threads cannot intersect – a situation which happens all too easily in the non-physical world of 3D modelling.

Starting from these principles and challenges, we will embark on two tutorials on digital weaving, where the second tutorial will build on the one before it. The first tutorial will construct a simple parametric ribbon that undulates smoothly along a curved spline. This will be the

basis for creating another parametric system, in the second tutorial, that will accept any NURBS surface as input and generate a matching woven surface made of weft and warp threads. As in any parametric system, we will enable the user to specify the parameters of the system, in this case the thread count in each direction, and the amount of undulation as well as the shape and size of the threads.

fig. 84 Aragon Pavilion, Saragossa, Spain (2008), Olando and Mendo Architects.

TUTORIAL A SIMPLE RIBBON

In this first tutorial on digital weaving, we will derive an undulating ribbon from any line or curve. The script allows the user to select a line from the scene, dynamically define the parameters of the ribbon and generate a sweep profile along the generated spline. The parameters for

the sweep profile (e.g. the sweep cross-section shape, size, etc.) can be adjusted independently using the built-in sweep modifier. This script will be created as a utility.

→ Open *3ds Max*, save and close any prior scenes, create a new empty scene. Create an undulating smooth line in the FRONT viewport. For a smooth line, make sure you choose *Bezier* as the drag type. Once you have created a curved line, choose **MAXScript** → **New Script** from the top menu. In the script window that opens, type the following algorithm:

```
1    utility Ribbon "Ribbon"
2    (
3        global mySplineShape
4        global myRibbon
5        global amplitude = 10
6        global steps = 20
7        global sweepMod
8
9        --filter all objects of class Spline or line:
10       fn spline_filt obj = ((classof obj == SplineShape) or (classof obj == line))
11
12       pickbutton selectSpline "Select Spline" width:140 filter:spline_filt
13       edittext selectedObject "Spline: " text:"NONE" readonly:true width:138
14       spinner steps_spinner "Steps: " range:[1,1000,steps] type:#integer
15       spinner amplitude_spinner "Amplitude: " range:[1,1000,amplitude]  type:#worldunits
16       button generate_button "Generate" enabled:true width: 140 height:50
17
18       on selectSpline picked obj do
19           (
20               --see if the user did not cancel the picking...
21               if obj != undefined do
22                   (
23                       -- display the name of the object on the button:
24                       selectedObject.text = obj.name
25                       mySplineShape = obj
26                   )
27           )
28       fn generateRibbon = (
29
30           if (mySplineShape == undefined) then
31               (
32                   return false
```

```
33              }
34
35          if (myRibbon != undefined) then
36          (
37              if (not (isDeleted myRibbon)) then
38              (
39                  sweepMod = myRibbon.modifiers["sweep"]
40                  delete myRibbon
41              )
42          )
43          myRibbon = SplineShape pos:[0,0,0]
44          addNewSpline myRibbon
45
46          for i = 0 to steps by 1 do
47          (
48              case of (
49                  (mod (i+2) 2 == 0): multFact = 1;
50                  (mod (i+2) 2 != 0): multFact = -1;
51              )
52
53              unitDist = 1.0/(float) steps
54              currentDist = abs ((float)i/(float)steps)
55
56              if (currentDist > 1) then
57              (
58                  currentDist = 1
59              )
60
61              pointPos = pathInterp mySplineShape 1 currentDist
62
63              tangent = normalize (pathTangent mySplineShape 1 currentDist)
64              offsetVect = (normalize (cross tangent y_axis) )* amplitude* multFact
65              offsetPos1 = pointPos + offsetVect
66
67              interpolationInValue = (currentDist - (unitDist/2))
68              if (interpolationInValue < 0) then
69                  (
70                      interpolationInValue = 0
71                  )
72
73              interpolationOutValue = (currentDist + (unitDist/2))
74              if (interpolationOutValue > 1) then
75                  (
```

```
76                    interpolationOutValue = 1
77                )
78
79              inpoint = pathInterp mySplineShape 1 interpolationInValue
80              outpoint = pathInterp mySplineShape 1 interpolationOutValue
81              invector = inpoint + offsetVect
82              outvector = outpoint + offsetVect
83
84              addKnot myRibbon 1 #bezier #curve offsetPos1 invector outvector
85          )
86
87          if (sweepMod == undefined) then
88          (
89              sweepMod = sweep()
90              sweepMod.currentbuiltinshape = 4
91          )
92          addmodifier myRibbon sweepMod
93          updateShape myRibbon
94      )
95
96      on amplitude_spinner changed amt do -- when spinner value changes...
97          (
98              amplitude = amt
99              generateRibbon();
100         )
101
102     on steps_spinner changed amt do -- when spinner value changes...
103         (
104             steps = amt
105             generateRibbon();
106         )
107
108     on generate_button pressed do
109         (
111             generateRibbon();
111         )
112 )
```

⟶ Save your script and then choose **Tools** ⟶ **Evaluate All** to run the script. You will find the script utility under the **Utilities** tab (hammer icon). Click on the **MAXScript** button and then choose **Ribbon** from the **Utilities** pull down menu (fig. 85).

⟶ Press the **Select Spline** button and click on the spline in your scene to select it. Its name should show up under that button. Next, click on the **Generate** button to generate an initial ribbon. You can then vary the parameters for amplitude and steps to dynamically change the ribbon. If you wish to change the sweep profile, click on the actual ribbon to select it, then choose the **Modify** tab. You will see the sweep modifier listed so you can change all its parameters there (fig. 86). You can still go back to the **Utilities** tab and the **Ribbon** utility to change the amplitude and the number of steps.

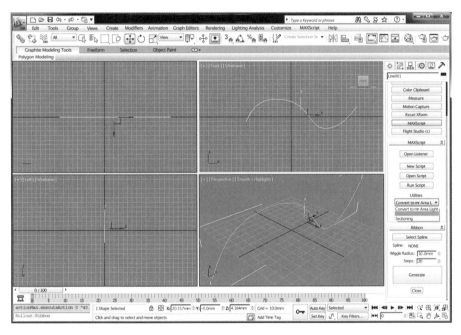

fig. 85 Ribbon Utility Script.

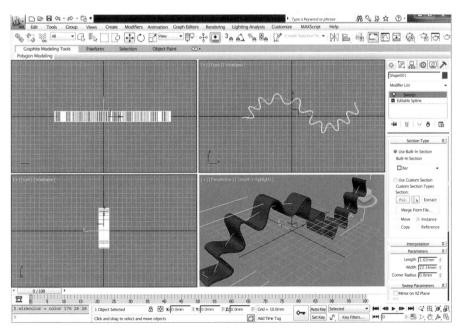

fig. 86 The sweep modifier.

A SIMPLE RIBBON/CONTINUED

Let's take a closer look at the script:

1	utility Ribbon "Ribbon"
2	(
3	global mySplineShape
4	global myRibbon
5	global amplitude = 10
6	global steps = 20
7	global sweepMod

We start by declaring a scripted utility called *Ribbon* and titled with the same name. The global variables are *mySplineShape* (this is the selected spline around which we will weave a ribbon); *myRibbon*, which is the resulting ribbon generated by the script; *amplitude*, which is the amount of undulation of the ribbon; *steps*, which are the number of undulations that the ribbon will have along the curve; and, finally, *sweepMod*, which is the sweep modifier that will sweep a cross-section of our choosing along the ribbon to create a 3D object with thickness.

9	--filter all objects of class Spline or line:
10	fn spline_filt obj = ((classof obj == SplineShape) or (classof obj == line))

Next, we declare a function called *spline_filt* that accepts an object and returns either *true* or *false* depending on the type (class) of the object. This function is used to restrict the user to selecting only splines or lines. Any other object will not be accepted as a selection in the next step.

12	pickbutton selectSpline "Select Spline" width:140 filter:spline_filt
13	edittext selectedObject "Spline: " text:"NONE" readonly:true width:138
14	spinner steps_spinner "Steps: " range:[1,1000,steps] type:#integer
15	spinner amplitude_spinner "Amplitude: " range:[1,1000,amplitude] type:#worldunits
16	button generate_button "Generate" enabled:true width: 140 height:50

Next, we declare a series of user interface elements that will be shown in a rollout once the user selects the **Ribbon** utility. The first, a pick button, is a special button that allows the user to select an object from the scene. One of its arguments is a filter that will refuse to select an object if the function returns *false*. This is where we specify our previously declared *spline_filt* function. Next, we specify a text field to display the name of the selected spline, two spinners for specifying the amplitude and the number of steps, and, last, a button that, when pressed, generates the ribbon.

28	fn generateRibbon = (
29	
30	if (mySplineShape == undefined) then
31	(
32	return false
33	)
34	
35	if (myRibbon != undefined) then

36	(
37	if (not (isDeleted myRibbon)) then
38	(
39	sweepMod = myRibbon.modifiers["sweep"]
40	delete myRibbon
41	)
42	)

We then declare the actual function to generate the ribbon. The function starts out by testing if the spline shape is undefined (i.e. whether the user has pressed the generate button before selecting a spline). In this case, the function does nothing but return the value *false*. Next, we check whether *myRibbon* is undefined and, if so, we check whether it exists. If it does exist (i.e. if it was generated in a previous cycle), we save its sweep modifier before deleting it to start fresh. We save the sweep modifier so that we can keep and reuse any prior customization the user has done to the default ribbon (e.g. changing the sweep shape or its size).

43	myRibbon = SplineShape pos:[0,0,0]
44	addNewSpline myRibbon

Next, we declare a new spline shape and we store it in a variable called *myRibbon*. We start by adding a new spline to *myRibbon* (a spline shape can be made of many sub-splines).

46	for i = 0 to steps by 1 do
47	(
48	case of (
49	(mod (i+2) 2 == 0): multFact = 1;
50	(mod (i+2) 2 != 0): multFact = -1;
51	)
52	
53	unitDist = 1.0/(float) steps
54	currentDist = abs ((float)i/(float)steps)
55	
56	if (currentDist > 1) then
57	(
58	currentDist = 1
59	)

In the next section, we start a loop from 0 to the desired number of steps. Within this loop, we compute whether we are at an odd or an even numbered cycle, by using the *mod* command, in order to specify a multiplication factor. Later in the code, this will be used to create the undulating effect of the ribbon. We then compute the normalized unit distance (which we can think of as a wave length) by dividing 1 by the number of steps. We also compute how far we have travelled along the ribbon's normalized length by dividing *i* by the number of steps (this will give us a number between 0 and 1). In order to avoid any decimal point inaccuracy we make sure that the current distance never exceeds 1.

| 61 | pointPos = pathInterp mySplineShape 1 currentDist |

The above line of code is perhaps the most relevant to this algorithm. The function *pathInterp* computes the location of a point on a path based on a parametric normalized distance (from 0 to 1).

63	tangent = normalize (pathTangent mySplineShape 1 currentDist)
64	offsetVect = (normalize (cross tangent y_axis))* amplitude* multFact
65	offsetPos1 = pointPos + offsetVect

Once we have computed the point on the curve, we need to compute the location of a second offset point, which will go either above or below the curve. The challenge here is that the point should be offset along a line perpendicular to the curve at that location (fig. 87). Therefore, we need to calculate the tangent at that location before specifying the perpendicular vector. This is done with an operation called the vector cross product, which examines two vectors and results in a third vector perpendicular to them.

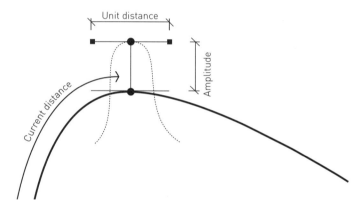

fig. 87 The basic parameters for curve interpolation.

67	interpolationInValue = (currentDist - (unitDist/2))
68	if (interpolationInValue < 0) then
69	(
70	interpolationInValue = 0
71	)
72	
73	interpolationOutValue = (currentDist + (unitDist/2))
74	if (interpolationOutValue > 1) then
75	(
76	interpolationOutValue = 1
77	)
78	
79	inpoint = pathInterp mySplineShape 1 interpolationInValue
80	outpoint = pathInterp mySplineShape 1 interpolationOutValue
81	invector = inpoint + offsetVect
82	outvector = outpoint + offsetVect

We then compute two additional values to specify handles for the Bezier curve tangent. These points are located half the unit distance on each side of the current point and then offset using the same offset vector. As we did before, we ensure that the values do not go outside the 0 to 1 limits.

84   addKnot myRibbon 1 #bezier #curve offsetPos1 invector outvector

Finally, we are able to add a *knot* (i.e. a vertex) to our ribbon spline. We specify this vertex as type *#bezier*, using the two vectors we have just computed, such that the curve is smooth and tangent to that vertex.

```
87          if (sweepMod == undefined) then
88          (
89              sweepMod = sweep()
90              sweepMod.currentbuiltinshape = 4
91          )
92          addmodifier myRibbon sweepMod
93          updateShape myRibbon
94      )
```

In this last step, we define a sweep modifier and add it to the shape. We leave the specification of the modifier to the user, who can modify the ribbon in the user interface.

In the remainder of the script, we respond to changes in values of the parameters by re-generating the ribbon in real-time (fig. 88). This is similar to prior tutorials.

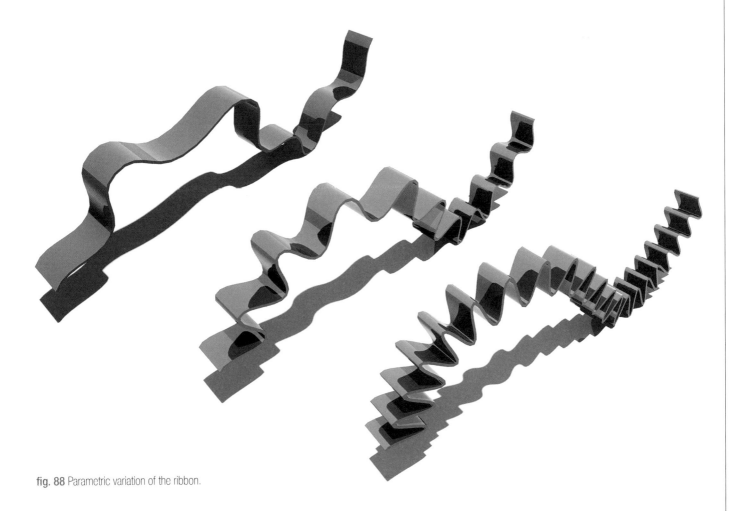

fig. 88 Parametric variation of the ribbon.

TUTORIAL WEAVING A NURBS SURFACE

In this second tutorial on digital weaving, we will derive a woven mesh from any NURBS surface. The script allows the user to select a NURBS surface and to specify the thread counts for the weft and the warp as well as the weave's amplitude, to create a mesh with smoothly interlaced weft and warp threads (fig. 89). These threads are created as single-line spline curves. A sweep modifier is then applied to them to create a thickened mesh. Applying the sweep modifier provides the user with the greatest flexibility in parametrically modifying the cross-section and size of the sweep as well as

other attributes in order to avoid self-intersection. Many of the algorithmic techniques in this script derive from the previous one. In particular, the distance along a curve is expanded in this script to the parametric *u* and *v* values, as we have seen in prior tutorials. The tangent at the curve in the previous tutorial is expanded to a *u-tangent* and a *v-tangent* in this tutorial. Luckily, *MAXScript* gives us built-in functions to calculate the *u* and *v* tangents at any location on the surface. These tangents will be essential to the calculation of a perpendicular (normal) vector to offset the warp threads in alternating directions.

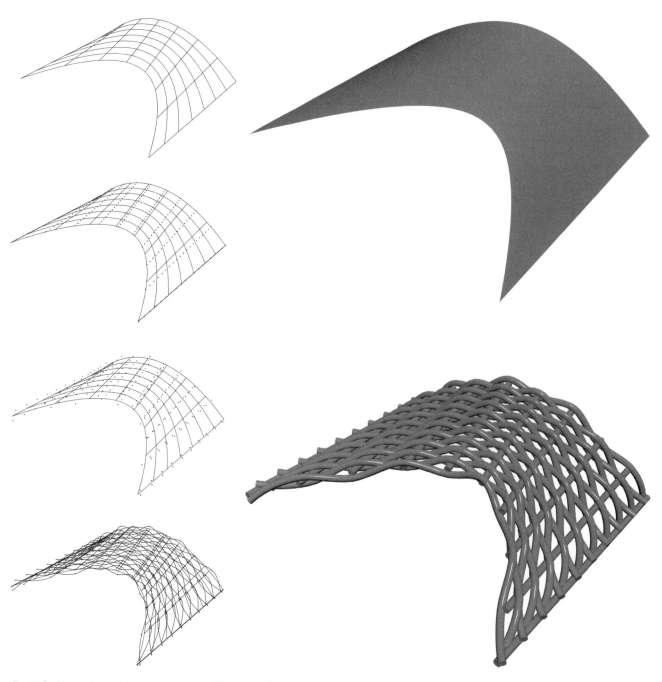

fig. 89 Deriving surface points, woven lines and solids from an initial surface.

$\rightarrow$ Open *3ds Max*, save and close any prior scenes, and create a new empty scene.
Create an undulating NURBS surface (if you need help with this, see the tutorial on
deriving a diagrid mesh from a NURBS surface on page 93). Once you have created
the surface, choose **MAXScript** $\rightarrow$ **New Script** from the top menu. In the script
window that opens, type the following algorithm:

```
1    utility Weave "Weave"
2    (
3        global selectedSurface
4        global myNURBSSurface
5        global myWeft
6        global myWarp
7        global weftThreadCount = 10
8        global warpThreadCount =10
9        global amplitude = 1
10       global multFact = 1
11       global weftSweepMod
12       global warpSweepMod
13       global hideNURBS
14       global swapUV = false
15       global closedInU = 0
16       global closedInV = 0

18       -- A function to filter all objects that are not of class NURBS Surface:
19       fn nurbs_filt obj = (classOf obj == NURBSSurf)

21       pickbutton selectNURBS "Select NURBS" width:140 filter:nurbs_filt
22       edittext selectedObject "NURBS: " text:"NONE" readonly:true width:138
23       spinner weftThreadCount_spinner "Weft: " range:[1,10000,weftThreadCount] type:#integer
24       spinner warpThreadCount_spinner "Warp: " range:[1,10000,warpThreadCount] type:#integer
25       spinner amplitude_spinner "Amplitude: " range:[0,10000,amplitude]  type:#worldunits
26       checkbox swapUV_cb "Swap" checked:false tooltip:"Swap U and V directions"
27       checkbox hideNURBS_cb "Hide NURBS" checked:false tooltip:"Hide Parent NURBS Surface"
28       button generate_button "Generate" enabled:true width: 140 height:50

30       on selectNURBS picked obj do
31           (
32               --see if the user did not cancel the picking...
33               if obj != undefined do
34                   (
35                       -- display the name of the object on the button:
36                       selectedObject.text = obj.name
37                       myNURBSSurface = getnurbsset obj #relational
38                       selectedSurface = obj
39                   )
```

```
40              )
41
42      fn generateWeave = (
43
44          if (myNURBSSurface == undefined) then
45              (
46                  return false
47              )
48
49          if (myWeft != undefined) then
50              (
51                  if (not (isDeleted myWeft)) then
52                      (
53                          weftSweepMod = myWeft.modifiers["sweep"]
54                          delete myWeft
55                      )
56              )
57
58          if (myWarp != undefined) then
59              (
60                  if (not (isDeleted myWarp)) then
61                      (
62                          warpSweepMod = myWarp.modifiers["sweep"]
63                          delete myWarp
64                      )
65              )
66
67          for m = 1 to myNURBSSurface.count by 1 do
68              (
69                  if ((superClassOf myNURBSSurface[m]) == NURBSSurface) then
70                      (
71                          -- Find the min and max values for the u and v range.
72                          minu = (myNURBSSurface[m].uParameterRangeMin)
73                          maxu = (myNURBSSurface[m].uParameterRangeMax)
74                          minv = (myNURBSSurface[m].vParameterRangeMin)
75                          maxv = (myNURBSSurface[m].vParameterRangeMax)
76
77                          case of (
78                              (myNURBSSurface[m].closedInU == true): (format "shape closed in U\n";closedInU = 1)
79                              (myNURBSSurface[m].closedInU == false): (format "shape open in U\n"; closedInU = 0)
80                          )
```

```
81
82              case of (
83                      (myNURBSSurface[m].closedInV == true): closedInV = 1
84                      (myNURBSSurface[m].closedInV == false): closedInV = 0
85              )
86
87              myWarp = SplineShape pos:[0,0,0]
88              for i = 0 to (warpThreadCount - 1) by 1 do
89              (
90                      case of (
91                              (mod (i+2) 2 == 0): xmultFact = 1;
92                              (mod (i+2) 2 != 0): xmultFact = -1;
93                      )
94
95                      xposition = (i/(warpThreadCount - 1) as float)
96                      if (xposition > 1) then
97                      (
98                              xposition = 1
99                      )
100
101                     addNewSpline myWarp
102
103                     for j = 0 to (weftThreadCount - 1 - closedInV) by 1 do
104                     (
105                             case of (
106                                     (mod (j+2) 2 == 0): ymultFact = 1;
107                                     (mod (j+2) 2 != 0): ymultFact = -1;
108                             )
109
110                             unitDist = (1/(weftThreadCount - 1) as float)
111                             yposition = (j/(weftThreadCount - 1) as float)
112                             uposition = (minu + (maxu-minu)*xposition)
113                             vposition = (minv + (maxv-minv)*yposition)
114
115                             case of (
116                                     (swapUV == false): pointPos = evalpos  myNURBSSurface[m] uposition vposition
117                                     (swapUV == true): pointPos = evalpos  myNURBSSurface[m] vposition uposition
118                             )
119
120                             uTangent = evalUTangent myNURBSSurface[m] uposition vposition
121                             vTangent = evalVTangent myNURBSSurface[m] uposition vposition
122                             offsetVect = (normalize (cross uTangent vTangent))*xmultFact*ymultFact*amplitude
123                             offsetPos = pointPos + offsetVect
```

```
124                        addKnot myWarp (i+1) #smooth #curve offsetPos
125                  )
126              if (myNURBSSurface[m].closedInV) then
127              (
128                  close myWarp (i+1)
129              )
130          )
131
132          if (warpSweepMod == undefined) then
133          (
134              warpSweepMod = sweep()
135              warpSweepMod.currentbuiltinshape = 4
136          )
137          addmodifier myWarp warpSweepMod
138          myWarp.rotation = selectedSurface.rotation
139          myWarp.scale = selectedSurface.scale
140          myWarp.pos = selectedSurface.pos
141          myWarp.name = selectedSurface.name + "-Warp" + (m as string)
142      Updateshape myWarp
143
144          myWeft = SplineShape pos:[0,0,0]
145          for i = 0 to (weftThreadCount - 1 - closedInV) by 1 do
146          (
147              yposition = (i/(weftThreadCount - 1) as float)
148              addNewSpline myWeft
149              for j = 0 to (warpThreadCount - 1 - closedInU) by 1 do
150              (
151                  xposition = (j/(warpThreadCount - 1) as float)
152                  uposition = (minu + (maxu-minu)*xposition)
153                  vposition = (minv + (maxv-minv)*yposition)
154
155                  case of (
156                      (swapUV == false): pointPos = evalpos  myNURBSSurface[m] uposition vposition
157                      (swapUV == true):pointPos = evalpos  myNURBSSurface[m] vposition uposition
158                  )
159
160                  addKnot myWeft (i+1) #smooth #curve pointPos
161              )
162              if (myNURBSSurface[m].closedInU) then
163              (
164                  close myWeft (i+1)
```

```
165                    }
166                  }
167                    myWeft.rotation = selectedSurface.rotation
168                    myWeft.scale = selectedSurface.scale
169                    myWeft.pos = selectedSurface.pos
170                    myWeft.name = selectedSurface.name + "-Weft" + (m as string)
171
172                    if (weftSweepMod == undefined) then
173                    (
174                        weftSweepMod = sweep()
175                        weftSweepMod.currentbuiltinshape = 4
176                    )
177                    addmodifier myWeft weftSweepMod
178                    updateShape myWeft
179                }
180            else
181            (
182                    format "Could not find a NURBS surface.\n"
183            )
184        )
185    )
186
187    -- Handle the user interface events.
188    on weftThreadCount_spinner changed amt do
189        (
190            weftThreadCount = amt
191            generateWeave();
192        )
193    on warpThreadCount_spinner changed amt do
194        (
195            warpThreadCount = amt
196            generateWeave();
197        )
198    on amplitude_spinner changed amt do
199        (
200            amplitude = amt
201            generateWeave();
202        )
203    on swapUV_cb changed state do
204        (
205            swapUV = state
206            generateWeave()
207        )
```

```
208          on hideNURBS_cb changed state do
209              (
210                  if (selectedSurface != undefined) then
211                  (
212                      case of (
213                          (state == true): hide selectedSurface
214                          (state == false): unhide selectedSurface
215                      )
216                  )
217              )
218          on generate_button pressed do
219              (
220                  generateWeave()
221              )
222      )
```

→ Save your script and then choose **Tools** → **Evaluate All** to run the script.
You will find the script utility under **Utilities** (hammer icon). Click on the
MAXScript button and then choose **Weave** from the **Utilities** pull down menu.

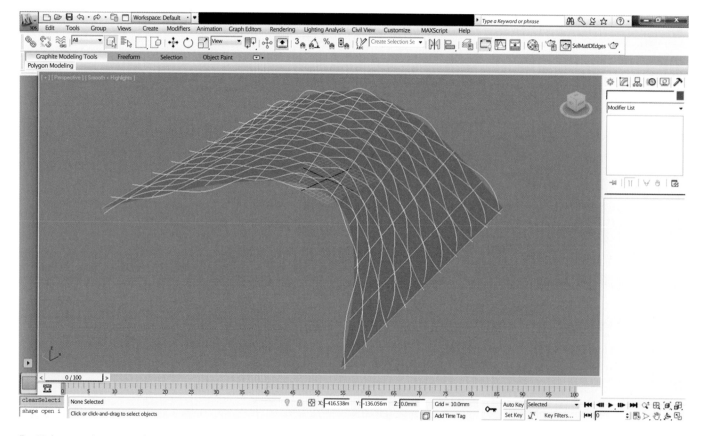

fig. 90 A parametric woven surface generated by the script.

→ Press the **Select NURBS** button and click on the NURBS surface in your scene to select it. Its name should show up under that button. Next, specify the number of weft and warp threads, and the amplitude of the undulation of the warp thread. Here you can also swap the direction of the threads and hide or show the selected NURBS surface. Once you are ready, click on the **Generate** button to generate an initial woven mesh (fig. 90). You can then vary the parameters for amplitude and steps to dynamically change the weave. If you wish to change the sweep profile, click on the actual weft or warp threads in the scene to select them, then choose the **Modify** tab. You will see the sweep modifier listed and you can change all its parameters there (fig. 91). You can still go back to the **Utilities** tab and the **Weave** utility in order to change the amplitude and the number of steps.

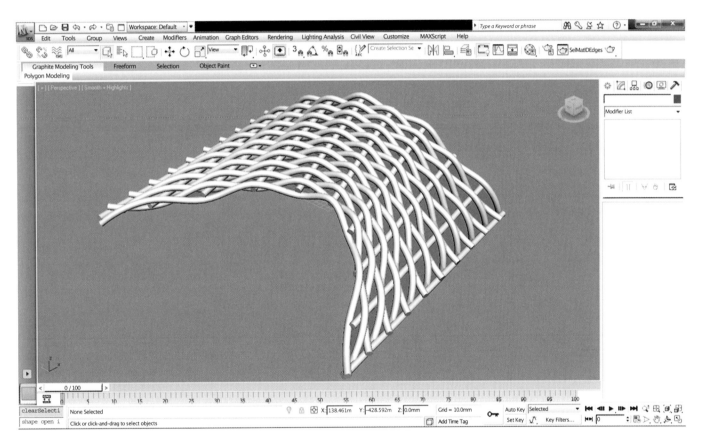

fig. 91 The sweep modifier.

Let's take a closer look at the script:

```
1    utility Weave "Weave"
2    (
3        global selectedSurface
4        global myNURBSSurface
5        global myWeft
6        global myWarp
7        global weftThreadCount = 10
8        global warpThreadCount =10
9        global amplitude = 1
```

10	global multFact = 1
11	global weftSweepMod
12	global warpSweepMod
13	global hideNURBS
14	global swapUV = false
15	global closedInU = 0
16	global closedInV = 0

We start by declaring a scripted utility called *Weave* and titled with the same name. The global variables are *selectedSurface* (the NURBS surface the user selects from the scene), *myNURBSSurface* (the internal representation of the NURBS surface), *myWeft* and *myWarp* (the generated splines for the weft and warp), the thread counts, the amplitude of the weave, a multiplying factor to decide on the direction of the offset, the weft and warp sweep modifiers, a Boolean variable for deciding if the NURBS surface is to be shown or hidden, a flag to switch the *u* and *v* directions, and two last variables to indicate if the NURBS surface is closed (joined end-to-end) or open (e.g. a sheet of paper).

19	fn nurbs_filt obj = (classOf obj == NURBSSurf)

This function is used as a filter to make sure only NURBS surfaces are selected for weaving.

21	pickbutton selectNURBS "Select NURBS" width:140 filter:nurbs_filt
22	edittext selectedObject "NURBS: " text:"NONE" readonly:true width:138
23	spinner weftThreadCount_spinner "Weft: " range:[1,10000,weftThreadCount] type:#integer
24	spinner warpThreadCount_spinner "Warp: " range:[1,10000,warpThreadCount] type:#integer
25	spinner amplitude_spinner "Amplitude: " range:[0,10000,amplitude] type:#worldunits
26	checkbox swapUV_cb "Swap" checked:false tooltip:"Swap U and V directions"
27	checkbox hideNURBS_cb "Hide NURBS" checked:false tooltip:"Hide Parent NURBS Surface"
28	button generate_button "Generate" enabled:true width: 140 height:50

Then we define the user interface: a pick button to select the NURBS surface from the scene, a text field to display the name of the selected surface, three spinners to input the values for the weft and warp thread counts and the amplitude of the warp, and two checkboxes, one to specify if the *u* and *v* need to be swapped and one for whether to hide the parent NURBS surface. Finally, we provide a button to generate the weave. Changing any value in the interface triggers a re-generation of the weave. This results in real-time updating and a smoother user experience, where the effect of changing a parameter can be seen instantly.

30	on selectNURBS picked obj do
31	(
32	--see if the user did not cancel the picking...
33	if obj != undefined do
34	(
35	-- display the name of the object on the button:
36	selectedObject.text = obj.name
37	myNURBSSurface = getnurbsset obj #relational

38	selectedSurface = obj
39	)
40	)

The callback function above is triggered once the user picks an object from the scene. The function copies the name of the object, retrieves *3ds Max*'s internal representation of the NURBS surface and stores a pointer to it in the variable *selectedSurface*.

42	fn generateWeave = (

We then start the main function to generate the weave.

44	if (myNURBSSurface == undefined) then
45	(
46	return false
47	)

If the surface is undefined, then stop the algorithm and return the value *false*.

49	if (myWeft != undefined) then
50	(
51	if (not (isDeleted myWeft)) then
52	(
53	weftSweepMod = myWeft.modifiers["sweep"]
54	delete myWeft
55	)
56	)
57	
58	if (myWarp != undefined) then
59	(
60	if (not (isDeleted myWarp)) then
61	(
62	warpSweepMod = myWarp.modifiers["sweep"]
63	delete myWarp
64	)
65	)

If the weft and warp exist and have not been deleted by the user, then, before deleting them, save a copy of their sweep modifiers to reuse for the new weft and warp.

67	for m = 1 to myNURBSSurface.count by 1 do
68	(

A NURBS can have many sub-surfaces. Loop through them one by one to weave each.

69	if ((superClassOf myNURBSSurface[m]) == NURBSSurface) then
70	(

A NURBS structure can be made of surfaces, curves and vertices. We make sure
we only weave surfaces by examining the superclass of the current surface.

72	minu = (myNURBSSurface[m].uParameterRangeMin)
73	maxu = (myNURBSSurface[m].uParameterRangeMax)
74	minv = (myNURBSSurface[m].vParameterRangeMin)
75	maxv = (myNURBSSurface[m].vParameterRangeMax)

We then find the parametric range for the surface (the minimum and maximum *u* and *v*
values).

77	case of (
78	(myNURBSSurface[m].closedInU == true): (format "shape closed in U\n";closedInU = 1)
79	(myNURBSSurface[m].closedInU == false): (format "shape open in U\n"; closedInU = 0)
80	)
81	
82	case of (
83	(myNURBSSurface[m].closedInV == true): closedInV = 1
84	(myNURBSSurface[m].closedInV == false): closedInV = 0
85	)

Next, we check if the NURBS surface is open or closed. This will help us to avoid
overlapping vertices if it is closed.

87	myWarp = SplineShape pos:[0,0,0]

We define a new spline shape for the warp.

88	for i = 0 to (warpThreadCount - 1) by 1 do
89	(

We create two nested loops to generate the warp. The outer loop iterates from 0 to
the warp tread count (minus 1).

90	case of (
91	(mod (i+2) 2 == 0): xmultFact = 1;
92	(mod (i+2) 2 != 0): xmultFact = -1;
93	)

We test if we are on an even or an odd iteration to reverse the direction of the warp.

95	xposition = (i/(warpThreadCount - 1) as float)
96	if (xposition > 1) then
97	(
98	xposition = 1
99	)

We then calculate the *xposition* as a factor from 0 to 1 based on the current iteration.
We will use *xposition* later to calculate the coordinates of the current point on the surface.

101	addNewSpline myWarp

We add a new spline to the *myWarp* spline structure.

103	for j = 0 to (weftThreadCount - 1 - closedInV) by 1 do
104	(

We then start the inner nested loop to go through the weft threads. We deduct 1 if it
is a closed NURBS surface to avoid overlapping vertices.

105	case of (
106	(mod (j+2) 2 == 0): ymultFact = 1;
107	(mod (j+2) 2 != 0): ymultFact = -1;
108	)

We then test if we are on an even or an odd inner iteration to set the direction of the
warp.

110	unitDist = (1/(weftThreadCount - 1) as float)
111	yposition = (j/(weftThreadCount - 1) as float)
112	uposition = (minu + (maxu-minu)*xposition)
113	vposition = (minv + (maxv-minv)*yposition)

Next, we calculate a normalized unit distance, a *yposition*, a *uposition* and a *vposition*.
The latter two positions will enable us to derive the coordinates of the current point on
the surface.

115	case of (
116	(swapUV == false): pointPos = evalpos myNURBSSurface[m] uposition vposition
117	(swapUV == true): pointPos = evalpos myNURBSSurface[m] vposition uposition
118	)

We detect whether the user wishes to swap the *u* and *v* directions and then we use the
built-in *evalpos* function to derive the coordinates of the current point on the surface,
based on the calculated *u* and *v* positions.

120	uTangent = evalUTangent myNURBSSurface[m] uposition vposition
121	vTangent = evalVTangent myNURBSSurface[m] uposition vposition
122	offsetVect = (normalize (cross uTangent vTangent))*xmultFact*ymultFact*amplitude
123	offsetPos = pointPos + offsetVect

We compute the *u* and *v* tangents at the current point. We then compute a vector perpendicular to these two tangents and add that offset to the current point (fig. 92).

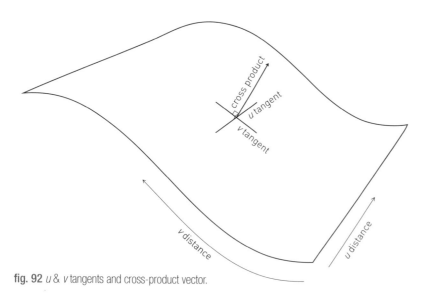

fig. 92 *u* & *v* tangents and cross-product vector.

124	addKnot myWarp (i+1) #smooth #curve offsetPos

We are finally ready to add a *knot* (vertex) to the spline. We specify the vertex to be smooth and part of a curve.

126	if (myNURBSSurface[m].closedInV) then
127	(
128	close myWarp (i+1)
129	)

If the curve is a closed NURBS, we close the spline as well.

132	if (warpSweepMod == undefined) then
133	(
134	warpSweepMod = sweep()
135	warpSweepMod.currentbuiltinshape = 4
136	)
137	addmodifier myWarp warpSweepMod
138	myWarp.rotation = selectedSurface.rotation
139	myWarp.scale = selectedSurface.scale
140	myWarp.pos = selectedSurface.pos
141	myWarp.name = selectedSurface.name + "-Warp" + (m as string)
142	Updateshape myWarp

In this section we apply the sweep modifier; position the warp with the same location, rotation and scale as the selected surface; give it a name; and update the shape on the screen.

| 144 | myWeft = SplineShape pos:[0,0,0] |

We are now ready to create the weft thread. The weft is simpler as it does not undulate.

| 145 | for i = 0 to (weftThreadCount - 1 - closedInV) by 1 do |
| 146 | (|

As we have seen before, we create a nested loop to draw all the weft threads and all the vertices on each thread. We deduct one iteration if the NURBS surface is closed.

| 147 | yposition = (i/(weftThreadCount - 1) as float) |

We then calculate the normalized *yposition*.

| 148 | addNewSpline myWeft |

Then we add a new spline that we call *myWeft*.

| 149 | for j = 0 to (warpThreadCount - 1 - closedInU) by 1 do |
| 150 | (|

The inner nested loop iterates through the number of warp threads. We deduct 1 if the NURBS surface is closed to avoid overlapping vertices.

151	xposition = (j/(warpThreadCount - 1) as float)
152	uposition = (minu + (maxu-minu)*xposition)
153	vposition = (minv + (maxv-minv)*yposition)

Next, we calculate the *xposition* and derive the *u* and *v* positions for the current point.

155	case of (
156	(swapUV == false): pointPos = evalpos myNURBSSurface[m] uposition vposition
157	(swapUV == true):pointPos = evalpos myNURBSSurface[m] vposition uposition
158	)

We check if the user wishes to swap the *u* and *v* directions, and then evaluate the position of the current point based on the current *u* and *v* positions.

| 160 | addKnot myWeft (i+1) #smooth #curve pointPos |

We are now ready to add a *knot* (vertex) to the current spline.

162	if (myNURBSSurface[m].closedInU) then
163	(
164	close myWeft (i+1)
165	)

If the NURBS surface is closed, we close the weft spline as well.

167	myWeft.rotation = selectedSurface.rotation
168	myWeft.scale = selectedSurface.scale
169	myWeft.pos = selectedSurface.pos
170	myWeft.name = selectedSurface.name + "-Weft" + (m as string)

Once we have created all the weft threads, we position the weft at the same location as the selected surface and give it a name.

172	if (weftSweepMod == undefined) then
173	(
174	weftSweepMod = sweep()
175	weftSweepMod.currentbuiltinshape = 4
176	)
177	addmodifier myWeft weftSweepMod
178	updateShape myWeft

We add the sweep modifier to the weft spline and update the shape on the screen.

180	else
181	(
182	format "Could not find a NURBS surface.\n"
183	)

The above is the *else* clause of the top *if* statement. That is, if the surface is not a NURBS surface, we simply display a message and stop the algorithm.

The last section of the code handles the user interface callback functions and triggers the *generateWeave()* function as needed.

By varying the number of threads and the parameters of the sweep profile, you can create almost endless variations and explore the structural qualities of the generated solution (fig. 93). The iterative, real-time nature of the script allows it to be used as a form-finding tool in the design process and moves us away from static modelling into truly parametric form generation (fig. 94).

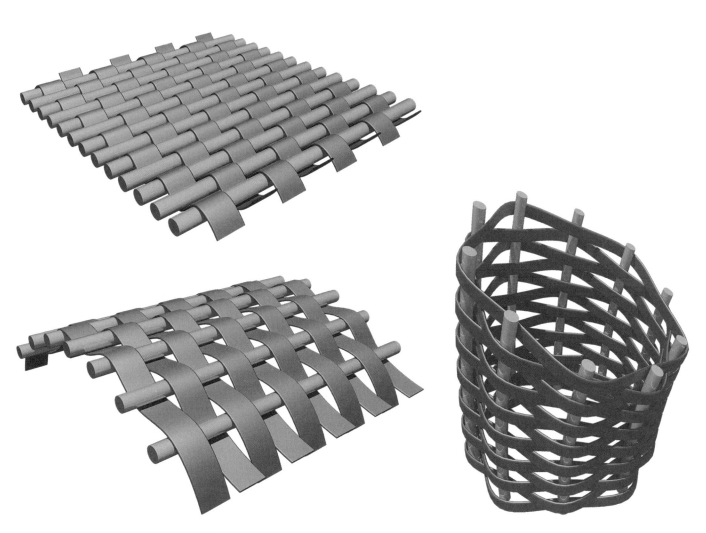

fig. 93 Example renderings of the weaving script.

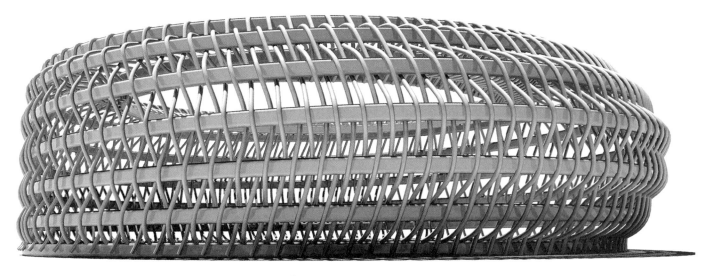

fig. 94 The weaving script is used to create an imaginary woven stadium structure.

Case study nonLin/Lin Pavilion, FRAC Centre, Orleans, France

Designer Marc Fornes/THEVERYMANY
Client FRAC Centre, Orleans, France
Design 2010
Construction 2011

A prolific and inventive designer, Marc Fornes produces large-scale installations and sculptural pieces of public art, but his work constitutes an investigation of fundamentally architectural issues, and the coral-like and floral creations that have come to identify his formal vocabulary raise questions that belong firmly in the discipline of architecture. As is the case with many other contemporary designers, Fornes is fascinated with the issue of the surface. He approaches it not as an undulating plane that simply embodies a formalistic treatment, but as a constituent member of his projects, with specific structural qualities and functional potentials and, of course, as a material with specific spatial and aesthetic possibilities.

The complex, organic curvatures incorporated in his installations serve as structural reinforcement; their form takes into consideration the material's natural stiffness as well as the conditions in which a particular project will be displayed. That is, the exact forms of his projects depend on whether they will be set on the floor, hung from a wall or ceiling, or placed in an interior or exterior space. Fornes approaches even this aspect of his work in a daring, experimental manner. In a composition for Union Square, New York, he selected thin, fragile

Above
General view of the pavilion fully assembled.

Opposite
Close-up view of the pavilion showing its star-like pattern.

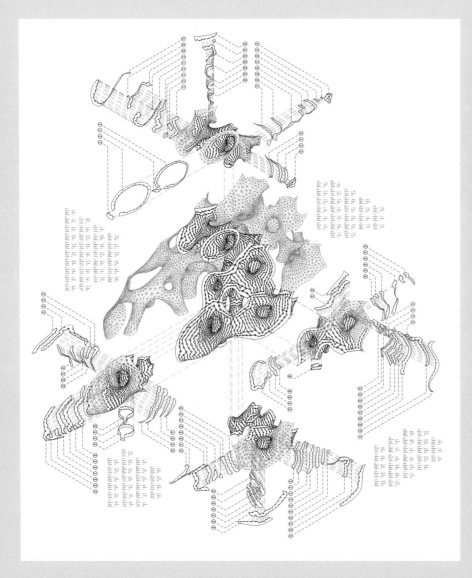

Above
View showing the forest-like character of the pavilion.

Left
Exploded axonometric drawing showing the pavilion's
various parts in preparation for digital fabrication.

sheets of walnut veneer, and sought to enhance
their strength by curving them in two directions.
While, unfortunately, the whole composition ended
up collapsing under its own weight, it was a true
test of the limits of material experimentation.

Fornes also addresses issues of utility
in his work. Due to their large scale, some of
his installations provide enclosures in which
traditional architectural elements (such as
walls, ceilings and openings) acquire new,
unconventional forms. Some of his other projects
have served utilitarian functions, such as the
centrepiece of a playground and a display for
jewellery. Fornes is very careful to note the
experimental, prototypical nature of his work, but
he has also stated that standardized production
of his projects is one of his objectives.

All of Fornes's projects begin with code.
His use of digital technologies is clearly visible
in the nonLin/Lin Pavilion, which is part of the
permanent collection of FRAC Centre in Orleans,
France. The elaborate form of the pavilion
originated from a 'Y' model, which transformed
in its dimensions as it was repeated in multiple
directions. Because this type of form cannot
be modelled with a bi-directional surface, an
important computational change was to move
away from (bi-directional) NURBS surfaces
and towards visualizing the project's form as a
topology. This approach allowed Fornes to follow
a cohesive sequence from the initial conception
to the final production of the project. Working with
custom computational protocols, he implemented
a form-finding parametric algorithm that allowed
surface smoothing and relaxation and which
resulted in the organic form of the pavilion.
The topological model was then put through
additional processes, including tessellation and
the derivation of planar developable surfaces, in
order to facilitate production. Finally, the model's

organization allowed Fornes to derive and re-
assemble the information and numerical data
necessary for the final production of the project.

The topological model for this project was
sufficiently powerful to generate a completed
pavilion consisting of 6,000 different strips of
aluminium, less than 1 mm thick, which are
connected to one another through 75,000 rivets
and are adorned with 150,000 star-shaped
holes. More important than the numbers,
however, are the architectural concepts that
the 10 m long pavilion is able to communicate
to its viewers. Issues of structural behaviour,
spatial enclosure, aperture and applied
ornamentation come together to compose a
comprehensive statement of future architecture.

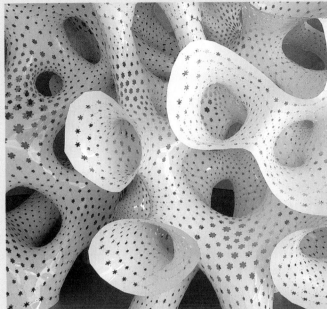

Above
The pavilion fully assembled at the site.

Above right
Close-up view of the extremities of the pavilion.

Below
View of the pavilion under construction.

Branching

Whether it is the limbs of a tree, the fibrous root system of an onion, human lungs or coralline algae, branching is a basic topological growth mechanism in nature for maximizing surface area, channelling resources and responding to structural forces (fig. 95). Branching systems in nature are self-similar and recursive and so tend to be fractal. To borrow the words of Benoit Mandelbrot, in a recursive branching system the geometry of the part is similar to the geometry of the whole. In reality, several forces or, more accurately, *tropisms* affect the overall growth direction and geometry of a branching system. The idiosyncratic form of a natural branching system, such

as a plant or tree (fig. 96), is determined by *phototropism* or *heliotropism* (seeking light and sun, respectively) and *gravitropism* (resisting the forces of gravity), as well as wind direction, physical obstacles, the availability of nutrients, and many other factors. In architecture, branching is most vividly illustrated in structural systems that use it to satisfy both practical and evocative design goals (figs. 97 and 98). We can also use hierarchical branching as an organizational instrument for ordering information, space, flow of resources or even the logic of a piece of software, as we have seen in previous algorithms.

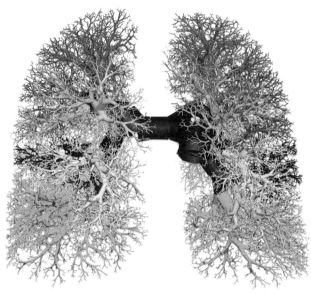

fig. 95 An anatomically based computational model of a pulmonary arterial network.

fig. 96 Windswept tree, south coast of England.

fig. 97 Branching columns at the Sagrada Familia church, Barcelona, Spain, Antoni Gaudí.

fig. 98 The Tote, Mumbai, India, Serie Architects.

TUTORIAL RECURSIVE BRANCHING

In the following tutorial, we will create a very simple yet parametrically flexible branching system using a recursive technique similar to those in prior tutorials. The logic of fractal recursion will be directly reflected in the recursive fractal geometry of the resulting design. The algorithm provides the possibility for either orthogonal/regular or randomized/organic branching, by allowing the user to specify ranges for parameters such as the number of branches at each recursive step, their angle of rotation and their length. For organic-looking results, the user can specify a range of numbers with minimum and maximum values, from which the algorithm chooses a random value. For a more regular result, the user can reduce the range all the way to the point where the minimum and maximum values are equal in order to force the algorithm to always choose a single value. There are many generative branching systems that are far more advanced than the basic algorithm presented here (e.g. ones that consider several tropisms), but the purpose of the following tutorial is to introduce you to the basics of generative branching algorithms. You can then use it as a stepping stone to a more refined and advanced script for creating more complex parametric constructs.

→ Open *3ds Max*, save and close any prior scenes, and create a new empty scene. Choose **MAXScript → New Script** from the top menu. In the script window that opens, type the following algorithm:

```
1    utility Branching "Branching"
2    (
3        global rootTree
4        global branchesArray = #()
5
6        -- Parameters
7
8        -- Branch Shape
9        global trunkHeight = 200
10       global trunkRadius = 2
11       global trunkSides = 12
12       global taperingFactorMin = 0.4
13       global taperingFactorMax = 0.6
14
15       -- Branching
16       global branchingDepth = 5
17       global branchingNumberMin = 4
18       global branchingNumberMax = 8
19
20       -- Offset/Translation
21       global offsetFactorMin = 0.0
22       global offsetFactorMax = 0.5
23
24       -- Unfolding/Rotation
25       global branchingXAngleMin = 10
26       global branchingXAngleMax = 15
27       global branchingZAngleMin = 2
28       global branchingZAngleMax = 6
```

```
29
30      -- Height/Scale
31      global heightFactorMin =  0.2
32      global heightFactorMax = 0.8
33
34      group "Branch Shape"
35      (
36          spinner trunkHeight_spinner "Height: " type:#worldunits range:[0.0001,100000,trunkHeight] toolTip:"Initial Trunk
            Height"
37          spinner trunkRadius_spinner "Radius: " type:#worldunits range:[0.0001,100000,trunkRadius] toolTip:"Initial Trunk
            Radius (at base)"
38          spinner trunkSides_spinner "Sides: " type:#integer range:[3,36,trunkSides] toolTip:"Number of Sides"
39          spinner taperingFactorMin_spinner "Taper Min: " type:#float range:[0.0,1.0,taperingFactorMin] toolTip:"Minimum
            Tapering Factor"
40          spinner taperingFactorMax_spinner "Taper Max: " type:#float range:[0.0,1.0, taperingFactorMax]
            toolTip:"Maximum Tapering Factor"
41      )
42
43      group "Branching"
44      (
45          spinner branchingDepth_spinner "Depth: " type:#integer range:[1,1000,branchingDepth] toolTip:"Total recursion
            steps"
46          spinner branchingNumberMin_spinner "Min: " type:#integer range:[0,100000,branchingNumberMin]
            toolTip:"Minimum number to branch out at each step"
47          spinner branchingNumberMax_spinner "Max: " type:#integer range:[0,100000,branchingNumberMax]
            toolTip:"Maximum number to branch out at each step"
48      )
49
50      group "Offset/Translation"
51      (
52          spinner offsetFactorMin_spinner "Min: " type:#float range:[0.0,100000,heightFactorMin] toolTip:"Minimum
            distance offset factor to slide child along parent"
53          spinner offsetFactorMax_spinner "Max: " type:#float range:[0.0,100000,heightFactorMax] toolTip:"Maximum
            distance offset factor to slide child along parent"
54      )
55
56      group "Unfolding/Rotation"
57      (
58          spinner branchingXAngleMin_spinner "X Min: " type:#float range:[0,360,branchingXAngleMin] toolTip:"Minimum X
            rotation angle of each branch"
59          spinner branchingXAngleMax_spinner "X Max: " type:#float range:[0,360,branchingXAngleMax] toolTip:"Maximum
            X rotation angle of each branch"
60          spinner branchingZAngleMin_spinner "Z Min: " type:#float range:[0,360,branchingZAngleMin] toolTip:"Minimum
```

```
        additional Z rotation angle offset"
61      spinner branchingZAngleMax_spinner "Z Max: " type:#float range:[0,360,branchingZAngleMax] toolTip:"Maximum
        additional Z rotation angle offset"
62      )
63
64      group "Height/Scale"
65      (
66          spinner heightFactorMin_spinner "Scale Min: " type:#float range:[0.0,100000,heightFactorMin] toolTip:"Minimum
            scale factor of child to parent"
67          spinner heightFactorMax_spinner "Scale Max: " type:#float range:[0.0,100000,heightFactorMax] toolTip:"Maximum
            scale factor of child to parent"
68      )
69
70      button generate_button "Generate" enabled:true
71
72      fn branch parent depth =
73      (
74          if (depth < branchingDepth) then
75          (
76              numberOfBranches = (random branchingNumberMin branchingNumberMax)
77              for i = 1 to numberofBranches do
78              (
79                  myBranch = copy parent
80                  myBranch.parent = parent
81                  myBranch.height = (parent.height)*(random heightFactorMin heightFactorMax)
82                  myBranch.radius1 = parent.radius2
83                  myBranch.radius2 = myBranch.radius1*(random taperingFactorMin taperingFactorMax)
84                  in coordsys parent move myBranch [0,0,parent.height]
85                  myRot = eulerAngles  (random branchingXAngleMin branchingXAngleMax) 0 0
86                  in coordsys parent rotate myBranch myRot
87                  myRot =  eulerAngles 0 0 (((360/numberOfBranches)*i) + (random branchingZAngleMin
                    branchingZAngleMax))
88                  in coordsys parent rotate myBranch myRot
89                  in coordsys parent move myBranch [0,0, ((random offSetFactorMin offSetFactorMax)*-parent.height)]
90                  myBranch.wirecolor = (color (255 - (255/branchingDepth*depth)) 0 0)
91                  append branchesArray myBranch
92                  branch myBranch (depth + 1)
93              )
94          )
95      )
96
```

```
97    fn deleteTree anArray=
98    (
99        for i = 1 to branchesArray.count by 1 do
100       (
101           if((isDeleted branchesArray[i]) == false) then
102           (
103               delete branchesArray[i]
104           )
105       )
106       branchesArray.count = 0
107   )
108
109   on generate_button pressed do
110   (
111       deleteTree branchingArray
112       rootTree = cone()
113       rootTree.height = trunkHeight
114       rootTree.radius1 = trunkRadius
115       rootTree.radius2 = rootTree.radius1*(random taperingFactorMin taperingFactorMax)
116       rootTree.sides = trunkSides
117       rootTree.heightsegs = 1
118       rootTree.wirecolor = (color 255 0  0)
119       append branchesArray rootTree
120       branch rootTree 1
121   )
122
123   on trunkHeight_spinner changed amt do
124   (
125       trunkHeight = amt
126   )
127
128   on trunkRadius_spinner changed amt do
129   (
130       trunkRadius = amt
131   )
132
133   on trunkSides_spinner changed amt do
134   (
135       trunkSides = amt
136   )
137
138   on taperingFactorMin_spinner changed amt do
139   (
```

```
140              taperingFactorMin = amt
141      )
142
143      on taperingFactorMax_spinner changed amt do
144      (
145              taperingFactorMax = amt
146      )
147
148      on branchingDepth_spinner changed amt do
149      (
150              branchingDepth = amt
151      )
152
153      on branchingNumberMin_spinner changed amt do
154      (
155              branchingNumberMin = amt
156      )
157
158      on branchingNumberMax_spinner changed amt do
159      (
160              branchingNumberMax = amt
161      )
162
163      on offsetFactorMin_spinner changed amt do
164      (
165              offsetFactorMin = amt
166      )
167
168      on offsetFactorMax_spinner changed amt do
169      (
170              offsetFactorMax = amt
171      )
172
173      on branchingXAngleMin_spinner changed amt do
174      (
175              branchingXAngleMin = amt
176      )
177
178      on branchingXAngleMax_spinner changed amt do
179      (
180              branchingXAngleMax = amt
```

181	)
182	
183	on branchingZAngleMin_spinner changed amt do
184	(
185	branchingZAngleMin = amt
186	)
187	
188	on branchingZAngleMax_spinner changed amt do
189	(
190	branchingZAngleMax = amt
191	)
192	
193	on heightFactorMin_spinner changed amt do
194	(
195	heightFactorMin = amt
196	)
197	
198	on heightFactorMax_spinner changed amt do
199	(
200	heightFactorMax = amt
201	)
202	)

→ Save your script and then choose **Tools → Evaluate All** to run the script. You will find the script utility under **Utilities** (hammer icon). Click on the **MAXScript** button and then choose **Branching** from the **Utilities** pull down menu. Select the desired parameters and then press the **Generate** button to view the result (fig. 99). Increasing the *depth* parameter creates a more detailed result, but also takes an exponentially longer time to complete (fig. 100). As mentioned earlier, forcing the minimum and maximum parameter ranges to be equal and using 90-degree angles creates a more orthogonal result. In contrast, allowing the script to choose a random value from a range of values creates a more organic-looking result (fig. 101).

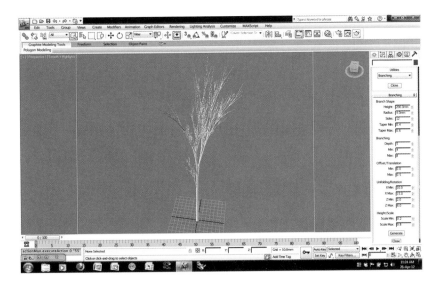

fig. 99 Branching utility script.

fig. 100 Recursive branching with depths 2, 3, 4, 5 and 6.

fig. 101 Orthogonal and organic branching by varying the values of parameters.

Let's take a closer look at the script. Here, we will not look at how to create the user interface and respond to user events, since this information is given in prior tutorials. Instead, we will concentrate on the actual recursive branching algorithm. For more information on recursion, please consult the prior section on recursion.

72	fn branch parent depth =
73	(
74	if (depth < branchingDepth) then
75	(

In this section, we define a recursive function called *branch* that accepts two arguments: a parent branch and the current depth level of the branching. We use the user-specified *branchingDepth* number as a maximum value beyond which this function will not execute its steps. This prevents the algorithm from infinite recursion.

76	numberOfBranches = (random branchingNumberMin branchingNumberMax)

We define a variable called *numberOfBranches*, which is a random number within the range specified by the user. This variable will determine how many children branches will sprout from the parent branch for this particular branching step.

77	for i = 1 to numberofBranches do
78	(

RECURSIVE BRANCHING/CONTINUED

Next, we start a *for loop*, which runs from 1 up to the generated number of branches, in order to create each branch in turn.

79	myBranch = copy parent
80	myBranch.parent = parent
81	myBranch.height = (parent.height)*(random heightFactorMin heightFactorMax)
82	myBranch.radius1 = parent.radius2
83	myBranch.radius2 = myBranch.radius1*(random taperingFactorMin taperingFactorMax)

We then start by creating a copy of the parent and setting it as the parent of this new branch. This will allow the user to move branches by dragging the root branch. The height (length) of the branch is set as a fraction of the height (length) of its parent based on a user-specified number or range. Since the branch is made out of a cone with a base radius and a top radius (*radius1* and *radius2*), we set the base radius of the child to be the same as the top radius of the parent. This ensures a smooth transition at the junction between branches. We then set the top radius of the child to be a fraction of its bottom radius based on a user-specified number or range.

84	in coordsys parent move myBranch [0,0,parent.height]

The *3ds Max* built-in term *in coordsys <node>* allows us to move the new branch using the coordinate system of its parent rather than the world's coordinate system. This is very important to the overall positioning and rotation of the new branches, as they need to be offset from their parent's coordinate system rather than that of the world. In the statement above, we simply slide the new branch so that its base matches the tip of its parent branch (i.e. we move it by exactly the height (length) of its parent).

85	myRot = eulerAngles (random branchingXAngleMin branchingXAngleMax) 0 0
86	in coordsys parent rotate myBranch myRot

The next step is to rotate the branch. We achieve this by first creating a rotation object for the X-axis and applying that rotation to the new branch.

87	myRot = eulerAngles 0 0 (((360/numberOfBranches)*i) + (random branchingZAngleMin branchingZAngleMax))
88	in coordsys parent rotate myBranch myRot

We repeat the process to create a second, Z-rotation. However, for the Z-rotation, we divide 360 by the desired number of branches to calculate the angle increment for each branch and we multiply that value by the current index of the iteration. For example, if we are to generate four branches, then we divide 360 by 4 to yield 90. Based on the formula above, the first branch will be rotated 90 degrees, the second branch will be rotated 180 degrees, the third will be rotated 270 and the fourth will be rotated 360 degrees. In addition to this rotation, the script allows for an optional random addition to the Z-rotation angle. If set, this will ensure that the branches are not regularly distributed around the parent branch.

89	in coordsys parent move myBranch [0,0, ((random offSetFactorMin offSetFactorMax)*-parent.height)]

fig. 102 Branching with an offset.

If the user has specified an offset factor, we slide the branch by that offset (or
a random number from a range) down along its parent branch. This parameter
yields a more organic and randomized branching of the model (fig. 102).

90 myBranch.wirecolor = (color (255 - (255/branchingDepth*depth)) 0 0)

In this purely cosmetic step, we assign a colour to the
branch based on its current branching depth.

91 append branchesArray myBranch

Next, we append the current branch to the array of branches. We keep track
of all the created branches by storing them in this array, so that we can
delete them once the user decides to vary the parameters and generate
a new tree. It is important to note that if you wish to keep the generated
tree, you must make a copy of it before generating a new one.

92 branch myBranch (depth + 1)

In this last step, the function calls itself, but this time with the parent argument
specified to be the current branch and the depth incremented by 1. The process then
starts again unless the depth has reached the user-specified maximum value.

The whole process starts when the user presses the generate button.
Please consult the callback function *on generate_button pressed* to
see how the root tree trunk is created and the branching processes
are started. The code is simple enough to be self-explanatory.

Case study PS_Canopy

Designer su11 architecture+design
Partners in Charge Ferda Kolatan, Erich Schoenenberger
Design Team Richard Baxley, Hart Marlow
Design and Construction 2009

Left
Side view rendering.

Opposite
Close-up of *petals* with varying apertures.

su11 architecture+design is a New York-based architecture firm. Their design investigations draw inspiration from an organic understanding of natural systems. One of their goals is to break down what they see as the 'categorical barrier' of traditional building components. In order to do this, they employ digital and parametric methodologies to produce what they call 'pluripotent structures': adaptive formal and structural organizations that can yield multiple possibilities while maintaining an overall cohesive consistency.

The work of biologist S.B. Carroll provides the theoretical framework for the firm's design explorations. According to Carroll, innovation in body parts does not depend on novel genes but rather on the 'modification of existing structures and on teaching old genes how to learn new tricks'.[1] Innovation, Carroll asserts, is achieved by switching so-called 'tool-kit genes' on and off at different times and places throughout the course of development. In order to adapt this

process to building, su11 employ traditional architectural concepts, including geometric principles, structural constraints and functional requirements, but they vary (activate or deactivate) localized relationships within those concepts in order to produce a multiplicity of novel designs. At the same time, like a body part, their designs must maintain an overall topological coherence.

The firm's design sensibility is exemplified in the PS_Canopy conceptual project, which was exhibited at the 2009 SIGGRAPH Generative Fabrication Conference in New Orleans, Louisiana, USA. PS_Canopy employed the metaphor of a flower, assigning utilitarian aspects such as interior height, shading and seating to different aspects of this biomimetic 'flower', which was then manipulated through parametric and modelling techniques to produce multiple variations of the proposed canopy.

For the design of the canopy, the firm used Bentley's *Generative Components* software to create a randomized point-branching, parametric

Above
Development of the branching algorithm.

Below
Parametric variation of *petal* aperture.

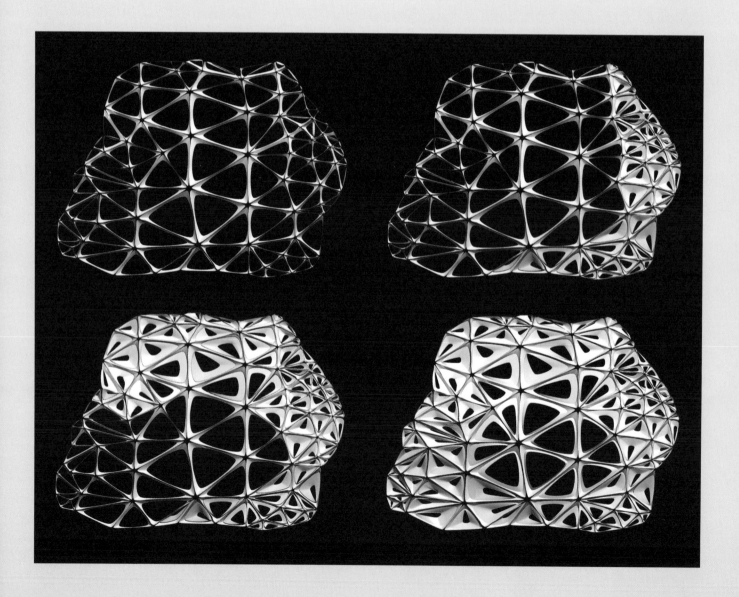

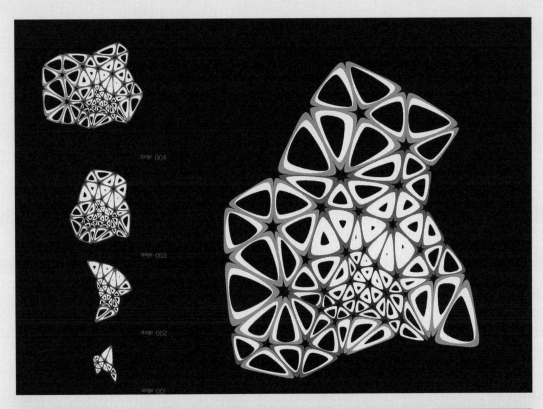

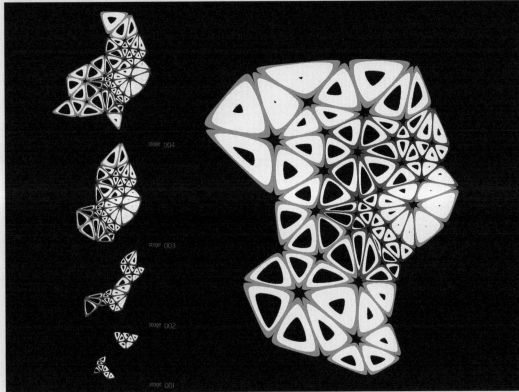

Top
Study of various conglomeration patterns.

Above
Second study of various conglomeration patterns.

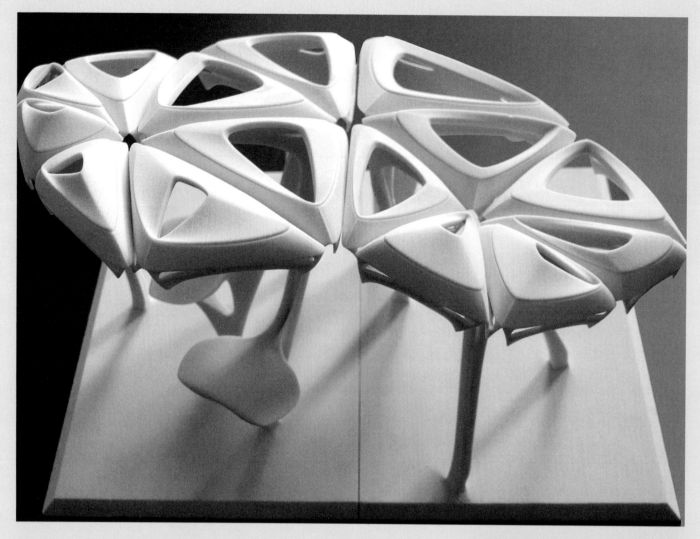

script that is akin to a type of fractal called L-Systems.[2] This script allowed the firm to create a master model in which scaling and clustering could be parametrically controlled. The initial network created by this script was then put through a process of triangulation, resulting in clusters of triangular cells that function as the basic geometric ingredient of the final canopy. Each cell was then populated with individual canopy pieces, which can either close, to provide a more continuous surface, or open, to become more structural. The designers continued to work with a floral metaphor through a second parametric model, which mapped stems, petals and leaves into the functional elements necessary for support, shading and seating. Thus, the *stem* constituted a vertical extrusion of a node and determined the height of the canopy; the opening or closing of the *petals* determined shading in different regions; and finally horizontal extrusions along the stems became *leaves*, which could function as seating or tables. The result

of this process was a geometric arrangement made up of points, lines and surfaces. In order to give this underlying structure its final 3D form and iconography, the firm used traditional digital meshing techniques that were inspired by nineteenth-century flower engravings. su11 continue to work with these ideas as they explore how elements can populate complex surface geometries, including façades. Developing a parametric system based on a branching floral morphology, they state, is critical to their design methodology because it helps them to 'visualize and conceptualize systems that focus on the transitory moments and details in a design project'.

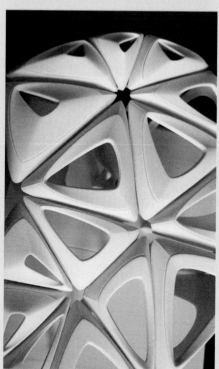

1 Carroll, S.B. (2006). *Endless Forms Most Beautiful: The New Science of Evo Devo*. W.W. Norton & Company.

2 Prusinkiewicz, P. and Lindenmayer, A. (1996). *The Algorithmic Beauty of Plants*. Springer-Verlag.

Opposite Above
3D printed model.

Opposite Below
Close-up view of 3D printed model.

Below
Front view showing *petals* (canopy), *stems* (structure) and *leaves* (seating and tables).

PART III NEXT STEPS

Towards a programming language for design

Traditionally, programming languages have been written for general-purpose problem solving of almost any type. Languages such as *LISP, FORTRAN, BASIC, C, C++, Objective-C, C#* and *Python* were not specifically written for designers. They were originated by computer scientists, looking to solve computing problems, who found they needed something more readable and logical than the numeric codes of native machine language and so invented these higher-order languages. As we saw in the chapter on algorithmic thinking, these languages share many properties. They all represent variables (which can be integers, float numbers or strings of characters). They all allow for logical flow control, using *if statements* or *for loops* that repeat a block of code instructions as many times as desired. In order to solve a domain-specific problem, however, programmers sometimes write a collection of functions (sometimes called libraries) or, in the case of object-oriented programming, a set of classes, objects and methods, which represent specific objects and functionalities. The question then becomes: do we have a language specifically invented for designers? The *Processing* language from MIT, which focuses on programming for visual design, comes close to that specification. While *Processing* can be used like any other traditional programming language (and many have done just that), it has gained popularity with designers and visual artists because of its specialized orientation towards graphics and the visual arts. There are very few languages that have been specifically written for designers and architects. Some of these, such as *AutoLISP, Maya Embedded Language* (*MEL*), *Rhinoscript, Grasshopper, Generative Components* (*GC*) and *MAXScript*, are suitable for geometric problems, because they contain built-in functions that create and edit geometric entities, and because they are linked to

computer-aided design and visualization systems (e.g. *AutoCAD, Rhino, Microstation* and *3ds Max*). While the situation may be different by the time you are reading this book, building information modelling (BIM) software such as *Revit* is in urgent need of a scripting language that is specifically geared to its core functionality (*Iron Python* is an independent effort to provide a scripting language for *Revit*, but is not supported by Autodesk, the makers of *Revit*). I predict that as the areas of BIM and parametric design mature, we will witness the arrival of design-specific languages that contain built-in knowledge of design elements and processes. In fact, we already have one language that moves us closer to the idea of a unified programming language for design. This language is called *DesignScript*. It was originated by Dr Robert Aish from Autodesk, who had previously originated *GC* while he was with Bentley. *DesignScript* has some similarities with *GC*, but unlike both *GC* and *Grasshopper* it goes beyond the visual association of parameters, with the aim of creating a hybrid and universal programming language for design. *DesignScript* aims to combine the power of *GC, Grasshopper* and *Processing* into one language that focuses on solving design problems. At a practical level, *DesignScript* starts with geometric form-finding operations (fig. 103), and then links those forms to parametric analysis software, such as Autodesk's *Robot* for structural analysis and *Green Building Studio* for energy and thermal analysis (fig. 104). *DesignScript* is a versatile language that promises to streamline the digital workflow of parametric design, so that eventually building performance analysis can directly influence geometric form exploration, which can then be directly translated into digital fabrication data. As Robert Aish explains, his team developed *DesignScript* with the objective of answering the following question: 'How can

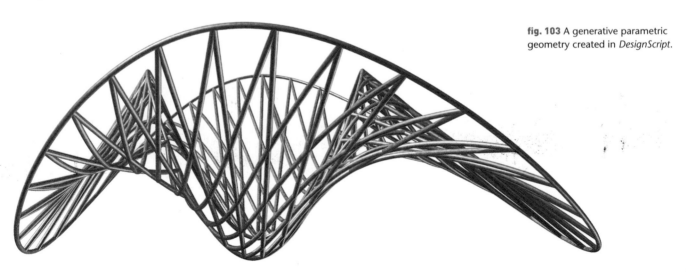

fig. 103 A generative parametric geometry created in *DesignScript*.

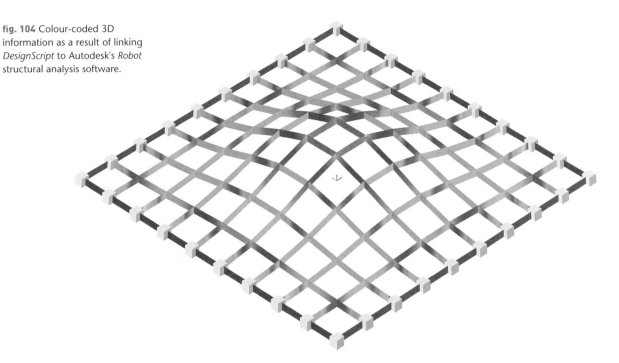

fig. 104 Colour-coded 3D information as a result of linking *DesignScript* to Autodesk's *Robot* structural analysis software.

the designer explore complex algorithmic geometric forms and build the lightest possible model, with the least effort, which will provide him with the most feedback, earliest in the design process?' From that mission statement, it is clear that *DesignScript* is a design-specific language rather than a general-purpose one. While the scope of this book does not allow for a full discussion of all the capabilities of *DesignScript*, in the next section we will look more closely at some of the features that make it a unique example of a language written specifically for designers. The optimistic assumption is that designers will more readily accept a programming language that focuses on design-specific needs and will use it to create sophisticated parametric models. To that end, we will compare *DesignScript* to *MAXScript*, in order to clarify the issues surrounding the introduction of the complexities of algorithmic thinking to designers and to explore areas of similarity and difference between the two scripting environments.

Imperative vs. Associative Programming

It is possible to understand programming as having two distinct traditions. First, there is the established tradition of *imperative* programming, as found in such languages as *Python*, *C#*, *Java* and *Processing*. Imperative languages are based on what is called explicit 'flow control', and they use special syntax such as the *for loop* and *if statement*. Second, there is the tradition of *associative* programming found in such systems as *GC* and *Grasshopper*. In these systems, 'flow control' is defined by a graph of dependencies, which shows relationships between variables – usually how variables are used within other operations or statements to define other variables. Because these relationships are represented by a visual

graph, they are not totally under the control of the user; in both *GC* and *Grasshopper* these relationships are partially or completely masked from the user, meaning that the concept of associative language is not made explicit. One strength of *DesignScript* is that it does makes associative programming explicit and, at the same time, combines it with imperative programming. This enables the user to consciously choose the appropriate style of programming to solve a particular type of computation design problem. Even more importantly, *DesignScript* allows associative and imperative programming to be combined in the form of a hybrid script, which can solve more interesting and complex design tasks than each type of programing can solve by itself.

Let's focus first on imperative programming. The word imperative comes from the Latin word *imperativus*, which means 'specially ordered'. Thus, as one can imagine, imperative programming languages execute their instructions in a specially ordered manner. Let us look at the following piece of imperative pseudo-code:

1	a = 1
2	b = 2
3	c = a + b
4	b = 4
5	print c

In the above code, a is assigned the value 1, b the value 2, and c is computed as the sum of a and b – thus it will be assigned the value 3. After that step, we change the value of b to 4. However, c has already been computed, and so the change in the value of *b* does not affect the value of *c*. Thus, when we print out the value of *c* it will continue to display the number 3. The code has been executed in an imperative manner from top to bottom.

If, however, we executed this code in *DesignScript*, the printed value of *c* would display 5 rather than 3. This happens because *c* was defined *associatively* as the sum of *a* and *b*, so a change in the value of these parameters necessitates a change in the value of *c*. This behaviour is like a spreadsheet computation where one cell's value can be derived from the values found in other cells, regardless of where the cells are in relation to one another. Incorporating associative behaviour in a scripting language requires a fundamental shift in our algorithmic thinking. For example, we can no longer casually store new values in variables later in our code, as this will affect all other variables that derive their value from these variables.

I mentioned earlier that both *GC* and *Grasshopper* are essentially associative programming systems, but with the associative notation masked by the graph-based user interface (UI). Interestingly, spreadsheet applications such as *Excel* are also associative programming systems, but again this fact is almost completely masked from the users by the traditional spreadsheet UI.

Associative scripting in *DesignScript* has an explicit purpose, which is to handle the relationships between variables, including variables that represent collections (an important concept, which we will examine closely in a moment). Sometimes it is important to iterate explicitly through such a collection using *for loops* and conditional *if statements*. For these functionalities, the *DesignScript* language offers the ability to switch to an imperative mode of programming using a special [Imperative] keyword. Code within the imperative block is executed sequentially, so modifications to a variable later within that block of code would have no effect on the code that preceded it.

The initial development of *DesignScript* has been focused on the language and the use of the language to generate geometry. Some aspects of the UI are still under development, specifically those involving interaction and the development of customised UIs. For the purposes of this book, the important point is that the *DesignScript* language has the concepts and syntax to capture such interaction, including selection, modification and customized controls. It is therefore not too difficult to imagine that, in the near future, these language facilities will be presented to the user in the form of a more intuitive user interface, enabling a truly fluid and interactive parametric design system. What *DesignScript* represents at the current stage is a solid foundation for a universal design-oriented programming language.

One of the most powerful aspects of *DesignScript* is *collections*. You have already learned about the concept of arrays: a list of values or objects that you can query, in order to retrieve and/or set its individual members. A *collection* in *DesignScript* is similar to an array, but it is, in a way, easier to use. Almost any parameter or variable in *DesignScript* can be either an individual object or value or a collection of objects or values. While in traditional imperative programming you have to iterate through an array to get access to an individual member of the array, in *DesignScript* this is done for you behind the scenes. Consider the following example: imagine that you wish to define a line that connects two points. In *DesignScript*, you would create point *A*, then point *B* and then define a line *L* that connects point *A* to point *B*. If any of these points move, line *L* will dutifully move in order to continue to connect them together because line *L* is associatively linked to points *A* and *B*. This in itself is the beginning of a powerful parametric construct. However, there is an even more interesting aspect to this associative behaviour when it is combined with the notion of a collection. If, later in the code, point *A* changes from a single point to a collection of multiple points, then line *L* will also automatically change, from a single line to a collection of multiple lines that

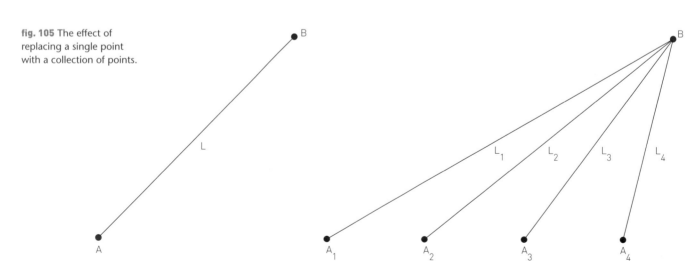

fig. 105 The effect of replacing a single point with a collection of points.

connect the single point *B* to all the points defined by the collection *A* (fig. 105). The developer of the script does not have to manually create multiple lines and then re-define the relationships between them and the control points. The power of collections and associativity also extends to functions. For example, if you have written a function that computes the distance between a point *A* and a point *B*, and later in the code point *A* becomes a collection of points, then *DesignScript* will repeatedly and automatically call this function for each point in the collection and compute the distance from each of those points to point *B*. Through the concept of replication *DesignScript* can handle not only two-dimensional but also three-dimensional collections. Replication *guides* are special additions to the syntax of the language that accept two or three one-dimensional collections and pair the members of these collections together to generate a one-, two- or three-dimensional collection. In these cases, *DesignScript* can either connect the first member of a collection to the first member of the second collection, and so on, or connect each member of the first collection to every member of the second collection. These concepts may be difficult to understand at first, but once you see a few visual examples of how they are implemented, their power and simplicity become apparent (fig. 106).

To illustrate the power of focusing on algorithm rather than on syntax, as well as to illustrate the power of associativity, collections and replication in *DesignScript*, we will undertake the re-writing of the diagrid and weaving tutorials in *DesignScript*. In the first tutorial, the diagrid script, we port the code almost as is from *MAXScript* to *DesignScript*, with minor syntactical modifications. However, the tutorial in *DesignScript* combines the two scripts in *MAXScript* into one universal diagrid class, which can generate either flat diagrids or doubly-curved diagrids that are derived from a host NURBS surface. The second tutorial, the weaving script, illustrates the ability of the replication and associativity concepts not only to reduce the coding burden, but also to clarify the code and link it more closely to design intent. As has been suggested several times in this book, once you have mastered algorithmic thinking and designed your algorithm in a logical and universal manner, you will be able to translate its syntax to other scripting environments. The necessary elements of an algorithmic approach are the clarification of design thinking, the establishment of the proper parametric associations and ensuring the precise expression in the appropriate language. This method of working enables efficient and creative exploration of the design space, regardless of the details of implementation.

```
1    // Import the Geometry library that allows us to
2    // create and display geometries
3
4    import("ProtoGeometry.dll");
5
6    // Generate three collections each with 10
7    // coordinates wth a range 0 to 9
8    // The default interval of the range is 1
9
10   x_coords = 0..9;
11   y_coords = 0..9;
12   z_coords = 0..9;
13
14   // Use replication guides to assign the x values
15   // to the first dimension, y values to the second
16   // dimension and z values to the third dimension.
17   // The result is a 3D matrix of points.
18
19   p = Point.ByCoordinates(x_coords<1>, y_coords<2>, z_
        coords<3>);
```

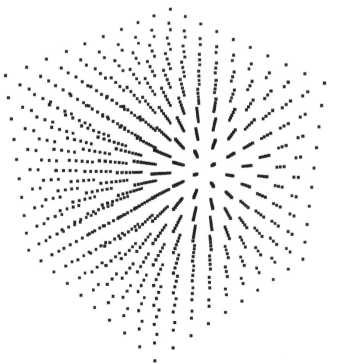

fig. 106 The effect of using replication guides to create 3D replication.

TUTORIAL DIAGRID

In rewriting the diagrid example for *DesignScript*, we will combine the two *MAXScript* tutorials (the simple diagrid mesh on a flat surface and the curved, NURBS-based diagrid mesh) into one integrated *diagrid class* that can generate both types on demand. Although this would be feasible in *MAXScript* through custom coding, because *MAXScript* does not explicitly implement the concept of a class, it would not be easy to do. However, when we shift to *DesignScript*, re-encoding the basic algorithm from *MAXScript* as an encapsulated class of diagrid objects makes our algorithmic thinking even more precise. This shift from a basic set of functions to an object-oriented mode of working will become clearer as you study and understand the following tutorial and compare it to the two *MAXScript* tutorials on pages 84 and 93. Much of the code you will see below should be already familiar to you: because the basic algorithm remains constant, code can be copied and pasted from *MAXScript* before minor modifications to syntax are made. Please note that the diagrid class in this new tutorial does not correctly handle closed surfaces, as the *MAXScript* one does. Once you have familiarized yourself with *DesignScript* syntax, a good exercise would be to apply what you learned from the *MAXScript* tutorial and expand the capabilities of the diagrid class in this tutorial to derive a diagrid from closed surfaces, such as cylinders and spheres.

→ We will assume that you have downloaded and installed *AutoCAD* and *DesignScript* on your computer. Launch *AutoCAD* and *DesignScript* and type the following script into the *DesignScript* window:

```
1    import("ProtoGeometry.dll");
2
3    class Diagrid
4    {
5        length : double;
6        width : double;
7        rows : int;
8        columns : int;
9        diagrid : SubDivisionMesh;
10       folded : double;
11
12       constructor ByLengthWidthRowsColumns(length : double, width : double, rows : int, columns : int, folded : double)
13       {
14           nr : int = rows * 2;
15           nc : int = columns;
16           unitLength = length / nr;
17           unitWidth = width / nc;
18
19           vertices = buildVertices(nr, nc, unitLength, unitWidth, folded);
20           faces = buildFaces(nr, nc);
21           diagrid = SubDivisionMesh.ByVerticesFaceIndices(vertices, faces, 0);
22       }
23
24       constructor BySurfaceRowsColumns(surface : Surface, rows : int, columns : int, folded : double)
25       {
26           nr : int = rows * 2;
27           nc : int = columns;
28
```

```
29              vertices = buildSurfaceVertices(surface, nr, nc, folded);
30              faces = buildFaces(nr, nc);
31              diagrid = SubDivisionMesh.ByVerticesFaceIndices(vertices, faces, 0);
32          }
33
34      def buildSurfaceVertices(surface, nr, nc, folded) {
35              vertices = { };
36              oddeven = 0;
37              deduct = 0;
38              offset = 0;
39              vertIndex = 0;
40              voffset = 0;
41              testing = [Imperative]
42              {
43                  for(i in 0..nr) {
44                  353 if (oddeven % 2 == 0)
45                      353     { offset = 0.0; deduct = 0;}
46                      353 else
47                      353     { offset = 0.5; deduct = 1;}
48
49                      353 for(j in 0..(nc - deduct)..1) {
50                      353     u = i / nr;
51                      353     v = (j + offset) / nc;
52                      353     cs1 = surface.CoordinateSystemAtParameter(u, v);
53                      353     ptemp = Point.ByCartesianCoordinates(cs1, 0, 0, folded*(j%2));
54                      353     vertices[vertIndex] = ptemp;
55                      353     vertIndex = vertIndex + 1;
56                      353 }
57                      353 oddeven = oddeven + 1;
58                  }
59              }
60              return = vertices;
61      }
62
63      def buildVertices(nr, nc, unitLength, unitWidth, folded) {
64              vertices = { };
65              testing = [Imperative]
66              {
67                  vertIndex = 0;
68                  deduct = 0;
69                  hoffset = 0.0;
70                  vx = 0.0;
71                  vy = 0.0;
```

```
72          for(i in 0..nr) {
73      353   if ((i % 2) == 0)
74      353       { hoffset = 0.0; deduct = 0; voffset = 2; }
75      353   else
76      353       { hoffset = 0.5; deduct = 1; voffset = -2; }
77      353       for(j in 0..(nc - deduct)) {
78      353           vx = (j + hoffset) * unitWidth;
79      353           vy = i * unitLength;
80      353           vertices[vertIndex] = Point.ByCoordinates(vx, vy, folded *(j%2));
81      353               vertIndex = vertIndex + 1;
82      353           }
83      353       }
84          }
85          return = vertices;
86      }
87
88      def buildFaces(nr, nc) {
89          faces = { };
90          testing = [Imperative]
91          {
92              v1 : int = 0;
93              v2 : int = 0;
94              v3 : int = 0;
95              i = 0;
96
97              // Create left and right triangular edges.
98              faceIndex = 0;
99              for(i in 1..nr..2) {
100     353         v1 = (i - 1) * (nc + 1) - ((i - 1) / 2) + 1;
101     353         v2 = (i - 1) * (nc + 1) - ((i - 1) / 2) + (nc + 1) + 1;
102     353         v3 = (i + 1) * (nc + 1) - ((i + 1) / 2) + 1;
103     353         faces[faceIndex] = { (v1 - 1), (v2 - 1), (v3 - 1) };
104     353         faceIndex = faceIndex + 1;
105     353         v1 = (i + 1) * (nc + 1) - ((i + 1) / 2) + nc + 1;
106     353         v2 = (i - 1) * (nc + 1) - ((i - 1) / 2) + nc + (nc + 1);
107     353         v3 = (i - 1) * (nc + 1) - ((i - 1) / 2) + nc + 1;
108     353         faces[faceIndex] = { (v3 - 1), (v2 - 1), (v1 - 1) };
109     353         faceIndex = faceIndex + 1;
110             }
111
112             // Create first set of triangles.
```

```
113         for(i in 1..nr..2) {
114     353 for(j in 1..nc..1) {
115     353     v1 = (i - 1) * (nc + 1) - ((i - 1) / 2) + j;
116     353     v2 = (i - 1) * (nc + 1) - ((i - 1) / 2) + j + 1;
117     353     v3 = (i - 1) * (nc + 1) - ((i - 1) / 2) + j + (nc + 1);
118     353     faces[faceIndex] = { (v1 - 1), (v2 - 1), (v3 - 1) };
119     353     faceIndex = faceIndex + 1;
120
121     353     if (j < nc)
122     353     {
123     353         v1 = (i - 1) * (nc + 1) - ((i - 1) / 2) + j + (nc + 1);
124     353         v2 = (i - 1) * (nc + 1) - ((i - 1) / 2) + j + 1;
125     353         v3 = (i - 1) * (nc + 1) - ((i - 1) / 2) + j + (nc + 2);
126     353         faces[faceIndex] = { (v1 - 1), (v2 - 1), (v3 - 1) };
127     353         faceIndex = faceIndex + 1;
128     353     }
129     353     }
130         }
131
132         // Create second set of triangles.
133         for(i in 3..nr + 1..2) {
134     353 for(j in 1..nc..1) {
135     353     v1 = (i - 1) * (nc + 1) - ((i - 1) / 2) + j + 1;
136     353     v2 = (i - 1) * (nc + 1) - ((i - 1) / 2) + j;
137     353     v3 = (i - 3) * (nc + 1) - ((i - 3) / 2) + j + (nc + 1);
138     353     faces[faceIndex] = { (v1 - 1), (v2 - 1), (v3 - 1) };
139     353     faceIndex = faceIndex + 1;
140     353     if (j < nc)
141     353     {
142     353         v1 = (i - 3) * (nc + 1) - ((i - 3) / 2) + j + (nc + 1);
143     353         v2 = (i - 3) * (nc + 1) - ((i - 3) / 2) + j + 1 + (nc + 1);
144     353         v3 = (i - 1) * (nc + 1) - ((i - 1) / 2) + j + 1;
145     353         faces[faceIndex] = { (v1 - 1), (v2 - 1), (v3 - 1) };
146     353         faceIndex = faceIndex + 1;
147     353     }
148     353 }
149         }
150         }
151     return = faces;
152     }
153 }
154
155 // Create a flat diagrid.
```

```
156   width1 = 30;

157   length1 = 30;

158   u1 = 10;

159   v1 = 10;

160   folded1 = 0;

161   flatGrid = Diagrid.ByLengthWidthRowsColumns(width1, length1, u1, v1, folded1);

162

163   // Create a diagrid derived from a host surface.

164   // Create points.

165   p1 = Point.ByCoordinates(40, 0, 0);

166   p2 = Point.ByCoordinates(70, 5, 10);

167   p3 = Point.ByCoordinates(35, 10, 20);

168   p4 = Point.ByCoordinates(60, 10, 0);

169   p5 = Point.ByCoordinates(40, 30, 0);

170   p6 = Point.ByCoordinates(70, 25, 10);

171   // Create lines that connect the points.

172   l1 = Line.ByStartPointEndPoint(p1, p2);

173   l2 = Line.ByStartPointEndPoint(p3, p4);

174   l3 = Line.ByStartPointEndPoint(p5, p6);

175   // loft between cross section lines to create a surface.

176   hostSurface = Surface.LoftFromCrossSections({ l1, l2, l3 });

177

178   //Hide the points, lines and host surface.

179   p1.Visible = false;

180   p2.Visible = false;

181   p3.Visible = false;

182   p4.Visible = false;

183   p5.Visible = false;

184   p6.Visible = false;

185   l1.Visible = false;

186   l2.Visible = false;

187   l3.Visible = false;

188   hostSurface.Visible = false;

189

190   // Create a diagrid on the host surface.

191   u2 = 8;

192   v2 = 10;

193   folded2 = 0;

194   surfaceGrid = Diagrid.BySurfaceRowsColumns(hostSurface, u2, v2, folded2);
```

→ Save your script and then press the **Play** button at the top of the *DesignScript* window in order to run the script. The script will then generate two diagrid meshes: a flat one and a doubly-curved one. You may need to zoom in on the extents of the resulting geometry in *AutoCAD* and rotate the view in order to see it in 3D. Once done, you should see the two resulting geometries (fig. 107).

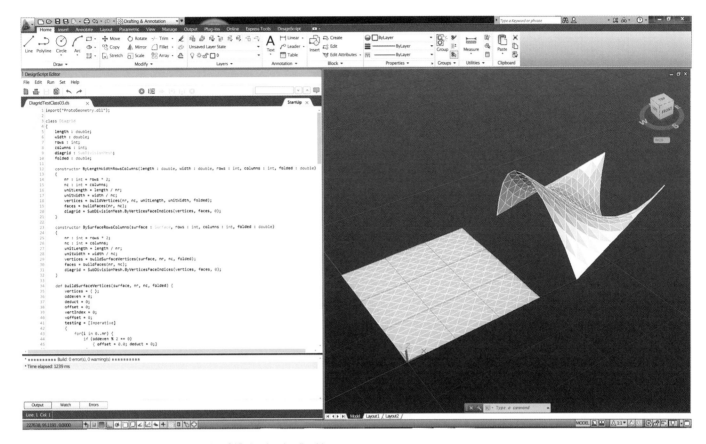

fig. 107 The *DesignScript* environment within *AutoCAD* showing the diagrid geometries.

Let's take a closer look at the script:

```
1    import("ProtoGeometry.dll");
```

The first step in the script is to import a dynamically linked library (dll) called *ProtoGeometry.dll*. This pre-packaged library includes the classes and functions needed to create and analyze the built-in geometrical entities in *DesignScript*.

```
3    class Diagrid
4    {
5        length : double;
6        width : double;
7        rows : int;
8        columns : int;
9        diagrid : SubDivisionMesh;
10       folded : double;
```

DIAGRID/CONTINUED

Next, we create our own new customized class of geometry that we call *Diagrid*. As stated earlier, a class in object-oriented programming software encapsulates attributes (parameters) and methods (functions) in one structure, so that you can logically ask it to do things such as to create copies or instances of itself, conduct operations on itself and give you information about its own state or parameters. In this case, the diagrid class has certain basic parameters, many of which should be familiar from the *MAXScript* tutorials. (Keep in mind that, in this case, the diagrid class creates both rectangular diagrids as well as ones that are derived from a host NURBS surface, and some of the parameters are particular to one type or the other.) For a flat diagrid, the class stores its own *length* and *width*. For both types of diagrids, the class stores the number of *rows* and the number of *columns* in the grid, as well as a pointer to the actual created diagrid object. The class also stores a new parameter, called *folded*, which is a numeric parameter with a value between 0 and 1; a value of 0 signifies a flat diagrid, while larger values signify a folded diagrid that resembles a piece of origami (fig. 108). (This was not implemented in the *MAXScript* tutorials, and a useful exercise might be to go back to that tutorial and add it in, after you have learned how it works in *DesignScript*.)

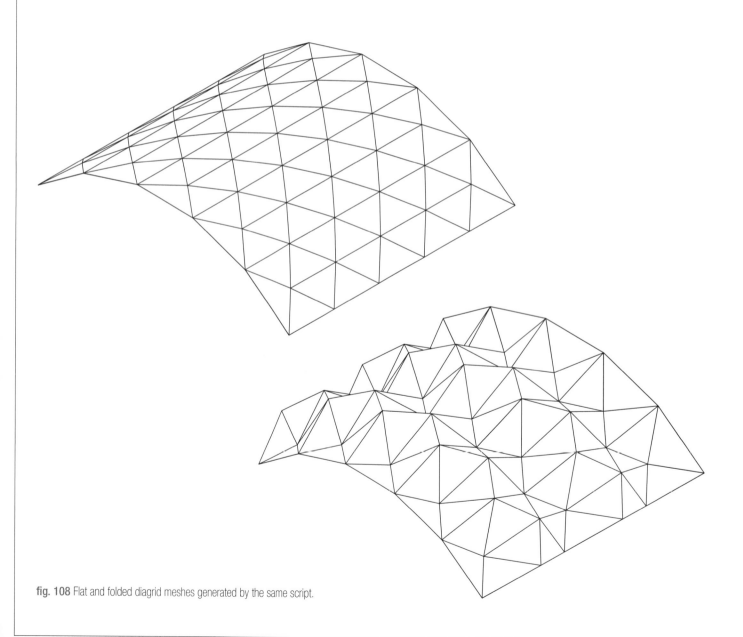

fig. 108 Flat and folded diagrid meshes generated by the same script.

```
12        constructor ByLengthWidthRowsColumns(length : double, width : double, rows : int, columns : int, folded : double)
13        {
14            nr : int = rows * 2;
15            nc : int = columns;
16            unitLength = length / nr;
17            unitWidth = width / nc;
18
19            vertices = buildVertices(nr, nc, unitLength, unitWidth, folded);
20            faces = buildFaces(nr, nc);
21            diagrid = SubDivisionMesh.ByVerticesFaceIndices(vertices, faces, 0);
22        }
```

In order to create the actual geometry, a class defines one or more special *constructor* methods. We call the first constructor method *ByLengthWidthRowsColumns*. As the name implies, this method can construct a rectangular diagrid, if you provide it with the desired length, width, number of rows and columns, and degree of folding. This method calculates the unit distances for width and length, and then calls one function to create a set of vertices and another function to create triangular faces from these vertices. These functions are the same as the ones implemented in *MAXScript* so we will not cover them in this tutorial. The final step in this method is to construct the diagrid by constructing an internal *DesignScript* geometry called *SubDivisionMesh*. We use one of its constructor methods, called *ByVerticesFaceIndices*, and we pass it the array of vertices and faces that we have created.

```
24        constructor BySurfaceRowsColumns(surface : Surface, rows : int, columns : int, folded : double)
25        {
26            nr : int = rows * 2;
27            nc : int = columns;
28
29            vertices = buildSurfaceVertices(surface, nr, nc, folded);
30            faces = buildFaces(nr, nc);
31            diagrid = SubDivisionMesh.ByVerticesFaceIndices(vertices, faces, 0);
32        }
```

The second constructor method builds a diagrid that is derived from a host surface. To maintain the consistency of the *DesignScript* naming convention, we call this constructor method *BySurfaceRowsColumns*. For the construction to be successful, the method needs to be given a host surface as well as the desired number of rows and columns for the diagrid. In a manner similar to that of the previous method, we build an array of vertices, but this time we use the function *buildSurfaceVertices*, rather than the simpler *buildVertices* function. It is important to note here that the *buildVertices* function is a direct translation from the first *MAXScript* tutorial (simple diagrid mesh) while the *buildSurfaceVertices* is a direct translation from the second tutorial (deriving a diagrid from a NURBS surface). A flat and a NURBS-based diagrid differ in their geometric coordinates but not in the topology connecting those coordinates. Thus, both constructor methods call the same function, *buildFaces*, in order to create the triangular faces that connect the vertices. Similarly, both constructor methods call the built-in *DesignScript* method to create a subdivision mesh.

34	def buildSurfaceVertices(surface, nr, nc, folded) {
63	def buildVertices(nr, nc, unitLength, unitWidth, folded) {
88	def buildFaces(nr, nc) {

The above three functions are the ones that have been directly imported from *MAXScript* and thus differ only in minor syntactical ways. The code in this tutorial has comments to help you better understand it, and you might also want to go back to the previous *MAXScript* tutorials to compare them directly.

| **52** | 353 | cs1 = surface.CoordinateSystemAtParameter(u, v); |
| **53** | 353 | ptemp = Point.ByCartesianCoordinates(cs1, 0, 0, folded*(j%2)); |

The above two lines of code are useful to examine in more detail; they achieve similar results to the *MAXScript* code but differ slightly in how those results are achieved. In addition, the code indicates how and where we added the folding parameter discussed above. In order to find the Cartesian coordinates of a point on a surface, we create a coordinate system, *cs1*, on that surface at the parametric points *u* and *v*. We then create another point, which is placed at the origin of *cs1* (giving us the *x* and *y* coordinates of that point on the surface). It is particularly useful to note that a coordinate system at a parametric point on a surface is always oriented such that its Z-axis is normal (perpendicular) to the surface at that point. Thus, to find a point that is offset from that surface along that Z-axis, we simply add a value to the *z* coordinate of that point. The use of (*j%2*) as a multiplier simply means that if *j* is even, then the modulus (*j%2*) is 0 and thus the derived point will be on the surface. If *j* is odd, then (*j%2*) will be 1 and thus we offset the point by the amount specified by the parameter *folded*. This allows us to offset every other row to achieve the folded effect.

155	// Create a flat diagrid.
156	width1 = 30;
157	length1 = 30;
158	u1 = 10;
159	v1 = 10;
160	folded1 = 0;
161	flatGrid = Diagrid.ByLengthWidthRowsColumns(width1, length1, u1, v1, folded1);

The above code, towards the end of the script, sets the desired parameters for the flat diagrid and then creates a new instance of the Diagrid class using its *ByLengthWidthRowsColumns* constructor method.

190	// Create a diagrid on the host surface.
191	u2 = 8;
192	v2 = 10;
193	folded2 = 0;
194	surfaceGrid = Diagrid.BySurfaceRowsColumns(hostSurface, u2, v2, folded2);

After creating a sample host surface and hiding it (since we are only interested in the resulting diagrid), the above code sets the desired parameters for the second grid and then creates a new instance of the Diagrid class, using its *BySurfaceRowsColumns* constructor method. Since the resulting geometry is created in *AutoCAD*, it can be easily exported to *3ds Max* or other rendering software (fig. 109).

In summary, the diagrid tutorial, as implemented in *DesignScript*, illustrates two main concepts: the generalization of algorithms and the advantages of object-oriented thinking. Having understood the geometric and topological properties of diagrids, it was relatively easy to translate the algorithm from the syntax used by *MAXScript* to that used by *DesignScript*. The translation was relatively easy because we maintained an imperative mode of programming, so the associative capabilities of *DesignScript* did not play a major role in this tutorial. However, we took advantage of *DesignScript*'s ability to encapsulate algorithms in an object-oriented manner and we combined what used to be two separate algorithms into one more universal class of objects that we can expand in modular ways. The next tutorial translation from *MAXScript* to *DesignScript* – the generation of a woven geometry based on a host surface – will illustrate how the combination of associative and imperative methods of scripting can fundamentally change our view of a design problem and more closely relate the algorithm to our intuitive understanding of its geometric and topological relationships.

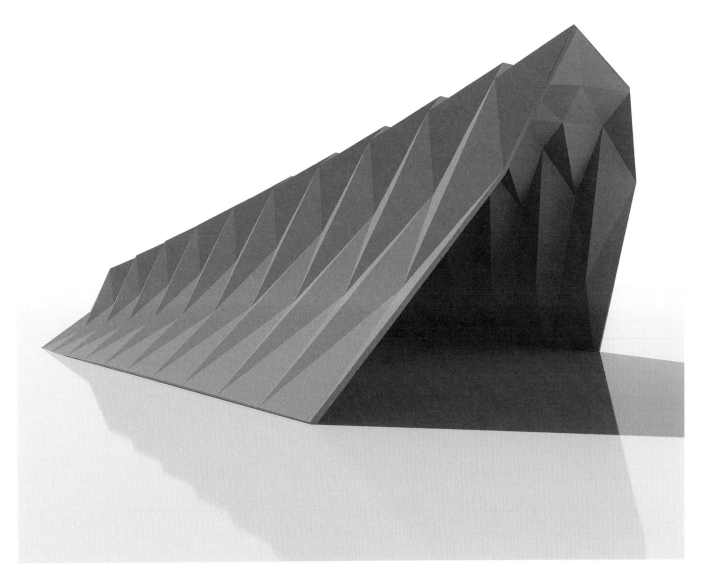

fig. 109 A rudimentary folded diagrid pavilion, created in *DesignScript* and exported to *3ds Max* for material mapping and rendering.

TUTORIAL WEAVING

For this tutorial, we will use the experience we gained from writing the weaving script in *MAXScript* to rewrite it in *DesignScript*. In doing so, we will take advantage of some of the powerful capabilities in *DesignScript*, such as replication and associative scripting.

⟶ Launch *AutoCAD* and *DesignScript* and type the following script into the *DesignScript* window:

```
1    import("ProtoGeometry.dll");
2    import("Math.dll");
3
4    // Create a host surface.
5    // Create points.
6    p1 = Point.ByCoordinates(3, 10, 2);
7    p2 = Point.ByCoordinates(-15, 7, 0.5);
8    p3 = Point.ByCoordinates(5, -3, 5);
9    p4 = Point.ByCoordinates(-5, -6, 2);
10   p5 = Point.ByCoordinates(9, -10, -2);
11   p6 = Point.ByCoordinates(-11, -12, -4);
12
13   // Create lines that join the above points.
14   l1 = Line.ByStartPointEndPoint(p1, p2);
15   l2 = Line.ByStartPointEndPoint(p3, p4);
16   l3 = Line.ByStartPointEndPoint(p5, p6);
17
18   // Create a surface from the above lines.
19   hostSurface = Surface.LoftFromCrossSections({ l1, l2, l3 });
20
21   // Create the weave.
22   // Define the number of threads for each direction.
23   weftThreads = 40;
24   warpThreads = 20;
25
26   // Define the amplitude scaling factor of the height of the warp.
27   amplitude = 0.3;
28
29   // Define the thread radius.
30   threadRadius = 0.25;
31
32   // Define the weft and warp parametric steps (from 0 to 1)
33   // based on the number of threads.
34   weftParam = 0..1..#weftThreads;
35   warpParam = 0..1..#warpThreads;
36
```

```
37    // Derive the weft and warp grid of points on the host surface.

38    weftPoints = hostSurface.PointAtParameters(weftParam<2>, warpParam<1>);

39    warpPoints = hostSurface.PointAtParameters(weftParam<1>, warpParam<2>);

40

41    def buildWarp(dummy) {

42        impCode = [Imperative] {

43            xMultFac = -1;

44            yMultFac = -1;

45            cs1 = CoordinateSystem.Identity();

46            for (i in 0..(weft-1)) {

47                if ((i % 2) == 0) {

48                    xMultFac = 1;

49                }

50                else {

51                    xMultFac = -1;

52                }

53                for (j in 0..(warp-1)) {

54                    if ((j % 2) == 0) {

55                        yMultFac = 1;

56                    }

57                    else {

58                        yMultFac = -1;

59                    }

60                    cs1 = hostSurface.CoordinateSystemAtParameters(weftParam[i], warpParam[j]);

61                    ptemp = Point.ByCartesianCoordinates(cs1, 0, 0, xMultFac*yMultFac*amplitude);

62                    warpPoints[i][j] = ptemp;

63                }

64            }

65        }

66        return = 1;

67    }

68

69    // Build the weave geometry (warp variable and "1" are unused dummy variables).

70    warp = buildWarp(1);

71

72    // Create the weft and warp BSpline curves from points.

73    weftCurves = BSplineCurve.ByPoints(weftPoints);

74    warpCurves = BSplineCurve.ByPoints(warpPoints);

75

76    // Create the weft and warp solid 'pipes'.

77    baseCircle = Circle.ByCenterPointRadius(Point.ByCoordinates(0, 0, 0), threadRadius);

78    warpSolids = baseCircle.SweepAsSolid(warpCurves);

79    weftSolids = baseCircle.SweepAsSolid(weftCurves);
```

80

81	// Hide the points, lines, curves, and host surface.
82	p1.Visible = false;
83	p2.Visible = false;
84	p3.Visible = false;
85	p4.Visible = false;
86	p5.Visible = false;
87	p6.Visible = false;
88	l1.Visible = false;
89	l2.Visible = false;
90	l3.Visible = false;
91	hostSurface.Visible = false;
92	warpPoints.Visible = false;
93	weftPoints.Visible = false;
94	warpCurves.Visible = false;
95	weftCurves.Visible = false;
96	baseCircle.Visible = false;

→ Save your script and then press the **Play** button at the top of the *DesignScript* window to run the script. You should see a woven surface (fig. 110).

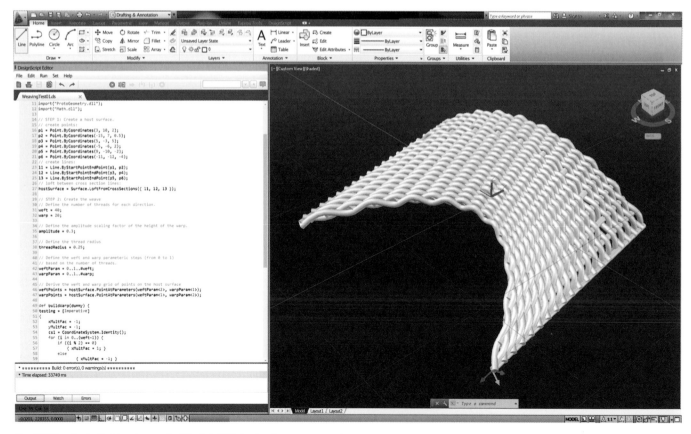

fig. 110 The *DesignScript* environment within *AutoCAD* showing the woven geometry.

The first step is to import two dynamically linked libraries (dll), which contain functions that allow *DesignScript* to create and edit geometry and to conduct mathematical operations.

Since the beta version of *DesignScript* does not allow the user to select a pre-existing geometry from the host CAD environment, this script creates its own host surface on which the woven pattern can be based.

4	// Create a host surface.
5	// Create points.
6	p1 = Point.ByCoordinates(3, 10, 2);
7	p2 = Point.ByCoordinates(-15, 7, 0.5);
8	p3 = Point.ByCoordinates(5, -3, 5);
9	p4 = Point.ByCoordinates(-5, -6, 2);
10	p5 = Point.ByCoordinates(9, -10, -2);
11	p6 = Point.ByCoordinates(-11, -12, -4);
12	
13	// Create lines that join the above points.
14	l1 = Line.ByStartPointEndPoint(p1, p2);
15	l2 = Line.ByStartPointEndPoint(p3, p4);
16	l3 = Line.ByStartPointEndPoint(p5, p6);
17	
18	// Create a surface from the above lines.
19	hostSurface = Surface.LoftFromCrossSections({ l1, l2, l3 });

The code above creates six points by specifying their Cartesian coordinates, then creates three lines, each joining one pair of two points. Finally, this section of code creates a lofted surface based on these three cross-sectional lines (fig. 111).

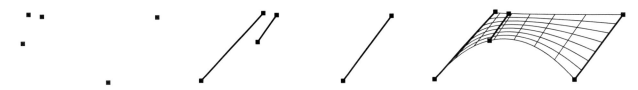

fig. 111 The process of creating a lofted surface from points and lines.

Next, the script starts the process of creating the weave.

23	weftThreads = 40;
24	warpThreads = 20;
27	amplitude = 0.3;
30	threadRadius = 0.25;

We define the desired input parameters: the number of weft and warp threads, the amplitude of the weave's undulation, and the thickness or radius of the threads themselves. These parameters can then be presented to the user as sliders or numerical input fields:

```
34   weftParam = 0..1..#weftThreads;
```

```
35   warpParam = 0..1..#warpThreads;
```

The above code may look like unfamiliar syntax. It is a simple definition of a range of values. For example, if we specify that $x = 0..10..\#2$ then x will be a collection of values ranging from 0 to 10 and varying in increments of 2. Thus, x would be equal to {0, 2, 4, 6, 8, 10}. If you recall, NURBS surfaces are parametric surfaces. A point on the surface can be located by traversing the u and v parameters of the surface. The parameters u and v vary from 0 to 1 where (0,0) signifies one corner of the surface and (1,1) signifies the opposite corner of the surface. In the above code we are doing something similar by creating the parameters for two collections, one for the weft and one for the warp, each with a range from 0 to 1, but we are also dividing each collection into the specified number of threads we want running in that direction.

```
38   weftPoints = hostSurface.PointAtParameters(weftParam<2>, warpParam<1>);
```

```
39   warpPoints = hostSurface.PointAtParameters(weftParam<1>, warpParam<2>);
```

Next, we derive a grid of points on the surface that are based on the range of the weft and warp parameters. The above code is a powerful example of both associativity and replication guides. The function *PointAtParameters* returns a 3D point on a surface based on a set of u and v parameters. However, because we pass it a collection of parameters, the function automatically returns a collection of points. Furthermore, because we wish to weave the surface in two directions that are perpendicular to each other (a weft and a warp), we use reversed replication guides (<1> and <2>) for each direction. Think of these guides as assigning the order of the points: in one case we order them first in rows and then in columns and in the second case we order them first in columns and then in rows. Later, when we ask *DesignScript* to thread a line through these points, it will respect the ordering of the points and thread horizontal lines in the first case and vertical lines in the second case. These two simply-constructed lines of code save us the burden of writing iterative *for loops* that would step through the weft and warp parameters in order to derive an ordered list of points. Code statements such as *give me back all the points on the surface at these parameters* are far more intuitive to a designer than a statement such as *for a variable that ranges from 1 to 10, step through each value of this variable and derive the point at the current value and add it to a collection and repeat the cycle.* The language constructs of *DesignScript*, while still esoteric to the uninitiated, bring us closer to a more design-oriented computer programming language.

```
41   def buildWarp(dummy) {
```

```
42       impCode = [Imperative] {
```

The next step is to move the control points above and below the surface in an alternating manner (based on odd and even row numbers) in order to create the wave-like pattern of the weave. For that, we write a function called *buildWarp* that we will call later in the code. Unfortunately, given the complexity and the procedural nature of what we need this function to achieve, the function reverts to traditional imperative coding very similar to the code written for the tutorial done in *MAXScript*. Thus, in this section we will not rehash how it works, but note that in order to instruct *DesignScript* to function in an imperative mode, we use the special [*Imperative*] keyword.

```
70    warp = buildWarp(1);
```

The above statement instructs *DesignScript* to call the *buildWarp* function that undulates the points. Since *DesignScript* is associative, all function calls need to be stored in a variable (*warp*) even if it is not needed anywhere else in the code.

```
73    weftCurves = BSplineCurve.ByPoints(weftPoints);
```

```
74    warpCurves = BSplineCurve.ByPoints(warpPoints);
```

Once the points have been moved, it becomes trivial to derive the undulating splines. *DesignScript* has built-in functions to create a *BSplineCurve* from a set of points. As mentioned earlier, the points are already ordered in two directions that are perpendicular to each other. Thus, there is no need for any nested *for loops* to iterate through them.

```
77    baseCircle = Circle.ByCenterPointRadius(Point.ByCoordinates(0, 0, 0), threadRadius);
```

```
78    warpSolids = baseCircle.SweepAsSolid(warpCurves);
```

```
79    weftSolids = baseCircle.SweepAsSolid(weftCurves);
```

In order to create solid pipes, we create a base circle with the specified thread radius parameter and sweep it as a solid using built-in functions. We pass to this function the curves we created in the prior step.

```
82    p1.Visible = false;
83    p2.Visible = false;
84    p3.Visible = false;
85    p4.Visible = false;
86    p5.Visible = false;
87    p6.Visible = false;
88    l1.Visible = false;
89    l2.Visible = false;
90    l3.Visible = false;
91    hostSurface.Visible = false;
92    warpPoints.Visible = false;
93    weftPoints.Visible = false;
94    warpCurves.Visible = false;
95    weftCurves.Visible = false;
96    baseCircle.Visible = false;
```

The last step is optional. It simply hides the geometries we have used to construct the weave, leaving visible only the final weft and warp solids.

As you would have noticed, compared to the *MAXScript* code, this code is significantly pithier and more understandable. The associativity of points, lines, surfaces and solids, as well as the power of replication guides, allow us to focus more intently on the design problem at hand. They also allow us to be more explicit about how various design elements relate to one another. While *DesignScript* is still in the very early stages of its development as a fully featured and interactive parametric system, it illustrates the pressing need to invent a higher-order universal language of computational design that allows us to shed some of the complexities of computer science concepts and couple the system more closely with our design intent.

A taxonomy of parameters

Parametric design is a process based on algorithmic thinking that enables the expression of parameters and rules that, together, define, encode and clarify the relationship between design intent and design response. It is only natural that computer-based parametric systems focus mainly on geometry and topology. After all, parametric systems are usually attached to, or built on top of, more traditional 3D solids modelling software. It is a good starting point for anyone interested in implementing a parametric approach to form-finding in his or her design workflow. Yet, at times, this can reduce the whole design process to a series of fantastic, self-congratulatory mathematical acts of acrobatics. As any other system, a parametric design system is defined by its input, algorithm, and output. We have matured in the area of geometric algorithms and can invent as well as physically build very complex geometry. The real challenge in parametric design is not how clever the algorithm is, or how complicated the output is, but in the selection of the initial input parameters. What parameters exist beyond the geometric one? Very few architects and software developers have taken on the challenge to classify, let alone invent, systems that can accept fundamentally different types of parameters. In order to truly connect parametric design to the everyday activities of designers, they need to understand and represent the same issues the designers are working with: geometry and topology, but also architectural components, materials, the environment and people. Below is an attempt to classify and explain these parameters, in the hope that it will serve as the foundation of future research projects with the goal of inventing more versatile tools to address this glaring deficiency in the current generation of parametric systems.

Mathematical parameters are the most basic type of parameter that are already understood by 3D modelling software: numbers, logical values and even strings of characters (which are represented internally using numbers). Many parametric systems, such as spreadsheets (which are undeniably powerful parametric systems in their own right), only need this level of parametric input in order to calculate very useful outputs.

Geometric parameters are higher-level entities that are built out of the lower-level mathematical parameters. Examples include points, lines, surfaces and solids. Most current 3D modelling software can represent and parametrically modify geometric constructs of various types.

Topological parameters describe how two or more entities relate to each other: connected to, above, below, is near to, looking at, is within, is outside of, etc. Most modern parametric systems excel at precisely these types of parameters. For example, a diagrid pattern is a topology that divides a surface in a consistent manner regardless of the exact geometry of the parent surface or the resulting pattern. This allows us to disassociate topology from geometry while maintaining the consistency of our design intents. Most of the examples in this book fall under this category. Topological parameters allow us to consider issues of form, composition and fabrication, and they open the possibility of further analysis as they more precisely define our design intent for how the parts relate to each other and to the whole.

Representational parameters describe and abstract entities outside themselves. Examples include computer representations of walls, windows or columns. Building Information Modelling (BIM) was invented in large part to address the need to represent 'real' objects. In BIM, a distinction is made between an isolated geometric construct such as a cuboid, and a brick wall, which knows how many bricks it has, its own weight, structural strength, cost, etc. Representational parameters allow us to describe some if not all of the physical properties of what we are modelling. They also allow us to aggregate that information so we can report overall values and quantities.

Material parameters build on mathematical, geometric, topological and representational parameters by adding and connecting several physical attributes: weight, tension, friction, elasticity, structural strength, U-value, reflection, refraction, etc. This class of parameter begins to remove us from the realm of self-referential geometric games and into the physical world of materiality. Good examples of parametric systems that accept and consider topological parameters are tensile membrane form-finders, biomimetic explorations, and particle and physics engines that can encode, almost at a cellular level, the physical properties, collision, velocity, gravity and structural stresses that a system is undergoing. Future systems for parametric design in architecture should encode materiality and physical parameters, as this will allow us to model, predict and thus parametrically explore the performative aspects of our design proposals before they are actually physically built. Analysis software that precisely models structural or thermal properties should more fully integrate the essential material and physical properties in our geometric and representational constructs, such that they fluidly react to, propagate and give us feedback on constraints and interactions within the overall parametric system in real or near-real time. For example, very few current parametric systems can represent the time-based effect of prolonged exposure to fire on a structural system or a particular building material. Physics-based computer games and bioengineering research, however, have reached that stage and we would be wise to learn from their techniques in the field of architecture.

Environmental parameters include the frequently invisible and fluid forces that surround us. Time, wind, thermal variation, vistas and views, the movement of light and shadow, magnetic fields, Wi-Fi and GPS signals, growth and erosion are all examples of environmental parameters. Not many of us can easily imagine the path of a shadow as it travels during the day or the undulations of a field of sunflowers as they follow the path of the sun; this is why we find time-lapse photography so fascinating. Interactive façades that respond to environmental conditions (usually the path of the sun) are a good start. However, we need a deeper understanding of the totality and complexity of environmental factors so that we can optimize our design solutions, given complex and competing constraints.

Human parameters form the seventh and most challenging class of parameters. Architecture's purpose is, after all, to shelter humans from the elements. While we share many physical attributes and needs, we also differ in profound ways both ergonomically and psychologically. If we are to create humane architecture and one that creates truly customizable spaces, we need to be able to model our clients, their intents and desires, and incorporate that information as parameters in our design systems. It is truly shocking that, in many cases, incorporating the human parameter in our design projects and renderings does not go beyond the inclusion of a scale model of a person. That is only a start; masterful architects know how to address and resolve multivalent parameters (fig. 112). We truly need to learn from the field of ergonomics and especially the advanced systems that office furniture, automobile and medical equipment manufacturers use to model human beings. A good development in our field is the increasing incorporation of simulated crowd systems. Sadly, while effective at simulated fire egress, the simplifying assumptions of such systems, which reduce the complexity of human behaviour to that of a robot, render them useless to predict common human behaviour such as where clusters of people might gather or pause on a sunny afternoon. As the computational capability of our systems grows, so will the sophistication of these simulations.

Incorporating all seven classes in a parametric design system is not only a tall order, but not always advisable given the design situation. Knowing how to abstract a situation and build a conceptual model in which extraneous parameters are excluded but essential ones

fig. 112 Le Corbusier's *Le Modulor* cast in concrete at the Unité d'Habitation (1965), Firminy, France.

are included is part of our irreplaceable skill as designers. Parametric modelling lets you capture that conceptual model and make it explicit. This shifts the conversation. The challenge is not one we can shy away from if we aim to be precise about our design intent and, perhaps more importantly, strive to understand the consequences of our decisions before we actually build them. Parametric systems are only one step in that endeavour.

Afterword by Brian Johnson

Congratulations! You have arrived at the beginning! Not the beginning of this book, but the beginning of your own ownership and mastery of the material covered here. There are just a few more words to review or consider before you go.

Patterns on the wall

In the preceding pages you've seen many examples of how the logic of geometry and the magic of creative intent can be combined and then embedded through code and variables into parametric design. These have been presented as a collection of 'patterns' – paradigms or prototypes, rather than recipes. How should you make the best use of this material? Pattern languages are not meant to ease design by reducing it to a matter of selection and arrangement. These patterns are the 'concept diagrams' of code, not a catalogue from which to pick and choose. They are the material from which to craft new solutions to new problems. Just as Christopher Alexander's patterns are meant to suggest the Platonic 'ideal forms' of good environmental design, the patterns presented here illustrate many of the ideal forms of parametric design. As in Plato's cave, the particular examples we see are always projections, reductions of the ideal necessitated by the available systems and syntaxes of expression, but their repeated emergence in new settings has demonstrated their persistence. Whether they serve your particular circumstance will depend on other issues.

Tectonics of code

The patterns are not the end of the story. Tectonics – the 'art and science of construction' – has a place in this discipline too, alongside the patterns. Buildings and scripts are both made of parts, put together to form systems, and the joints are often quite important. Thinking about parts and systems and their impact on designs is often challenging for students. Learning to 'see' (sometimes literally) the important parts can be critical. Constraints arising from systems are often viewed as negatives by beginner students, but are seen as opportunities by more mature designers. Parametric design is one way of learning to think about parts and systems and the opportunities inherent in their various logics.

Consider the design of a mechanism of some sort. We know that two points define a line. But does the line represent a rubber band connecting two points in space? Or is it supposed to be a piece of steel with a bolt in each end? The difference is whether the script preserves or enforces the constancy of length in the steel, or allows the points to move as if it's a rubber band. If one end of the steel is fixed in place, the other end must always be the same distance away. That is, it must

fall on the circle defined by the distance between bolt holes. The ideal parametric system allows us to explicitly manifest the physical truths of the mechanism as well as the geometric intentions of the designer (fig. 113).

Remember that, as some materials cause corrosion when used together, some computations need special handling as well. A classic in the realm of computational geometry can be found in the 'inverse' trigonometry functions (arcSine and arcCosine). Computing the arcsine of the sine of an angle doesn't always get you back to where you started. Test your details and use them in the right context.

Be careful of assumptions. Computers work with numbers, but don't generally understand units. If you prompt for a dimension, specify the units in which it should be entered. If your software system supports multiple base units, state up front what your assumptions are, or find out how your script can enquire and convert appropriately between units.

Praxis

As with any craft, the application of code to design requires experience, insight and practice, as well as care, judgement and attention to detail. Gain experience and confidence by using these patterns. Don't just copy the code, work with the code to understand the 'ideal form' or combine it with other fragments and then use that to create your own designs.

Not all code is created equal, even if the results are equivalent. Occam's Razor says you should be suspicious of messy code, but density and cleverness of expression can be misleading as well, if it masks what's really going on. If clear expression isn't apparent in the result, it may indicate muddied thinking in the intent or a weak understanding of fundamentals. Good code can be elegant!

Add comments to your code, to remind yourself what clever or mundane thing your code is doing. Your code won't have the benefit of the explanations this book provides to remind you what your script is doing and why. Use meaningful names for variables wherever possible. Reading your own scripts some months after you created them can be a humbling experience.

Watch for repeating units, within a design or across multiple designs. These are the signs of an emerging pattern, an opportunity to leverage your creativity and save time, or perhaps a chance to give back to the community of practice into which you are now entering.

Parametric Designs and Designing

Available direct-manipulation drafting or modelling programs are efficient editors of geometry, but good design involves a complex interplay of ideas, relationships and intent. Geometry is just the most visible product of the design process. Parametric design tools offer you the opportunity to express and explore design intent itself, not just the geometry of a project. These tools present the opportunity to engage the deep questions about the influences that shape your individual designs, and about what it means to design, elevating design discourse generally. Parametric design, along with sophisticated building information models and digitally enhanced construction techniques, will be a core component of practice in the 21st century.

fig. 113 *Glimpse the Future.* Hinting at things to come, this parameterized, sinusoidal displacement of points along one edge of a set of surface strips was generated by a *Processing* script. The resulting gill-like surface is thickened and rendered with a backlight.

Glossary

Algorithm
A step-by-step procedure for solving a problem. An algorithm usually takes an input, performs a process and creates an output.

Argument
In computer programming, a piece of information or a variable that is passed on to a function as input to that function.

Associative Programming
This type of programming differs from traditional (imperative) programming in that it associates variables with one another, such that a change in one variable automatically triggers an update in other variables that are associated with it.

Boolean Algebra
Named after George Boole, Boolean algebra deals with the algebra of only two integers: 0 and 1. These can also be thought of as *false* and *true*. These values can be combined in conjunction (AND), disjunction (OR) and complement (NOT). Using these Boolean operations, an algorithm can compute logical expressions and handle set theory. The term is also used in 3D modelling as the operation of union (addition), intersection and subtraction of solids.

Bounding Box
The smallest cuboid in which all the points of a geometrical object lie. It is useful for knowing the maximum and minimum extents of an object.

Building Information Modelling (BIM)
A computer-aided method of conducting design, construction, facility management, renovation and even demolition. It relies on an integrated information model of the project that encodes not just the geometry of the project, but other aspects of it, such as spatial relationships, building components, manufacturers' data, etc.

CNC
An abbreviation for Computer Numerical Control. A CNC machine interprets geometric data as a series of machine operations that act on raw material. CNC machines such as routers and milling machines are used for digital fabrication.

Coordinate System
In geometry, a coordinate system uses one or more numbers to determine the location of a point. A 3D Cartesian coordinate system, named after René Descartes, uses a set of three intersecting axes (x, y, z) that are usually perpendicular to one another. Their point of intersection is called the origin. A Cartesian coordinate system uses coordinates along the x, y and z axes to determine the location of points in 3D space.

Cross Product
In geometry, an operation performed on two vectors that results in a third vector that is perpendicular to the plane formed by the first two vectors. A cross product is useful when trying to find the direction of a location on a surface.

CV
An abbreviation for Control Vertex. A CV is a point that is used to compute the geometric shape of a NURBS surface. Think of a CV as a magnet that pulls on a surface. The location and weighting assigned to several CVs determine the final curvature of the surface.

Developable Surface
A surface that can be unfolded without distortion and manufactured from flat sheets. Developable surfaces are useful for easing digital fabrication.

Encapsulation
In object-oriented programming, a class of objects that contains within itself both methods and attributes. Encapsulation allows for a more structured and modular method of computer programming.

Fibonacci Series
A sequence of numbers named after Leonardo de Pisa, a thirteenth-century mathematician known as Fibonacci. A Fibonacci sequence starts with the numbers 0 and 1 and then each subsequent number is the addition of the previous two. Fibonacci series occur in nature (notably, in certain plants, in the arrangement of leaves on the stem, known as *phyllotaxis*) and are used by architects as a system for achieving elegant proportions.

Flowchart
In computer programming, a diagram that represents an algorithm. Computer programmers use flowcharts to test the logic and robustness of their algorithms and to explain them to others.

Genetic Algorithm
In computer programming, a genetic algorithm (GA) uses the metaphor of natural evolution to search for the fittest solution to a problem. A GA represents the input data as a population that can breed a new generation. Genetic crossover and mutation is cyclically used to improve the fitness of the next generation until the population reaches an overall satisfactory solution.

Global Variable
A variable in an algorithm that can be accessed and modified by all its functions.

Golden Rectangle
A rectangle whose sides form a golden ratio. Golden rectangles and spirals are closely related to Fibonacci numbers. A distinctive feature of this shape is that it is fractal. In particular, when a square shape is removed from the original rectangle, the remaining rectangle also forms a golden rectangle.

GUI
An abbreviation for Graphical User Interface. Basically, this is the set of all the visual elements (windows, buttons, menu items, sliders, etc.) that allow a user to interact with a computer.

Imperative Programming

A style of computer programming in which statements or instructions are made that change the current state. Imperative programming is usually contrasted with declarative or associative programming, which declares the relationships between variables, but does not specify the sequences of how a state change should take place.

Modifier

In *3ds Max* and similar 3D modelling software, an encapsulated method that modifies a base object. A bend modifier, for example, bends an object. Several modifiers can be applied to an object in sequence, forming a modifier stack.

Normal

In geometry, normal basically means 'perpendicular to'.

Normalized Vector

In mathematics, a vector that maintains the same direction as the original, but has a length of 1.

NURBS

An abbreviation of Non-Uniform Rational Basis Spline (or Surface). A NURBS is a mathematical model for generating and representing curves and surfaces.

Object-Oriented Programming

Object-Oriented Programming (OOP) is a programming style that represents concepts as objects that encapsulate *attributes* and *methods*. Attributes describe the features of the object and methods are functions and procedures that can act on the object when called. OOP has many advantages over traditional programming methods mainly in maintaining modularity, readability and extensibility of the computer code.

Parametric Design

A process based on algorithmic thinking that enables the expression of parameters and rules that, together, define, encode and clarify the relationship between design intent and design response.

Pi (π)

A mathematical constant that is the ratio of a circle's circumference to its diameter. It is approximately equal to 3.1415926.

Primitive

In 3D modelling, a basic geometry such as a cube, cylinder or sphere.

Radian

A unit of angular measurement. One radian is equal to $180/\pi$ degrees.

Rollout

In *3ds Max*, a group of user interface elements that can be hidden or shown (rolled out) on demand.

Script

Usually a short algorithm written to solve a problem. A script is usually interpreted and executed immediately rather than compiled and linked.

Spinner

In *3ds Max*, a user interface element that allows a user to either type in a value or use up and down arrows to change the value.

Sweep Profile

In *3ds Max* and similar 3D modelling software, a 2D shape that gets extruded along a line, creating an extruded solid object.

Tessellate

In geometry, a process of tiling a repeating a geometric shape on a surface with no overlaps and no gaps.

Topology

In mathematics, topology describes how things are connected to each other without regard to their actual geometry.

Transformation

A process of changing the geometry of a shape or object. Standard transformations include translation (movement), rotation and scaling.

Transformation Matrix

A matrix of numbers that encapsulate standard transformations. Transformation matrices allow the combination of several transformations through matrix multiplication.

Translate

In geometry, to translate an object is to move it from one location to another location. Translation, rotation and scale are called standard transformations.

Tropism

In botany, the direction an organism takes in response to external factors such as light, gravity, wind or water.

Vector

In geometry, a line with a magnitude (distance) and a direction.

Visual Programming Environment

In computing, a visual programming environment allows users to create computer programs by manipulating and linking elements graphically rather than by specifying them textually. *Grasshopper* is an example of a visual programming environment.

Bibliography

Aish, R. and Woodbury, R. (2005). 'Multi-level Interaction in Parametric Design'. *Smart Graphics, Proceedings of the 5th International Symposium, SG 2005, Frauenwörth Cloister, Germany, August 22–24, 2005*, 151-162. Springer.

Alexander, C. (1974). *Notes on the Synthesis of Form*. Harvard University Press.

Alexander, C. (1978). *A Pattern Language: Towns, Buildings, Construction*. OUP USA.

Antonelli, P. and Legendre, G. (2011). *Pasta by Design*. Thames & Hudson.

Aranda, B. and Lasch, C. (2006). *Tooling (Pamphlet Architecture)*. Princeton Architectural Press.

Arnold, K. and Gosling, J. (1996). *The Java Programming Language*. Addison-Wesley Publishing Company.

Batty, M. (2007). *Cities and Complexity: Understanding Cities with Cellular Automata, Agent-Based Models, and Fractals*. MIT Press.

Beckmann, J. (ed.) (1998). *The Virtual Dimension: Architecture, Representation and Crash Culture*. Princeton Architectural Press.

Beesley, P. *et al* (eds.) (2006). *Responsive Architectures: Subtle Technologies 2006*. Riverside Architectural Press.

Benedikt, M. (ed.) (1992). *Cyberspace: First Steps*. MIT Press.

Bovill, C. (1996). *Fractal Geometry in Architecture & Design*. Birkhäuser.

Bridges, A. (1996). *The Construction Net: Online Information Sources for the Construction Industry*. E & FN Spon.

Burden, E. (2000). *Visionary Architecture: Unbuilt Works of the Imagination*. McGraw–Hill.

Burrowes, K.S. *et al* (2011). Pulmonary Embolism: Predicting Disease Severity. *Philosophical Transactions of the Royal Society*. Vol. 369, 4255–4277.

Burrowes, K.S., Hunter, P.J. and Tawhai, M.H. (2005). 'Anatomically Based Finite Element Models of the Human Pulmonary Arterial and Venous Trees Including Supernumerary Vessels'. *Journal of Applied Physiology*. Vol. 99, 731–738.

Burry, J. and Burry, M. (eds.) (2010). *The New Mathematics of Architecture*. Thames & Hudson.

Burry, M. (2011). *Scripting Cultures: Architectural Design and Programming (Architectural Design Primer)*. John Wiley & Sons.

Carroll, S.B. (2006). *Endless Forms Most Beautiful: The New Science of Evo Devo*. W.W. Norton & Company.

Ceccato, C. *et al* (eds.) (2010). *Advances in Architectural Geometry 2010*. Springer.

Coates, P. (2010). *Programming.Architecture*. Routledge.

Daniele, T. (2009). *Poly-modeling with 3ds Max: Thinking Outside of the Box*. Focal Press.

Del Campo, M. and Manniger, S. (2011). 'Performative Surfaces: Computational Form Finding Processes for the Inclusion of Detail in the Surface Condition. Computational Design Modeling', *Proceedings of the Design Modeling Symposium, Berlin, 2011*. Springer, 225-238.

Derakhshani, R. and Derakhshani, D. (2011). *Autodesk 3ds Max 2012 Essentials*. John Wiley & Sons.

Eglash, R. (1999). *African Fractals: Modern Computing and Indigenous Design*. Rutgers University Press.

Ehn, P. (1989). *Work-Oriented Design of Computer Artifacts*. Arbetslivscentrum.

Evans, R. (2000). *The Projective Cast: Architecture and Its Three Geometrics*. MIT Press.

Flake, G.W. (2000). *The Computational Beauty of Nature: Computer Explorations of Fractals, Chaos, Complex Systems and Adaptation*. MIT Press.

Fornes, M. (2011). *11 FRAC Centre*. Accessed at http://theverymany.com on 4 April 2012.

Gamma, E. *et al* (1994). *Design Patterns: Elements of Reusable Object-Oriented Software*. Addison Wesley.

Garcia, M. (2009). *The Patterns of Architecture: Architectural Design*. John Wiley & Sons.

Grobman, Y. and Neuman, E. (eds.) (2011). *Performalism: Form and Performance in Digital Architecture*. Routledge.

Harris, J. (2012). *Fractal Architecture: Organic Design Philosophy in Theory and Practice*. University of New Mexico Press.

Hauer, E. (2004). *Erwin Hauer: Continua – Architectural Screens and Walls*. Princeton Architectural Press.

Hensel, M. and Menges, A. (2008). *Versatility and Vicissitude: Performance in Morpho Ecological Design*. John Wiley & Sons.

Hensel, M. Menges, A. and Weinstock, M. (2004). *Emergence: Morphogenetic Design Strategies*. John Wiley & Sons.

Hensel, M. Menges, A. and Weinstock, M. (2010). *Emergent Technologies and Design: Towards a Biological Paradigm for Architecture*. Routledge.

Hensel, M., Menges A. and Weinstock M. (eds.) (2006). 'Techniques and Technologies in Morphogenetic Design'. *AD Profile* 180, Wiley-Academy.

Hesselgren, L. *et al* (2012). *Advances in Architectural Geometry 2012*. Springer.

Holme, A. (2002). *Geometry: Our Cultural Heritage*. Springer.

Iwamoto, L. (2009). *Digital Fabrications: Architectural and Material Techniques*. Princeton Architectural Press.

Kieran, S. and Timberlake, J. (2004). *Refabricating Architecture: How Manufacturing Methodologies are Poised to Transform Building Construction*. McGraw-Hill.

Kolarevic, B. (ed.) (2003). *Architecture in the Digital Age – Design and Manufacturing*. Taylor & Francis.

Kolarevic, B. and Klinger, K. (eds.) (2008). *Manufacturing Material Effects*. Routledge.

Kolarevic, B. and Malkawi, A. (eds.) (2004). *Performative Architecture: Beyond Instrumentality*. Routledge.

Krawczyk, R. (2009). *The Codewriting Workbook*. Princeton Architectural Press.

Lawson, B. (1990). *How Designers Think: The Design Process Demystified*. Butterworth Architecture.

Leach, N., Turnbull, D. and Williams, C. (eds.) (2004). *Digital Tectonics*. Wiley-Academy.

Legendre, G. (2011). *Mathematics of Space: Architectural Design*. John Wiley & Sons.

Lima, M. (2011). *Visual Complexity: Mapping Patterns of Information*. Princeton Architectural Press.

Littlefield, D. (ed.) (2008). *Space Craft: Developments in Architectural Computing*. RIBA Publishing.

Liu, Y. (2007). *Distinguishing Digital Architecture: 6th Far Eastern International Digital Architectural Design Award*. Birkhäuser.

Lunenfeld, P. (ed.) (1999). *The Digital Dialectic: New Essays on New Media*. MIT Press.

Lynn, G. (1999). *Animated Form*. Princeton Architectural Press.

Mandelbrot, B. (1982). *The Fractal Geometry of Nature*. W.H. Freeman & Co Ltd.

McCullough, M. (1996). *Abstracting Craft: The Practiced Digital Hand*. MIT Press.

McCullough, M. (2004). *Digital Ground: Architecture, Pervasive Computing, and Environmental Knowing.* MIT Press.

McLuhan, M. (1994). *Understanding Media: The Extensions of Man.* MIT Press.

Menges, A. (2012). *Material Computation: Higher Integration in Morphogenetic Design.* John Wiley & Sons.

Menges, A. and Ahlquist, S. (eds.) (2011). *Computational Design Thinking.* John Wiley & Sons Ltd.

Mitchell, W. (2003). *ME++: The Cyborg Self and the Networked City.* MIT Press.

Mitchell, W. and McCullough, M. (1995). *Digital Design Media.* Van Nostrand Reinhold.

Moussavi, F. *et al* (2009). *The Function of Form.* Actar and Harvard Graduate School of Design.

Moussavi, F. (2011). 'Parametric Software is no Substitute for Parametric Thinking', *Architectural Review.* October 2011, 39.

Moussavi, F. and Kubo, M. (eds.) (2006). *The Function of Ornament.* Actar and Harvard Graduate School of Design.

Murdock, K. (2011). *3ds Max 2012 Bible.* John Wiley & Sons.

Negroponte, N. (1970). *The Architecture Machine.* MIT Press.

Negroponte, N. (1995). *Being Digital.* Vintage Books.

Neumann, O. and Beesley, P. (eds.) (2007). *FutureWood: Innovation in Building Design and Manufacturing.* Riverside Architectural Press.

Otto, F. (2008). *Occupying and Connecting: Thoughts on Territories and Spheres of Influence with Particular Reference to Human Settlement.* Axel Menges.

Otto, F. and Rasch, B. (1996). *Finding Form: Towards an Architecture of the Minimal.* Axel Menges.

Oxman, N. (2007). 'Get Real: Towards Performance-Driven Computational Geometry'. *International Journal of Architectural Computing,* Vol. 5, Iss. 4, Multi-science, 663–684.

Oxman, N. (2007). 'Material-based Design Computation: An Inquiry into Digital Simulation of Physical Material Properties as Design Generators'. *International Journal of Architectural Computing,* Vol. 5, Iss. 1, Multi-science, 26–44.

Oxman, N. (2010). 'Structuring Materiality: Design Fabrication of Heterogeneous Materials'. *AD/Architectural Design,* Vol. 80, Iss. 4, Wiley-Academy.

Oxman, R. (2008). 'Performance Based Design: Current Practices and Research Issues'. *International Journal of Architectural Computing,* Vol. 6, Iss. 1, Multi-science, 1–17.

Oxman, R. and Oxman, R. (2010). *The New Structuralism: Design, Engineering and Architectural Technologies (Architectural Design).* John Wiley & Sons.

Pawlyn, M. (2011). *Biomimicry in Architecture.* RIBA Publishing.

Pearson, M. (2011). *Generative Art: A Practical Guide Using Processing.* Manning Publications.

Perella, S. (ed.) (1998). *Hypersurface Architecture (Architectural Design).* John Wiley & Sons.

Plauger, P.J. (1992). *The Standard C Library.* Prentice Hall.

Pottmann, H. *et al* (2007). *Architectural Geometry.* Bentley Institute Press.

Prusinkiewicz, P. and Lindenmayer, A. (1996). *The Algorithmic Beauty of Plants.* Springer-Verlag.

Rahim, A. (2000). *Contemporary Processes in Architecture.* AD Profile 145, Wiley-Academy.

Rahim, A. (ed.) (2002). *Contemporary Techniques in Architecture.* AD Profile 155, Wiley-Academy.

Rajchman, J. (1998). *Constructions.* MIT Press.

Reas, C. (2010). *Form+Code in Design, Art, and Architecture (Design Briefs).* Princeton Architectural Press.

Reas, C. and Fry, B. (2007). *Processing: A Programming Handbook for Visual Designers and Artists.* MIT Press.

Reas, C. and Fry, B. (2010). *Getting Started with Processing: A Hands-on Introduction to Making Interactive Graphics.* Make.

Rowe, P. (1995). *Design Thinking.* MIT Press.

Sakamoto, T., Ferre, A. and Kubo M. (eds.) (2008). *From Control to Design: Parametric/Algorithmic Architecture.* Actar.

Schodek, D. *et al* (2005). *Digital Design and Manufacturing: CAD/CAM Applications in Architecture and Design.* John Wiley & Sons.

Schön, D. (1983). *The Reflective Practitioner: How Professionals Think in Action.* Basic Books.

Schumacher, P. (2004). *Digital Hadid: Landscapes in Motion.* Birkhäuser.

Schumacher, P. (2009). *Parametricism–A New Global Style for Architecture and Urban Design, AD/Architectural Design – Digital Cities,* Vol. 79, Iss. 4, July/August 2009.

Schumacher, P. (2011). *The Autopoiesis of Architecture: v. 1: A New Framework for Architecture.* John Wiley & Sons.

Schumacher, P. (2012). *The Autopoiesis of Architecture: v. 2: A New Agenda for Architecture.* John Wiley & Sons.

Semper, G. (2011). *The Four Elements of Architecture and other Writings.* Cambridge University Press.

Sheil, B. (2012). *Manufacturing the Bespoke: Making and Prototyping Architecture.* John Wiley & Sons.

Sherwood, S. (2011). *The Shape of Things to Come: Marc Fornes Conducts a Spatial Experiment for the FRAC Centre in Orleans, France.* Accessed at http://www.interiordesign.net on 4 April 2012.

Snodgrass, A. and Coyne, R. (2006). *Interpretation in Architecture: Design as a Way of Thinking.* Routledge.

Spiller, N. (1998). *Digital Dreams: Architecture and the New Alchemic Technologies.* Whitney Library of Design.

Spuybroek, L. (ed.) (2009). *Research and Design: The Architecture of Variation.* Thames & Hudson.

Spuybroek, L. (2011). *Textile Tectonics – Research and Design.* NAI Publishers.

Szalapaj, P. (2005). *Contemporary Architecture and the Digital Design Process.* Elsevier Architectural Press.

Taimina, D. (2009). *Crocheting Adventures with Hyperbolic Planes.* A K Peters/CRC Press.

Tedeschi, A. (2011). *Parametric Architecture with Grasshopper.* Le Penseur.

Terzidis, K. (2003). *Expressive Form: A Conceptual Approach to Computational Design.* Routledge.

Terzidis, K. (2006). *Algorithmic Architecture.* Architectural Press.

Tschumi, B., and Cheng, I. (eds.) (2003). *The State of Architecture at the Beginning of the 21st Century.* The Monacelli Press.

Umemoto, N. and Reiser, J. (2006). *Atlas of Novel Tectonics.* Princeton Architectural Press.

Weinstock, M. (2010). *The Architecture of Emergence: The Evolution of Form in Nature and Civilization.* John Wiley & Sons Ltd.

Weishar, P. (1998). *Digital Space: Designing Virtual Environments.* McGraw-Hill.

Woodbury, R. (2010). *Elements of Parametric Design.* Routledge.

Index

Page numbers in *italics* refer to picture captions

Picture credits

Images are by the author except on the pages specified below:

7 (fig. 2) Beeeh Photography
8 (fig. 3) Etan J. Tal
10 (fig. 5) Scottish Doors (Ross Sampson)
12–19 SPAN (Matias del Campo & Sandra Manninger)
26 THEVERYMANY (Marc Fornes)
28 (fig. 9) MATSYS Design (Andrew Kudless)
29 (fig. 10) Frankie Roberto
29 (fig. 11) Andreas Tille
30 (fig. 12) Stephen Lee
36–37 Populous (David Hines)
38 Roly Hudson
39 Populous (David Hines)
40 Roly Hudson
41 Populous (David Hines)
42 (fig. 24) Nevit Dilmen
42 (fig. 25) Rocío Ruiz
47 Studio Mode (Ronnie Parsons and Gil Akos)
48 (fig. 38) Tomas Castelazo
58 (fig. 44) Pentocelo
64–67 Studio Mode (Ronnie Parsons and Gil Akos)
69 (fig. 50) Alexis Monnerot-Dumaine
69 (fig. 51) Richard Bartz
69 (fig. 52) Gnomz007 and Túrelio
78–79 Images © Ty Cole. Caliper Studio (Stephen Lynch, Jonathan Taylor, Michael Conlon and Nicholas Desbiens)

80–81 Caliper Studio (Stephen Lynch, Jonathan Taylor, Michael Conlon and Nicholas Desbiens)
82 (fig. 58) Michael Rygel
104–109 HYBRIDa scp (J. Truco and S. Felipe)
110 (fig. 71) Henri-Georges Naton
110 (fig. 72) Srini G. via Wikimedia Commons
110 (fig. 73) Dr Jocelyn via http://biocharproject.org
110 (fig. 74) Dawn Endico
111 (fig. 75) NASA
111 (fig. 76) Tom Pawlofsky
124–125 Neri Oxman
126 (fig. 83) PfarreLiesing
127 (fig. 84) Olando and Mendo Architects
128 (fig. 85) Sergis via Wikimedia Commons
152–155 THEVERYMANY (Marc Fornes)
156 (fig. 95) Kelly Burrowes
156 (fig. 96) R. Neil Marshman
157 (fig. 97) Zhang Wenjie
157 (fig. 98) Serie Architects (Photographer: Edmund Sumner)
168–173 su11 architecture+design (Ferda Kolatan & Erich Schoenenberger)
174 SPAN (Matias del Campo & Sandra Manninger)
176 (fig. 103) Autodesk (Robert Aish, Patrick Tierney, Luke Church)
177 (fig. 104) Autodesk (Robert Aish, Patrick Tierney, Luke Church)
197 (fig. 112) www.mr-erno.blogspot.com
199 (fig. 113) Brian Johnson

Acknowledgements

I could not have completed this book without the invaluable help of my family, friends and colleagues. I would like to offer my sincerest gratitude to Dr Robert Woodbury who gave of his generous time to read the book and provide a thoughtful foreword to it. I am also very grateful to the friendship and insight that Professor Brian Johnson offered me over the many months leading to the publication of this book. Brian kindly agreed to provide the afterword for this book, but I am also grateful for his patient advice laced with humour in the numerous e-mail exchanges we had about this book and parametric design in general. My thanks also go to three old friends, Dr Theodore Hall, Dr Scott Johnson and Jeremy Kargon. Ted is truly a walking encyclopedia of algorithmic knowledge. If I am ever at a loss on how to solve a problem, I can always rely on his help. Through years of friendship, Scott has offered me invaluable advice on issues of digital design, building-information systems and representation. Jeremy, on the other hand, collaborated with me on the first visual online archive on the Internet before the World-Wide Web was invented. Over the years, he remained a loyal friend always pushing me in new directions. I am also deeply grateful to Professor Harold Borkin and Professor James Turner, my Ph.D. advisors, who taught me how to think algorithmically and how to code early on at the University of Michigan. I will always be indebted to them for the knowledge they imparted on me. My heartfelt gratitude goes to Carl Luckenbach who, apart from sponsoring my application for U.S. citizenship, offered me my first digital design job in practice and allowed me to realize the amazing potential of using digital tools to communicate design intent. My thanks also go to Neil Katz of SOM who read a draft of the book and provided many invaluable comments. There is no space in this book to individually thank the many researchers, designers and programmers who have selflessly contributed inspirational ideas and open source code online for all of us to learn from. I am also immensely grateful to those who contributed images and descriptions of their work for inclusion in this book.

I would also like to thank my colleagues as well as my students at the Welsh School of Architecture at Cardiff University who warmly welcomed me and provided the intellectual and collegial environment that enabled me to dedicate the time and effort needed to complete this book. In particular, I would like to sincerely thank Professor Richard Weston, who recommended me to Laurence King Publishing, for his friendship and for stimulating discussions about all things digital and parametric.

I offer my deep gratitude to the team at Laurence King Publishing, especially Philip Cooper, Liz Faber and Sara Goldsmith, for their wise advice, tireless efforts and patience while they waited for the completed manuscript.

Finally, I would like to give a very heartfelt thanks to my two daughters, Maye and Sarah, for their unconditional love and especially to my wife, Dr Vassiliki Mangana. Her unwavering support over the years gave me the strength to continue working on several projects when I would have otherwise given up. Her expertise as a historian of architecture was invaluable in helping me properly research, understand and describe the case studies in this book.